ology

evised Edition

Zdenek Salzmann

Anthropology

Revised Edition

Harcourt Brace Jovanovich, Inc.

New York, Chicago, San Francisco, Atlanta, Dallas

ZDENEK SALZMANN taught anthropology at the high school level for many years. From 1966 to 1968, Dr. Salzmann taught anthropology at Phillips Exeter Academy. Previously, he was instructor in anthropology and then headmaster of the Verde Valley School in Sedona, Arizona. At Verde Valley, anthropology is a required part of the curriculum and involves annual field trips to Mexican villages and nearby Indian reservations. Dr. Salzmann received a Ph.D. from Indiana University in 1963. He has contributed articles in anthropology and linguistics to many scholarly journals. He served as an acting consultant to the Anthropology Curriculum Study Project of the American Anthropological Association. Currently, Dr. Salzmann is a member of the Department of Anthropology at the University of Massachusetts.

FIGURES: Graphic Arts International

ALL MAPS: Harbrace

COPYRIGHT ACKNOWLEDGMENTS

TEXT: **pp. 94–95,** adapted from *Human Races* by Stanley M. Garn (1961, 1965) by permission of the author and Charles C. Thomas, Publisher, Springfield, Ill.

ILLUSTRATIONS: **p. 49,** adapted from Figure 20–1, page 363 of *Biological Science: An Inquiry into Life* by the Biological Sciences Curriculum Study, copyright © 1963 by the American Institute of Biological Science, Washington, D.C., reprinted by permission of the Biological Sciences Curriculum Study; **p. 70,** Jack J. Kunz, Time-Life Books, *The Primates,* copyright © 1965 Time, Inc.; **p. 71,** adapted from Figure 31–18, page 811 of *Life: An Introduction to Biology,* 2nd ed., by Simpson and Beck, copyright © 1957, 1955 by Harcourt, Brace & World, Inc.; **pp. 79, 81, 82,** adapted from page 357 of *Vertebrate Paleontology,* 2nd ed., by Alfred S. Romer, copyright © 1945 by The University of Chicago Press; **p. 112,** Tree-Ring Chronology Building (after Stallings), from "Dendrochronology" by Bryant Bannister, in *Science in Archaeology,* ed. by Brothwell and Higgs, Basic Books, Inc., Publishers, New York, 1963.

ISBN   0-15-371107-8

Contents

Contents

Drawings and Charts

Tables

Maps

Unit Illustrations

UNIT I

UNIT II

UNIT III

ARCTIC OCEAN

GREENLAND

ALASKA

ICELAND

NE

RING
RAIT

NORTH SE.

HUDSON
BAY

CANADA

UNITED
KINGDO
DE

IRELAND

BEL
FRAN

UNITED STATES
OF AMERICA

ATLANTIC OCEAN

PORTUGAL SPAIN

MOROCCO

GULF OF
MEXICO

MEXICO

SPANISH
SAHARA

ALGE

CUBA

DOMINICAN
REPUBLIC

O HAWAII

BR.
HONDURAS
GUATEMALA HONDURAS
EL SALVADOR NICARAGUA
COSTA RICA

HAITI
JAMAICA

PUERTO RICO

MAURITANIA

MALI

SENEGAL
GAMBIA

UPPER
VOLTA

CARIBBEAN SEA

PACIFIC OCEAN

TRINIDAD & TOBAGO

GUYANA

PANAMA

VENEZUELA

SURINAM
FRENCH GUIANA

SIERRA LEONE
GUINEA

IVORY
COAST

LIBERIA

DA
TOGO

COLOMBIA

GHANA

ECUADOR

GULF
GUIN

PERU

BRAZIL

BOLIVIA

PARAGUAY

CHILE

URUGUAY

ARGENTINA

TIERRA
DEL FUEGO

ANTARCTIC OCEAN

UNIT 1

The Study of Man

An Introduction to Anthropology

The world in which man lives holds
countless wonders for him to contemplate
and to try to understand. Yet perhaps the
most remarkable creation in this world is
man himself. Anthropology is the study of
man. It examines man both as a creature of
nature and as a creator of culture. It is
concerned with human evolution in the
distant past, with men living in the present,
and with mankind's future. It considers of
equal importance the ways of peoples living
in the uncharted jungles of mountainous
New Guinea and the ways of peoples living
in populous and technologically advanced
nations.

This unit provides an introduction to
anthropology. It defines the scope of our
study; it introduces the concept of culture,
which is central to anthropological
thinking; and it introduces other terms
and concepts that are essential to an inquiry
into human nature and human culture.

1

Chapter **1**

The Scope and Nature of Anthropology

A man is sitting quietly concealed behind thick tropical brushes on a jungle floor in Thailand. He moves only to make adjustments on the apparatus—microphones and high-fidelity recording unit—that he has set up to record the sounds made by gibbons in their tree abodes and at their feeding places. The man wishes to record and to classify the calls of gibbons according to the emotions they express. What is his business? He is an anthropologist.

A group of men and women are busily engaged in clearing layers of collected debris off a mound of earth. Their work is slow and methodical. Suddenly, all look up at the sound of a spade striking stone. Are these men and women about to uncover an Arab village of the eighteenth century? Roman fortifications built to defend an outlying area of the ancient Roman Empire? a site hitherto known only from occasional mention in the prophetic books of the Old Testament? Only time will

tell—time and a great deal of systematic effort by the group of anthropologists involved.

Seated among a group of villagers who appear by manner and dress to belong to an age long past is a man quite obviously of the twentieth century. He is speaking with the people around him and at intervals appears to be taking notes on the conversation in progress. Occasionally he asks someone to repeat his remarks more slowly and proceeds to record the person's words verbatim. What is the man doing? He, too, is an anthropologist, engaged in obtaining the most accurate description possible of the lifeway of a people remote from modern civilization.

If people following such diverse occupations may all be termed anthropologists, what then is anthropology? The word itself may provide the best answer. "Anthropology" derives from two Greek words: *anthrōpos*, meaning "man," and *logos*, meaning "word" or "account." **Anthropology** may be simply but effectively defined as the study of man. Since anthropologists study mankind from two basic points of view, the biological and the cultural, two main branches of anthropology are recognized: physical anthropology and cultural anthropology.

Physical Anthropology

Physical anthropology may be defined as that branch of anthropology which is concerned with human evolution and physical variation. All scientists today agree that man is a member of the animal kingdom. Not only does man closely resemble other members of the order of primates to which he himself belongs—the gorillas, chimpanzees, other apes, and monkeys—but he shares basic anatomical features with such diversified animal species as cats, frogs, and sparrows.

The whale's flipper, the bird's wing, and the human arm may seem to have very little in common. Yet the evidence of science shows them to be closely related structurally, suggesting that they are all derived from a common ancestral form. Even more striking are the resemblances between man and the other primates. Anthropologists have devoted a great deal of effort to comparing the fossils of early man with the body structures of these other primates. Using the fossil record —incomplete as it is—anthropologists speculate about the appearance of man's early ancestors and about the evolutionary process that led to the development of modern man.

But physical anthropologists are concerned with more than just man's place in the scheme of biological evolution. Of equal interest to them are variations in the physical appearance of different groups of people. According to certain inherited physical traits —including hair and skin color, and the shape of the skull—early anthropologists classified mankind into a number of racial groups. Modern anthropologists are less interested in giving names to racial groups than in discovering what accounts for the physical differences among peoples. This leads modern anthropologists to study carefully both the fundamental processes involved in human heredity and the adjustments the human body makes to different environmental and dietary conditions. Recognizing that there are physical variations among men, anthropologists stress the relative unimportance of these differences when compared to the overall likeness of mankind.

Cultural Anthropology

Cultural anthropology is the study of human culture and its development. The term "culture" refers to the whole of mankind's learned behavior. It includes in its meaning how people act, what they say and think, and everything they make either with their hands or by means of machines. You may have heard "culture" used in everyday speech to mean refinement. People who are well educated or sensitive in taste are often spoken of as being "cultured." Anthropologists use the term "culture" in a much broader sense; to them all that man learns from the moment of his birth and most of man's actions during the course of his lifetime constitute learned behavior, or "culture." All men possess culture, although the cultures of whole groups of people often differ strikingly from each other. The possession of culture is the distinct mark of being human.

Cultural anthropology studies such widely varying human activities as the performance of religious rituals, the making of tools, and the telling of humorous tales. So broad is the field of cultural anthropology, in fact, that it has become divided into several specialized areas of study.

Linguistics

One of the most important aspects of any culture is its language. The possession of language is common to all human groups. The handing down of information from father to son, from teacher to student, from generation to generation, cannot well be imagined without the use of language, whether spoken or recorded by some system of writing. The scientific study of language in its various aspects is called **linguistics**.

Archaeology

The reconstruction of a past way of life through the careful study of its remains is the goal of **archaeology**. The cultures of prehistoric and historic peoples fall within the scope of archaeology. Most often the archaeologist must depend upon mute material evidence—buildings and monuments or objects dug up from the ground—in his reconstruction of a past culture. But some early cultures have been studied with the aid of their written records. Sumerian clay tablets, Egyptian papyrus scrolls, and runic in-

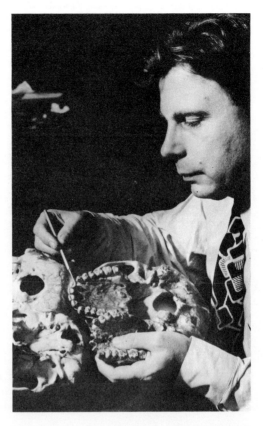

The physical anthropologist learns through the careful observation of anatomical details. This anthropologist is pointing to a gap between teeth that is characteristic of apes but absent in modern man. The skull he holds belongs to an early man discovered in Java.

scriptions on stone all enhance our knowledge of the early cultures with which they were associated. The archaeologist who can supplement the materials he digs up from the ground with information gleaned from the written records of a culture is working in the field of **classical archaeology**. The archaeologist who must reconstruct a past way of life through the evidence of material remains only is working in the field of **prehistoric archaeology**.

Ethnology and Ethnography

The study of the behavior of different groups of people, whether small tribes numbering in the hundreds or populous nations of many millions, is the branch of cultural anthropology called **ethnology.** Ethnological work may involve either a thoroughgoing analysis of one culture over a period of time, or a comparison of several cultures. If an anthropologist is primarily concerned with describing the culture of a particular society at a particular time—generally the time of his visit to the society—he is contributing to the division of ethnology called **ethnography.** Ethnology and archaeology are closely related, archaeology being an extension of ethnology into the remote past.

Other Specialized Branches of Anthropology

Aside from the broad divisions just mentioned, anthropology embraces additional fields of special interest. Some anthropologists explore the relationships among the different religious systems of mankind, a study known as comparative religion. Other anthropologists study the folklore of different peoples—that is, the myths, legends, songs, and dances preserved by different peoples over many generations. Still other anthropologists probe into the attitudes and motivations that characterize members of different cultures. They may seek to discover, for instance, what makes some groups of people competitive and others more cooperative. This

Modern ethnographers believe that the surest way to obtain accurate information about human cultures is through firsthand information. Here, an anthropologist is gathering facts about a native tribe of Australia.

area of anthropology is known as the study of culture and personality.

From this very sketchy survey, it should be evident that few other branches of knowledge are as comprehensive as anthropology. This should come as no surprise, if one keeps in mind the fact that anthropology ranges over a many-sided topic —man and his works.

The Relationship of Anthropology to Other Branches of Knowledge

The broad scope of anthropology requires the support of many specialized fields of knowledge. In order to place human development properly within the entire scheme of biological evolution, the anthropologist must have some knowledge of zoology. **Zoology** is the science that treats of the animal kingdom. The anthropologist also needs to be familiar with the sciences of **anatomy**, the study of the structures of organisms, and **physiology,** the study of how animals and plants function under varied conditions. The genetic principles underlying human heredity and physical variation are also of great importance in the study of anthropology.

In order that the anthropologist and his close associate, the archaeologist, may assign human fossil remains and excavated artifacts to a particular period of the earth's history, they must make use of the findings of geology and paleontology. **Geology** is the science that studies the history and structure of the earth. **Paleontology** is the science that studies past forms of life as preserved in fossil remains. In recent years, some dating of organic fossil remains has been done in chemical laboratories using the **carbon-14 method.** This ingenious method of gauging the past is based on the fact that all living plants and animals contain radioactive carbon 14; and that upon death these organisms decrease their content of carbon 14 at a regular, known rate. By measuring the amount of carbon 14 against the number of regular carbon atoms in a fossil organism, scientists can sometimes determine age accurately up to about 60,000 years. Other methods of dating used by anthropologists include the analysis of soil composition around archaeological sites and the estimation of the age of wood remains by reference to their rings of growth.

The cultural anthropologist, too, needs to draw on other branches of knowledge in his study of human culture. In order, for instance, to understand the dietary and medicinal uses of plants by a certain people, he should know something about the plants themselves. The anthropologist who records and analyzes the music of a particular group of people must understand musical theory and be familiar with varying forms of musical expression. And the anthropologist who seeks to understand the relationship between culture and personality must know a great deal about human psychology. The point here is a simple but essential one: a clear understanding of man's social institutions, such as the family; of his material culture, whether simple or highly technical; and of his nonmaterial preoccupations, such as his religious and political traditions, can only be achieved with the aid of several other branches of knowledge.

A tape recorder is an indispensable tool of the anthropologist dealing with people who lack a writing system. Here, an African village chief is narrating tribal legends.

Anthropology as a Science

It is not easy to classify anthropology among the conventional divisions of the sciences. The physical anthropologist, insofar as he concerns himself with human biology, is a natural scientist. The cultural anthropologist is a social scientist or a behavioral scientist. He is interested in man's social institutions and in the relationships of individuals as members of a society. And, on the basis of his findings, he hopes to be able to generalize about human behavior.

Regardless of what his special field of interest is, an anthropologist is a scientist. This statement implies that, by training and temperament, he is given to describing observable facts

concerning human behavior, to classifying these facts, to establishing connections among them, and to deriving general principles from them. A generalization based upon sufficient evidence—for example, the statement that the amount of job specialization in a society depends upon its size—not only is helpful in explaining man's past, but also may have important predictive value.

Anthropology combines both the descriptive and the historical methods. It uses the descriptive method when it studies the present means of subsistence of an African tribe or nation. At the same time, it uses the historical method when it studies past factors, such as colonization, which may have influenced this group's present source of livelihood. Just as the future course of humanity has its roots in the present, so mankind today cannot be studied intelligently without looking into the past.

The History of Anthropology

In one sense, anthropology is very old —as old as man's speculations concerning his own nature. As a science, however, anthropology is still in its youth. It is only within the last hundred years that the study of human evolution and human culture has become an academic subject in its own right. It is only within our own century that the scientific method has been applied vigorously to the study of man and his cultures.

Among the pioneers in physical anthropology were the philosopher Aristotle, the historian Herodotus, and the Hippocratic physicians, all of ancient Greece. Some two thousand years ahead of modern biology, Aristotle assigned man a natural place among the animals. Herodotus made some interesting racial observations about the inhabitants of Greece, North Africa, and Asia Minor. The physicians of the Hippocratic school of medicine pondered such matters as the effect of the natural environment upon the human body.

The study of cultures also had its beginnings among the ancients. As chronicler of the Persian Wars, Herodotus gave a great deal of attention to the customs of various peoples with whom he came in contact during his extensive travels about the ancient world. His observations were in many instances unscientific, either made secondhand or colored by prejudice. Yet his eye for the differing customs of mankind has sometimes earned him the title, "father of anthropology." The Roman poet Lucretius should also be cited in any discussion of the beginnings of anthropology. Lucretius dealt at length with the origin of society and the process of cultural development in his epic poem *On the Nature of Things*.

The study of man and his cultures suffered a long lapse from ancient times until the early modern era. Then, stimulated by the discovery of new continents inhabited by strange peoples, European interest in other cultures began to quicken. As early as the sixteenth century, a Jesuit missionary named Bernardino de Sahagún carefully recorded various customs of the Aztec Indians of conquered Mexico. Not only did Sahagún describe these customs, but he had helpers draw accompanying illustrations for his massive volumes on the Aztec way of life. During the eight-

eenth century another Jesuit, Father Lafitau, made a study of Iroquois Indian culture and contrasted it to cultures of ancient times. These studies by Sahagún and Lafitau may be considered forerunners of modern cultural anthropology.

During the eighteenth century, advances were also being made in physical anthropology. Various schemes for the classification of human races were developed. Among these was a system devised by a German scholar named Johann Friedrich Blumenbach, who classified mankind into five races on the basis of skin color and variations in skull shape.

Anthropology had taken some giant steps forward. But the greatest leap forward in anthropological study occurred during the latter half of the nineteenth century. Within a brief

The archer stringing a bow on this ancient vase discovered in the Crimea is a Scythian— a member of a warring tribe that lived north of the Black Sea in the time of Herodotus. By appearance, costume, and military preoccupation, the warrior fits almost exactly Herodotus's description of the Scythians.

The first step in the creation of an Aztec feathered mosaic was to paste feathers to a leaf of paper (left). Apprentices helped the master craftsman to prepare the paste (center). The craftsman used a bone scraper to shape the feathers into the desired mosaic pattern (right). These illustrations appear in Sahagún's massive sixteenth-century work on Aztec culture.

span of years, several major studies of various aspects of human culture were published. The authors of these studies—E. B. Tylor, Lewis Henry Morgan, and Sir James Frazer among them—might be termed the "founding fathers" of modern cultural anthropology. The publication of their works, each of which emphasized the idea that human cultures make progress, roughly coincided with the appearance of Sir Charles Darwin's classic work on biological evolution, *The Origin of Species.* The great importance of Darwin's work for anthropology was to stimulate the search for fossil evidence of early man.

As the need for intelligent understanding of man's ways the world over has become more apparent, the importance of anthropology has gained increasing recognition. The Chinese philosopher and teacher Confucius said: "Men's natures are very much alike; it is their habits that put them far apart." Twenty-five hundred years later, one is tempted to paraphrase this statement and say: "All men are very much alike; it is

their ignorance of one another that sets them apart." One may hope that the broad, unbiased view of mankind which anthropology offers may help to reduce the fears and prejudices that mark the relationships among many peoples today.

The Value of Studying Anthropology

What are the benefits to be derived from the study of anthropology? To begin with, the study of anthropology will deepen your acquaintance with man and his works. Anthropology will enable you to go beyond the relatively short span of recorded history, taking you as far back in time as the fossil and archaeological evidence permits. The study of anthropology should help you to see human development within the context of the evolutionary change that characterizes all of nature. Moreover, since anthropologists do not limit their discussion of man to a nation or a continent, you will learn about man in a variety of cultural circumstances. Nonliterate hunters and food gatherers, no less than men living in great metropolises, will become your acquaintances. The late anthropologist Clyde Kluckhohn best expressed the intellectual value of the study of anthropology when he wrote: "Anthropology holds up a great mirror to man and lets him look at himself in his infinite variety."

Applied Anthropology

The findings of anthropology may also be of immediate value. Their most common use so far has been in helping to clear up situations of misunderstanding between people of different cultural backgrounds. For example, medical workers serving a group of people who do not understand the premises of modern medicine have been significantly aided by the services of anthropologists. An anthropologist may be able to explain to such people in their own terms what a doctor is trying to accomplish by his unfamiliar actions. He may also help to make the doctor more acceptable to his patients by advising against actions that could arouse their suspicion or dislike.

As another example, not so long ago lack of anthropological advice resulted in near tragedy for the entire population of a western Pacific atoll. When the United States government decided to use Bikini Atoll for atomic bomb tests in 1946, it removed the Bikinians to the island of Rongerik without fully investigating the many problems involved in this transplantation. In their new environment, the Bikinians were soon in a hopeless situation and near to starvation. Only at this point were the services of an anthropologist familiar with the area engaged. The Bikinians, he discovered, were suffering not only from a scarcity of food but also from tribal disorganization caused by separation from their paramount chief. Worse yet, their will to survive was being undermined by their traditional belief that Rongerik had been the home of a malign spirit. On the anthropologist's recommendation, the Bikinians were eventually removed to a more suitable location. But the cost in human dignity had been high.

In recent years, more and more people throughout the world have recognized the need for better understanding of other cultures. One expression of this lies in the growing amount of travel and exchange of information among cultures. Many people feel that a better understanding of the nature of cultural differences, of the genetic and environmental bases of racial differences, and of the historical roots of modern ideological controversies is imperative if the crises facing mankind are to be solved peacefully. If understanding between cultures can breed toleration, anthropology has major contributions to make to the creation of world peace.

SUMMARY

Anthropology is the study of man and his culture. Physical anthropology deals with man from a biological point of view, and seeks to explain the nature of human evolution and physical variations. Cultural anthropology is concerned with all of man's learned behavior, or his culture. Among those who work in cultural anthropology are archaeologists, who study man's past; linguists, who study that which above all makes culture possible—human speech; and ethnologists, who study cultures throughout the world. The broad scope of anthropology makes contact with many other branches of knowledge not only fruitful but very necessary. A student may expect to benefit in many ways from the study of anthropology. Above all, he should learn from it respect for all human cultures, which are in fact but the many reflections of man in his "infinite variety."

Chapter Review

Terms in Anthropology

anatomy	cultural anthropology	paleontology
anthropology	ethnography	physical anthropology
archaeology	ethnology	physiology
carbon-14 method	geology	prehistoric archaeology
classical archaeology	linguistics	zoology

Questions for Review

1. Define "anthropology." What are the two main branches of anthropology?
2. What is the physical anthropologist interested in learning about man?
3. What is the cultural anthropologist interested in learning about man?
4. Define "linguistics." Why are languages an important concern of the cultural anthropologist?
5. What is the distinction between classical archaeology and prehistoric archaeology?
6. How is ethnology related to ethnography? What is the relationship between ethnology and archaeology?
7. What are some of the specialized branches of knowledge that assist an anthropologist in performing his work?
8. What is a "scientist"? What kind of scientist is the anthropologist?
9. What are some of the important milestones in the development of anthropology into a science?
10. How did the application of anthropological knowledge save the Bikinian people from destruction? How else do you think the study of anthropology may contribute to better understanding among peoples of the world?

Chapter **2**

The Concept of Culture

Suppose that someone described to you a society in which each member is assured of a place to live, proper nourishment, and a suitable occupation. You are told, moreover, that this society is characterized to a high degree by the division of labor. Certain members of the society provide food, shelter, and care of offspring for the whole society. Other members are responsible for the defense of the society. Does this strike you as a well-organized form of social life? Now add to this description the facts that reproduction in this society is the function of two members only and that the occupations of all members of this society are determined from birth. This should be a sufficient hint to tell you that what is being described is not a human society at all. What then is it? And how do the bases for social behavior in this society differ from those within a human society?

The Bases of Insect Behavior

What has been described above is the organization of a termite society.

This description may be taken as more or less typical of the organized life of all the social insects, including bees and ants.

A typical termite society is differentiated into several groups, or **castes,** based upon occupation. The members of the society who build and maintain the structure that houses it, attend to the young, and feed and clean all other members of the society belong to the worker caste. Members of the soldier caste provide for the defense of the society against its enemies. Among some species of termites, both worker and soldier castes may be even further differentiated. For example, the heads of some soldier termites are drawn out into a snoutlike projection from which a sticky fluid can be ejected for defensive purposes.

The reproductive function within a termite society is served solely by two members, the king and the queen. Although soldier and worker termites are of both sexes, they are incapable of producing offspring except in special circumstances. The king and the queen remain always in the royal cell, where the queen, made fertile by the king, lays eggs at the rate of several thousand a day during her lifetime of ten or more years.

What is the basis for behavior in a termite society? Insect life, even when social, is governed by **instincts**—biologically inherited patterns of complex behavior that help the members of a given species to adjust to their environment. The behavior of each of the castes within a termite society is guided by instinct. For instance, a termite soldier acts—and may even look—like a soldier from the moment it hatches. Similarly, a termite worker instinctively begins its pattern of food gathering, provision of shelter, and care of offspring. Little, if any, modification of hereditary patterns of behavior takes place within a termite society. The success of the termites and other social insects in forming and maintaining large communities is due, it is true, to highly complex instinctive behavior. But it is still instinct only.

Human Behavior and Human Society

There are obvious advantages to a society in which important tasks are performed by members who are especially equipped to deal with them. And in this respect, the life of the social insects strongly resembles human societies. But here the similarity ends. For in human societies, an individual is not born physically equipped or with an instinctive preference for a particular occupation. In human societies, an individual is generally free to choose his occupation, and does so at the beginning of adult life. It is only then that an individual receives the specialized training needed to per-

form his work. Moreover, an individual may change his occupation again and again during the course of his lifetime.

In coping with the natural environment, both human and social insect groups seem to derive their greatest effectiveness from living in societies and dividing important tasks among their membership. But there is a fundamental difference in the source of social behavior in these two types of societies. What is this difference?

Although scientists today hold varying opinions about the extent to which human actions are guided by instinct, they are at least this much in agreement: as compared with other animal species, man is remarkably free of behavior patterns that are purely instinctive, or hereditary. There are certain automatic actions, such as grasping and sucking, that may be observed in all newborn human infants. But these actions are so simple as to be called **reflexes,** rather than instincts. Moreover, their usefulness is limited to a fairly short period of time, after which they give way to socially influenced responses called forth by the circumstances into which an infant is born.

It is true that man has certain bodily needs, or **drives,** that must be satisfied if he is to survive. But one noteworthy thing about man's drives—which include hunger, thirst, and the sex urge—is the extent to which they are modified by different peoples. All men feel hunger; man must eat in order to live. Yet the manner in which hunger is satisfied varies greatly from one society to another. Food that forms the staple diet of one society may be forbidden to the members of another society, who will starve before

Moslem and Hindu soldiers in the Indian army mutinied against their British officers in 1857. The mutiny was sparked by rumor that the soldiers' rifle cartridges—which had to be held in the teeth while loading—were greased with cow and pig fat. The cow is held sacred by Hindus; the meat of pigs is prohibited to Moslems. The picture below shows Mahatma Gandhi during one of his fasts in protest against more recent British rule in India.

they violate this food prohibition. You have probably heard of cases of long fasting for religious or political reasons. The leader of India's modern struggle for independence, Mohandas (Mahatma) Gandhi, kept strict fasts for months on end in protest against British rule in India.

The point is this: man is relatively free of behavior patterns that are determined biologically, or are instinctive. Rather, practically all of man's behavior is learned after birth from other members of the society into which he is born. While the success of an insect society in maintaining itself is based upon instinct, man's

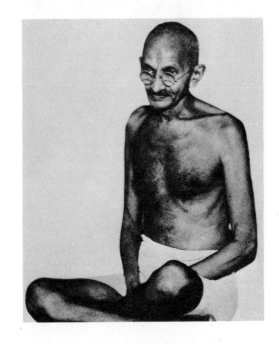

success in not only maintaining but also improving his society is based upon the human capacity to learn. While the insect is a creature of instinct, man is a creature of culture.

Culture, a Culture, Civilization

The term "culture" was earlier defined as "the whole of mankind's learned behavior." Let us now expand this definition slightly: **culture** refers to the enormous whole of learned, socially influenced behavior that has characterized mankind during the entire course of its history. A further distinction, that between culture in general and "a culture" in particular, now becomes necessary. **A culture** refers to the traditional ways of doing things in a particular society—that of the Navaho people, for example. The difference between "culture" and "a culture" is the difference between a general concept, such as automobile, and a specific example thereof, Thunderbird.

Anthropologists make very common use of the terms "culture" and "a culture." They make use also of an important term borrowed from history. In history, the term **civilization** is customarily used to describe a particular stage in the cultural development of a society. This stage is generally marked by the keeping of written records, the building of large cities, and the use of advanced techniques in agriculture, industry, and the arts. You may have heard the term "civilization" used to suggest that a culture is superior in quality to other cultures. For the most part, anthropologists are reluctant to judge cultures qualitatively. Rather, they measure a culture in terms of how well it satisfies the particular needs of the society. Anthropologists tend, therefore, either to apply the terms "culture" and "civilization" synonymously, or to use the term "civilization" to refer to cultures that have attained a high degree of complexity.

Some Other Definitions of Culture

There are many definitions of culture. Some appear to differ so greatly from others that you may well wonder whether any reasonable agreement exists as to what culture really is. However, a brief survey of the major types

Acquiring the skills necessary for harvesting cacao is an important aspect of the cultural training of these two young African boys. They belong to a West African society whose subsistence is based on farming.

The process of acquiring culture may be expanded in the classroom. These young American schoolchildren are just beginning the formal education that will prepare them for adult life in their complex society.

of definitions of culture will show that their differences lie in emphasis rather than in substance.

Some definitions of culture attempt to list its most representative parts. They are usually influenced by the classical definition of culture made in 1871 by E. B. Tylor: "Culture, or civilization . . . is that complex whole which includes knowledge, belief, art, morals, custom, and any other capabilities and habits acquired by man as a member of society." One could add to this list political organization, material objects of human manufacture, language, religion, and many other characteristics that distinguish one society of men from another. However, to attempt to define culture by listing all of its component parts

would be an impossible task.

Another group of definitions stresses the fact that most cultural habits are handed down from generation to generation. A good, representative definition of this type comes from Clyde Kluckhohn: "By 'culture' anthropology means the total life way of a people, the social legacy the individual acquires from his group."

Still other definitions emphasize various aspects of culture: a particular culture represents a specific solution of man's efforts to adjust to his natural environment and to fulfill his basic needs; a culture consists of all that one learns from other members of one's society; culture is all that has been created or conceived of by man as a member of society; culture is that characteristic of man that separates him from all other animals.

No one of these definitions is necessarily better than the others. Taken together, they suggest the complexity of what the anthropologist refers to simply as "culture."

Culture as a Mold

The definition of culture used throughout this study stresses the fact that culture is learned behavior, influenced by the society to which one belongs. All newborn infants are, in fact, natural heirs to a particular cultural heritage—that of their family and their society. The language in which a child is talked to and which he progressively learns is an important part of this heritage. So are the material objects which the child learns to handle, such as toys and utensils. And so are the songs, tales, dances, and rituals that the child learns from the adult members of his society.

Let us assume that a newborn boy of white, French-speaking parents is left in the care of a Yagua couple. (The Yagua are Indians who live in the Amazon region of northeastern Peru.) What would be the way of life of this boy if he grew up among the Yagua people, uninfluenced by his own parents' culture? His clothing would consist of a bandlike headgear, a long neckpiece, a skirt, armbands, knee bands, and bracelets, all made from the dyed fibers of a native palm tree. He would carry a decorated walking stick and wear a necklace made of the claws or teeth of a jaguar, if he had killed one himself. His staple food, meat, would be obtained from the animals native to the area—deer, monkeys, wild turkeys, bats, and certain types of lizards. He would consider as great delicacies the meat of giant anteaters, turtle eggs, hummingbirds, and certain kinds of ants cooked in honey.

The boy would become very skillful in the use of blowgun and spear in hunting. He would also learn to set a variety of snares, traps, pitfalls, and deadfalls to secure game. During festivals, he would consume large quantities of a fermented drink made from manioc root that had been thoroughly chewed by the old women of the group in order to bring about fermentation. Occasionally, he would start a fire by means of sparks from flint stone. He would be proficient in playing a simple flutelike instrument or a panpipe, which is a kind of harmonica. By the age of sixteen, he would probably have married and perhaps have already fathered children. Naturally, his native language would be Yagua.

In only one respect would this boy be different from other Yagua tribesmen. He would have inherited his physical features from his biological parents and consequently would be recognizable among the Yagua people by such minor characteristics as the shape of his cheeks and the form of his upper eyelids. Culturally, he would be a Yagua. And similarly, had the same boy been reared among the Hottentot people of South Africa, he would have become culturally, although not physically, a Hottentot.

Although cases of the above kind are rare, we are all aware of how little time it takes for immigrants to the United States to become "Americanized." The often-used term "melting pot" essentially refers to this molding influence of American culture upon the people who live in it. Nor is the molding process peculiar to American culture. All cultures, from the simplest to the most complex, exert profound influences upon the people who possess or adopt them.

Cultures Are Dynamic

A common pitfall awaiting those who try to describe a culture is to create the impression that the culture is fixed and unchanging. Nothing could be farther from the truth; all cultures are dynamic. The rate of cultural change may vary from one society to another, or from one institution within a society to the next, but no culture stands still.

Complex and technologically advanced societies often undergo change so rapidly that the effects are readily apparent not only from generation to generation, but even within the space of a decade. As one example, within only a few years the spread of television in the United States profoundly changed the manner in which Americans spend their free evening hours. It also affected the daily activities of a large number of American children. A good index of the newly emerging elements in any culture is the language. Who, fifteen years ago, had ever heard of an "astronaut," a "miniskirt," or a "teaching machine"?

Cultural change proceeds at a much slower pace in societies that are only slightly affected by new technological developments. Nevertheless, change in such societies does take place, even if it goes largely unnoticed. In all societies, certain aspects of culture tend to resist change more than others. Religion is a good example of those aspects of human culture that are largely resistant to change.

The process by which a society undergoes cultural change as a result of prolonged contact with another culture is known as **acculturation.** "Acculturation" may describe a case where two cultures mutually exert influence upon each other. Or it may describe a case in which one culture has a strong impact on another, without experiencing any adjustment of its own cultural patterns. At the present time, many societies throughout the world are undergoing profound modification through prolonged contact with more technologically advanced societies. The study of acculturation, as a result, is gaining importance among students of cultural anthropology.

This Yagua boy is identifiable by his bandlike headgear, his palm fiber skirt and armbands, and the painted markings on his face. Yagua boys of this age are already skilled at hunting and setting snares.

Populous India can only benefit from the use of tractors and other Western farm machinery to increase its agricultural output. This kind of cultural influence—which benefits a nation's economy—is an example of the good effects of acculturation.

Ethnocentric Attitude

People brought up to act, talk, and think in certain ways often come to feel that their way of behaving is the only natural and sound one. Such people might find themselves in difficulty arguing with an anthropologist. Eating honey, a material elaborated out of the nectar of flowers in the stomachs of bees, seems reasonable enough to most Americans. They learn to do so in early childhood. Likewise, Americans eat hen's eggs in many forms and could hardly imagine a diet without them. There is thus no logical reason why the American diet should not include ant eggs. Yet most Americans do not eat ant eggs and consider them repugnant as food. On the other hand, there are groups of people who eat ant eggs as a matter of course. And there are peoples who do not eat hen's eggs or, if they do, prefer to eat them rotten. From the point of view of the anthropologist, no one taste can be judged better than any other.

Closely associated with the feeling that one's own ways and values are eminently reasonable is the notion, present to some extent in all societies, that other peoples tend to behave in a childlike or even a contemptible manner. This tendency to look upon other cultures with disfavor and to consider one's own culture inherently superior is termed an ethnocentric attitude, or **ethnocentrism.**

The ancient Greeks, in their cultural conceit, divided all of mankind into two groups—Greeks and barbarians. Among the barbarians, whose name was derived from the Greek *barbaros,* meaning "foreign, rude, ignorant," they included the Romans. The Eskimo people refer to themselves by the term *Innuit,* which means "the people" and carries the connotation of uniqueness and superiority.

The Cherokee Indians of the Great Smoky Mountains have a myth by which they explain the origin of the human races. In the beginning, the myth relates, the Creator fashioned three human forms from a doughlike material and placed them in an oven. The form removed from the oven first was underdone but served well enough as the ancestor of the white people. The form that was well timed and richly browned gave descent to the Cherokees. Admiring this perfect form, the Creator forgot about the third form until he smelled it burning. This overdone form became the ancestor of the Negro people.

Many Americans are ethnocentric. Some Americans, when traveling in foreign countries, find other cultures lacking in the things they are used to. For example, they may complain loudly about the local food or the plumbing standards. Yet these same people tend to be impatient when anyone visiting the United States is less than enthusiastic about American ways of living. The proper way to judge another culture is by trying to find out how well it serves the people who live in it.

History has demonstrated often enough that there is great potential danger when any nation or people feels superior to any other. A feeling of ethnic superiority may become the first step in justifying treatment of others that is not in accordance with the full respect due all human beings.

Ethnic Appreciation

The argument that ethnocentrism may be useful inasmuch as it promotes patriotism rests on a false assumption: that in order for one to love his own country, he must dislike other countries and their peoples. It is indeed necessary that members of any society have respect for its institutions. Such an attitude of **ethnic appreciation** is necessary if the society is to continue and prosper. But respect for one's own way of life should not come at the expense of disdain for other cultures. Nor should it blind one to faults in need of correction within one's own society. An honest attitude of ethnic appreciation will not harbor such mistaken "patriotism."

SUMMARY

The term "culture" refers to the enormous whole of learned, socially influenced behavior that has characterized mankind from earliest times to the present. Culture depends upon man's capacity to learn, to accumulate knowledge, and to transmit this knowledge to succeeding generations. Culture provides the common bonds by which human societies, as opposed to the societies of other animals, are held together.

Although the possession of culture characterizes mankind as a whole, cultures vary from one human society to another. The fact that people generally see the world through glasses tinted with the preferences and prejudices of their own culture results in only partial and fragmented appreciation of all of mankind's accomplishments. Appreciation of one's own cultural heritage should provide only the starting point in any attempt to really comprehend the meaning of being human.

Chapter Review

Terms in Anthropology

acculturation	culture	ethnocentrism
a culture	drive	instinct
caste	ethnic appreciation	reflex
civilization		

Questions for Review

1. What is the fundamental difference between a termite society and a society of men?
2. What role does instinct play in determining the behavior of the social insects? of man?
3. What examples does this chapter give of how man's basic drives may be modified by culture? What examples can you think of to illustrate the modification of human drives?
4. Why do anthropologists find it necessary to distinguish between "culture" and "a culture"?
5. How is the term "civilization" used in anthropology?
6. What is indicated by the fact that there are so many different definitions of the term "culture"?
7. How does this chapter illustrate the powerful hold a culture may exert over the members of a society?
8. What do anthropologists mean when they assert that cultures are dynamic?
9. Define "acculturation." What examples of the process of acculturation can you cite from American history?
10. How do the attitudes of ethnocentrism and ethnic appreciation appear alike? How do they in fact differ? Provide examples of each from American society.

Chapter **3**

Studying Cultures

The general concept of culture may be defined in a sentence or a short paragraph, but the analysis of a particular culture requires very careful study. When studying a particular culture, one must remember that the culture which members of any society share consists of far more than the observable behavior associated with their economic pursuits, ritual and family life, or leisure-time activities. Behind the choices that humans must constantly make in the ever-changing variety of circumstances there is a complex system of rules or standards. These rules or standards must be followed, unless one is to stand out from the group as an odd and ill-fitting individual. These rules are applied largely on a subconscious level, in much the same way that one uses his native language without consciously thinking about it. The similarity is so striking, that many modern anthropologists have compared the analysis and description of a culture to the analysis and description of a language.

Besides the difficult task of getting "inside the heads" of the people one studies, other problems face the students of man. Just as any individual is a member of a society into which he was born or which he subsequently adopts as his own, all societies belong to one vast community of mankind. And just as individual members of a society meet and interact, so do various human groups come into contact, directly or indirectly, and through this contact modify or change each other's cultures.

The study of cultures and societies on a worldwide scale poses a number of basic questions. What are some of the kinds of social and political units into which mankind is organized? What are some of the reasons for cultural similarity other than direct culture contact? And how does an anthropologist look at those peoples whose humble way of life has earned them the disparaging label "primitive"? These and other questions will be discussed in this chapter.

Human Units of Common Bonds

Unlike political states with recognized boundaries, cultures are not always well defined geographically. One distinct culture may blend with another by slight, scarcely perceptible degrees. Nevertheless, man's need to form and maintain bonds with other men on various levels of complexity provides the anthropologist with the criteria to study cultures.

Territorial, or geographical, units provide the most common basis for human social and political organization. Beginning at the bottom of the organizational pyramid, the basic territorial unit is the **household,** consisting of a family group of varying size. Anthropologists further distinguish between two basic types of households, the sedentary and the nomadic.

Whenever some hundred or more people are settled as a group, anthropologists speak of a **village.** Still larger units of concentrated population are customarily termed **towns** or **cities.** To an anthropologist, the difference between a village and a town or city is not so much due to the number of inhabitants as to the influence exercised in a given area by reason of political power or market facilities.

A group of wandering people comparable in size to a village make up a **band.** The Crow Indians of the American Great Plains were organized into several bands, each one politically independent of the others. However, the Crows recognized their unity as one people by virtue of kinship bonds and a common culture and language. A similar relationship today characterizes some of the wandering peoples of Saharan Africa.

When a number of bands or villages share a common territory, language, and culture, they are usually referred to as a **tribe.** Several tribes loosely joined together, either for mutual protection or for aggressive purposes, form a **league** or **confederacy.** A good example of such an alliance in North America was the league of the Iroquois tribes, who inhabited what is now the central portion of the state of New York. Similarly, when the United States was formed, it operated as a league of semi-independent states joined under the Articles of Confederation.

Society, Nation, and Ethnic Group

It is necessary now to draw some distinctions between the major units of human social and political organization, both of which are commonly based upon territorial groupings of mankind. When a group of people, regardless of size, share a common culture and a sense of common identity, they are referred to as a **society.** The term "society" describes not only the group but also the system of interpersonal relationships among its members. A band, a village, a tribe, or a large nation may constitute a society. It is equally appropriate to speak of "Yagua society" and of "American society," disregarding the differences in size and complexity between the two. While societies function within territorial units, it is possible for a society to exist even when its parts are geographically removed from each other. An example of this is modern Pakistani society, whose membership is divided between East and West Pakistan.

A tribe or a people organized into a relatively sizable and complex society may be termed a **nation.** More characteristic of a nation than a common racial or cultural background is, however, the existence of a central government operating over a well-defined territory. It is possible for a nation to include people of very different cultural backgrounds speaking different languages. This is especially true of nations superimposed by force on existing societies and of many of the newly independent nations of the world, whose boundaries often were artificially created by the ruling colonial powers of the nineteenth century. Such nations may eventually become well-integrated societies, or they may be rent apart by conflicting pressures from within.

A term used rather loosely by anthropologists to designate a human group identifiable either racially or culturally, or both, is **ethnic group.** A number of ethnic groups have preserved their identity over several centuries without actually living together as one people sharing one government. A good example is the Armenian people, who are distinctly recognizable as a cultural group but have lacked independent national status since the early centuries of the Christian era. Another example is the Lapps, a reindeer-herding people whose cultural traditions vary little throughout the several nations they inhabit—Norway, Sweden, Finland, and the Soviet Union.

Persian rugs are a good index to the subcultures within Iranian society. Each of the several tribes of Iran possesses traditional rug patterns that are easily recognizable.

Analyzing Cultures

The relationship between society and culture has been defined from two different standpoints in this book. "Society" was defined as a group of people sharing a common culture and a sense of common identity. "Culture" has been defined both as the whole of mankind's learned, socially influenced behavior (culture in general), and as the traditional ways of doing things in a particular society ("a culture"). We are now ready to see how anthropologists proceed in their analysis of cultures.

Societies, particularly large ones, usually consist of various groups of people sharing different regional, economic, religious, or other interests. Whenever any group within a society develops interests sufficiently different as to be distinct from the overall cultural pattern, anthropologists speak of a **subculture.** A good example of a regional subculture in the United States is the South, which has retained over the years some distinctive patterns of speech, behavior, and belief. Another subculture in the United States today is that of teen-agers, who, since World War II, have grown both in influence and in identity. Since generalizations about so vast a society as the United States may easily become vague, if not completely meaningless, the more specific concept of the subculture is valuable to anthropologists.

Another concept useful to anthropologists in analyzing cultures is that of the culture trait. Any single characteristic of a culture, such as a pattern of behavior or typical object in use, is referred to as a **culture trait.** Eating with chopsticks is one culture trait, using a knife and fork another, and scooping food with a tortilla still another. Each of these traits helps to characterize the eating habits of a different group of people. For a waiter to set a glass of water in front of a patron before he orders his meal is a trait typical of the United States but is not a custom in European countries. Throwing rice over a newly wed couple is also an American culture trait, as is the bride's tossing her bouquet among the unmarried girls present. Elsewhere, marriage customs differ. For instance, in some countries to be married on a rainy day is considered a good rather than a bad omen. Culture traits may be described in terms of several aspects, including their form, their function, and their meaning. All the culture traits exhibited within a society help to make up the total culture.

A number of closely related culture traits centering around a particular interest shared by certain members of a society is termed a **culture complex,** or a **trait-complex.** Camping during summer vacation, an amusement which is gaining rapidly in popularity among Americans, is an example of a culture complex. The many traits associated with camping include an increased variety of camping equipment, the development of many new camp grounds in national parks or other scenic areas, and a growing attitude that camping is a good way to develop both self-reliance and a greater appreciation of nature. Another culture complex involving many young Americans surrounds the sport of surfing. Among the traits that characterize this complex are the skills involved in surfing, the necessary equipment, and a special vocabulary.

In analyzing cultures, anthropologists go beyond the description of cultural patterns that characterize a particular society. "Culture" was earlier defined, in one sense, as the adjustment a society makes to its natural environment. Whenever several neighboring societies have made similar adjustments, thereby sharing a number of trait-complexes in common, anthropologists speak of a **culture area.** Many such culture areas exist in the world today.

A culture area that formerly existed on the North American continent was the vast territory inhabited by the Plains Indians tribes. This culture area, which extended roughly from the Mississippi River to the Rocky Mountains, became home to over a score of nomadic tribes in the centuries after the Spaniards introduced the horse on the North American continent. All of the Plains Indian tribes hunted the buffalo for meat and skins, lived for the most part in large conical tents called "tepees," valued personal bravery highly, and performed an elaborate annual religious rite known as the sun dance. Because the various Plains Indian

The Algerian Bedouin (above) and the Moroccan shepherd (below) have similar ways of life. Both have chosen sheep raising as the best means of supporting themselves in their harsh desert environment. Moreover, both speak Arabic and belong to the Moslem religion. Because they—and their societies—share many important cultural patterns, anthropologists describe them as belonging to the same culture area.

tribes held these trait-complexes in common, they are spoken of as belonging to the same culture area.

The Concept of the Ethnographic Present

One of the consequences of the growth and expansion of many large nations during the past few centuries has been the disappearance or total assimilation of small tribes of people who stood in the way of expanding populations. Hundreds of small societies with distinctive cultures and languages of their own have disappeared. What we know about these societies is based upon the incomplete, and frequently biased, reports of explorers

and settlers who first encountered these peoples, missionaries who endeavored to convert them to Christianity, and colonial administrators who were assigned to deal with them.

Anthropologists are anxious to learn what the cultures of such peoples were like before they either disappeared completely or underwent profound changes as a result of the pressures put upon them. In these efforts, anthropologists seek not only to learn more about man's ways in the past but also to gain understanding of the processes of cultural change, in particular that of acculturation.

Today, acculturation is taking place on every major continent, and especially wherever primarily agricultural societies are experiencing the powerful impact of Western technological civilization. In Alaska, the Eskimos must learn to adjust to increasing numbers of settlers and their different ways. In Africa, the leaders of many newly independent nations emulate Western civilization in their efforts to reduce tribalism and promote national unity.

The United States has witnessed the disappearance of many of the original Indian societies of North America. Our knowledge of their cultures is based upon what was learned over several centuries of contact with them. Even when speaking of Indian cultures still in existence, anthropologists may describe them as they existed at some time in the past. For instance, when anthropologists speak of the aboriginal, or native, cultures of the various Algonquian tribes of southern New England, they are describing them as they existed during the seventeenth century; when they refer to the Plains Indian cultures,

they are describing a way of life that was at its height during the first half of the nineteenth century.

When anthropologists refer to the cultures of such societies as though they were still fully functioning, although the conditions described are those of a former period, they are making use of a time reference known as the **ethnographic present.**

Inventions and Diffusion

The fact that man has been able to adjust successfully to a wide variety of environmental conditions, ranging from frigid Arctic wastes to the scorching deserts of Australia's interior, is an eloquent testimony to his inventiveness. How has man been able to do this? One example is provided by the Eskimos, who for centuries have used frozen skins for sled runners whenever more suitable material was unavailable. At times, the Eskimos have actually doubled the usefulness of these runners by rolling up fish or other raw meat into the skins before freezing them. When no longer needed for runners, the skins were thawed and fed to the sled dogs, the meat consumed by the masters.

Another example of keen inventiveness is provided by the natives of central Australia, who because of the stark simplicity of their material culture are frequently referred to as contemporary "Stone Age people." Yet these people have survived occasional droughts when no water was available by the ingenious method of digging up bushes or small trees and burning the leafy parts to release sap from the roots.

Human culture may be looked

This house built from the scrap materials of modern industrial civilization is a good example of human inventiveness. Its owner has at least provided himself with shelter from wind and rain.

upon as an accumulation of **basic inventions,** or inventions that involve the application of new principles, and of **secondary inventions,** which derive from the basic principles. The bow, the wheel, and the harnessing of atomic energy are examples of basic inventions. The catapult, the cart with wooden-disk wheels, and radio-cobalt treatment of disease are all secondary inventions, based upon the primary innovations just mentioned.

The study of history reveals that quite frequently similar inventions have been made independently in widely separated parts of the world. For example, the concept of zero appears to have been invented at least twice, once by the Maya Indians of Central America and once by Hindu scholars of India. Systems of writing have also been invented at least twice, first in the Near East and later among the Mayas. Such parallel inventions by groups not in contact with one another are instances of **independent invention.**

While parallel inventions of similar objects and concepts do occur, it is the spread of useful inventions and ideas from one group to another that is primarily responsible for the modification of a society's culture, or **cultural change.** Yet it may come as a surprise to most Americans that many of the objects with which they come into daily contact, such as cotton, linen, wool, pajamas, beds, chairs, shoes, ties, glass, paper, soap, coins, pottery, knives, and hundreds of others, are of ancient and widely diffuse origin. The migration and borrowing of culture traits, whether they be tools, manufacturing processes, or ideas, is referred to as **diffusion.**

As we study the cultural record of mankind, we are reminded that Western civilization is a product of innumerable inventions contributed over thousands of years by peoples from all over the world. Moreover, one can show that the nature and complexity of any civilization relates to historical and environmental circumstances rather than to some inborn endowment which a population may claim to possess. Thus, the Aztec, the Hopi, and the Ute Indians differed in their cultural achievement, although they descended from the same parent group and only later migrated to their historical locations.

Following the example of their new neighbors, the Aztec people developed such a highly advanced civilization that Cortés termed their capital in the Valley of Mexico "the Venice of the New World." While in their Southwestern pueblos, the Hopis developed a peaceful and sedentary culture. And the Utes, under the stimulus of the adjacent Plains Indians, changed from simple hunters and gatherers to skillful horsemen who hunted buffalo and raided their neighbors. Today, any group of people can bridge the cultural distance from the bush to the jet age within one generation, if the necessary educational and economic means are available.

Over the last two million years, an unbroken series of changes has brought man's culture from the simplicity of pebble tools and hammerstones to the awe-inspiring complexity of journeys to the moon. To be sure,

in early prehistoric times changes occurred slowly. Then, some ten thousand years ago, the first major revolution in the history of human culture took place—the domestication of plants and animals and the subsequent rise of the first cities. About five thousand years later, the second revolutionary breakthrough in man's cultural development came—the invention of writing. Since then the pace of change has been steadily quickening until it now proceeds at a staggering rate. And because modern communications and transportation have brought all parts of the globe into virtually instant contact, changes occurring anywhere become subject to potential adoption everywhere.

But this enormous scope and rate of cultural contact and change quite frequently results in friction or conflict. This friction develops not only between societies but also among the various segments within a single society. In the United States one acknowledges this conflict whenever one speaks of the generation gap, or the failure of various population groups to share fairly in the country's wealth. The problems are just as pressing on the international scene, particularly in those countries which are attempting to become modern industrial nations within just a few decades.

Toward the Study of Complex Societies

We have seen that the rate of cultural change today is enormous. And because the study of man is one of the important concerns of Western culture, we might expect that anthropology would also be subject to change. This is indeed the case, and a shift over the past several decades has been noticeable. The time when the term "anthropology" stood for the study of the exotic is largely gone. This change partly reflects the fact that the forces of modernization have been so strong and widespread that even tribal peoples isolated for thousands of years have not been able to escape them. Moreover, anthropologists have come to realize that a comprehensive study of man must not exclude a large part of the world population which has long been living in the backyard of industrial centers —the peasants.

The late anthropologist A. L. Kroeber defined **peasantry** as constituting part-societies with part-cultures. According to him, peasants are "definitely rural—yet live in relation to market towns; they form a class segment of a larger population which usually contains also urban centers, sometimes metropolitan capitals. . . . They lack the isolation, the political autonomy, and the self-sufficiency of tribal populations; but their local units retain much of their old identity, integration, and attachment to soil and cults." Traditional peasant economies are important in most of those new nations which are presently beginning intensive industrialization. A better understanding of peasant lifestyles should help smooth their transition into the modern world.

Anthropologists are also beginning to study the urban scene. The study of contemporary American society, with its varied ethnic minorities and its sprawling urban centers, is only in its beginnings. Here, the anthropologist can contribute to the other concerned social scientists his broadly comparative and cross-cultural approach.

However, the most important prospect of **urban anthropology,** or the study of ethnic minorities and their life-styles in urban areas, is that the causes of the deterioration of the social and natural environment may be identified. And measures may be undertaken to restore man's well-being.

The Concept of "Primitive" in Anthropology

It is likely that the term "primitive" will continue to be applied to peoples whose economy is based upon hunting and food gathering or, more broadly, to peoples whose cultures appear relatively uncomplex when compared with those of advanced technological societies. But one should at least be aware of what the term "primitive" does not and should not imply when used in anthropology.

The term "primitive," if used to describe any recent human group, should not imply a lower stage of mental development and, consequently, inborn inferiority. This is one of the worst abuses of the term. It has been shown repeatedly that the mentality of so-called "primitive" men does not differ substantially from that of men who call themselves "civilized." Cases of individuals from the humblest cultural backgrounds who have learned to perform tasks characteristic of advanced technological societies are so numerous as to leave no doubt concerning this point.

Accordingly, anthropologists avoid the use of such terms as "primitive," "savage," and "backward" to describe peoples whose cultures are not highly advanced in a technological sense. Since many of these peoples do not make use of a writing system, some anthropologists use the term "nonliterate" to describe their cultures. **Nonliterate,** as opposed to "illiterate," suggests the lack of a writing system rather than the failure to learn to read and write in a society where literacy is the norm. Since many nonliterate peoples are rapidly becoming literate, even this term should be used only with the greatest care.

The Concept of "Race"

The term "race" has in popular usage acquired so many different meanings that it has become one of the most widely misunderstood words in the English language. Expressions such as "French race," "white race," "Jewish race," "Islamic race," "Slavic race," and "Aryan race" are good examples of the indiscriminate use of the term to describe national, biological, religious, linguistic, and even mythical groupings. Since for many people the term "race" is tinged with prejudice or favoritism, such careless employment of this term can easily lead to abuses.

Anthropologists have been using the term **race** to describe biological groupings only. Traditional classifications have been based upon certain physical traits held in common. Quite recently, anthropologists have begun moving toward a conception of "races" as breeding populations more or less isolated from each other genetically. But even this more flexible view of race is now being questioned. There is a noticeable increase in the mobility of individuals the world over—marriage

patterns are rapidly changing and large-scale migrations of population groups occur, whether occasioned by wars, economic pressures, or other factors. As a result, the concept of race as a distinct human type may be more and more difficult to apply. The question inevitably arises as to whether the concept of race has any real validity—that is, is it useful to classify and reclassify mankind in the first place?

However anthropologists may define "race," they agree that its only proper use is in a biological sense. A further discussion of the uses and abuses of this term will follow in Chapter 8, "The Races of Mankind" on page 89.

SUMMARY

The terms "culture" and "society," when used generally, present no special difficulties. But for the discussion of particular human groups and their cultural characteristics, the anthropologist must employ a variety of additional terms and concepts. Some of these, dealing with the various levels of social complexity and with processes contributing to cultural change, belong to the basic vocabulary of anthropology.

Just as any vital field of inquiry, anthropology has been undergoing changes in direction and emphasis. As a result, the study of peasantry began to claim a significant portion of the anthropologist's interest. More recently still, the social problems of complex societies, and of urban areas in particular, are being studied by younger anthropologists.

Two concepts associated with

human groups require special explanation. The concept of "primitive" as applied to recent human societies and cultures is shunned by most modern anthropologists as misleading. Equally misused is the term "race," which anthropologists urge be used for biological groupings of mankind only.

Chapter Review

Terms in Anthropology

band	ethnic group	secondary invention
basic invention	ethnographic present	society
city	household	subculture
confederacy	independent invention	town
cultural change	league	tribe
culture area	nation	urban anthropology
culture complex	nonliterate	village
culture trait	peasantry	
diffusion	race	

Questions for Review

1. Distinguish between a tribe, a society, a nation, and an ethnic group. What are some examples of each? Can you think of a human group which is an example of several of these categories?
2. Why is the concept of the subculture useful in describing complex societies? What characteristics of teen-agers do you think warrant calling them a subculture within American society?
3. Why may one expect a "generation gap" to develop during a period of rapid cultural change?
4. What are some of the subcultures in American society and what are their differentiating characteristics? What are the features which these subcultures share?
5. Provide your own examples of second-ary inventions derived from basic inventions.
6. How would you describe the difference between the processes of "diffusion" and "acculturation"?
7. How would you counter the assertion that the degree of cultural accomplishment of a people is a direct reflection of their inborn endowment?
8. What are some of the areas of interest which cultural anthropologists have recently begun to emphasize? Why do they consider them important?
9. Why do anthropologists caution against the use of the term "primitive" when referring to present-day human societies and cultures?
10. From the manner in which "race" is defined in this chapter, in what branch of anthropology would you expect to find it discussed?

Man and Nature

An Introduction to Physical Anthropology

Man has always sought to understand his place in nature. Early man's awareness of his kinship with other living things is reflected both in his myths and in his religion. A more scientific approach to man's relationship to the rest of living nature began with Aristotle's classification of man as the highest form of animal life. Modern man, equipped with the necessary scientific tools, has gone much further in documenting his relationship to all forms of life. He is aware that his family tree encompasses all of living nature, even if the relationship among the various branches has not yet been fully ascertained.

This unit provides an introduction to physical anthropology. It explores what is known about man's place in living nature; it focuses upon the available evidence of man's immediate ancestry; and it examines the variations present in the human species today.

Chapter **4**

The Origin of Life

It is a natural tendency of man to consider himself of central importance in the world of nature. And yet man is a relative newcomer in the scheme of living things on earth, or so the scientific evidence seems to tell us. The fossil evidence discovered to date suggests that man's oldest human ancestors appeared on earth at the very earliest between one and two million years ago. One million years would seem to be a very impressive age for man to have achieved—until we consider that the sparrow's ancestry probably dates back about fifty million years and that the simple horseshoe crab is thought to have little changed his appearance and demeanor for at least two hundred million years.

How old is the earth itself? One scientific estimate places the age of the earth at about five billion years. The very simplest forms of living things are believed to have appeared close to three billion years ago. This means that the earth must have existed for two billion years with no living things inhabiting it, with no movements visible upon its surface. If this

is so, what then happened to give rise to life on earth? What were the origins of the earliest forms of life? What is man's place in the infinite variety of nature?

Three Theories of the Origin of Life

There have been three main theories as to the origin of life on earth. Some people assert that life came into existence supernaturally, by an act of divine creation. Others believe that life was introduced on earth from another heavenly body on which it had arisen previously. Still others contend that life came into being from nonliving material. The type of discussion in which we are engaged places the first of these three theories outside the limits of our discussion. The second theory also does not concern us, since it attempts only to explain how life that had originated elsewhere in the universe was introduced onto our planet; it leaves the question of how life actually began virtually unanswered. The third theory—that life arose out of nonliving material—has undergone an important transformation within this century. The modern version of this theory is what will concern us throughout this chapter.

The Original Theory of Spontaneous Generation

The idea that living organisms may proceed under certain circumstances from lifeless matter, known as the theory of **spontaneous generation,** has had a long history in Western thought. It was professed in its original form by such outstanding scholars as Aristotle, Sir Isaac Newton, and the French philosopher-scientist René Descartes. In essence, the original theory of spontaneous generation held that not only very simple animals and plants but even such relatively complex organisms as mice and frogs could and did derive from certain nonliving environments known to be favorable to them. Thus, plant lice were thought to arise from the dew on plants, maggots from putrefying meat, frogs from the mud of marshes, and mice from accumulated refuse or filth.

This theory of spontaneous generation first came under attack during the seventeenth century by an Italian physician, Francesco Redi. Redi proved by a simple experiment that maggots are not generated by decaying meat but are due to blowflies that have previously laid eggs on the meat. Subsequent experiments by other investigators, including Lazzaro Spallanzani in the eighteenth century and Louis Pasteur in the nineteenth, finally discredited completely the original theory of spontaneous generation.

The Modern Theory of Life's Origin

As a result of the refutation of the original theory of spontaneous generation, scientists found themselves left without any reasonable scientific explanation of life's origin. Only recently have many scientists throughout the world developed an acceptable new theory concerning the origin of life. Interestingly enough, this new theory once again accepts the possibility that life may have arisen from lifeless matter. Does this mean that science has returned to a position it fully abandoned a hundred years ago? Not at all, for the modern theory of spontaneous generation differs from the original in an essential respect.

The new theory of the origin of life holds that there is no evidence whatsoever that living matter can arise from lifeless material under present conditions on the earth. On the other hand, this new theory does assume that early in the earth's history, and for a very long period of time, there existed conditions under which living matter could have derived from nonliving materials.

The new theory concerning the origin of living matter is a product of many minds. It represents a synthesis of much that scientists have discovered during the last hundred years in fields ranging from astronomy to zoology. The first scientist who brought the many pieces of evidence together was a Russian biochemist, A. I. Oparin. During the 1930's, Oparin wrote a book on the subject of the origin of life that has since become a classic of biological literature. Moreover, since the publication of this book, Oparin's views have been further elaborated both in the United

States and in other countries. How have Oparin and others accounted for the emergence of living forms on earth? Before examining their ideas in more detail, let us consider what we mean when we talk about "life."

The Nature of "Life"

While it may seem simple enough to distinguish living organisms from nonliving matter, a sharp definition of just what "life" is—of where nonliving matter leaves off and what we term "life" begins—needs to be agreed upon before proceeding any further with our discussion.

Living organisms have much in common with their nonliving environment. All matter is composed of countless atoms arranged into many definite combinations, or molecules. A number of the same kinds of atoms —that is, atoms of the same chemical elements—are found in both living and nonliving matter. Thus, atoms of oxygen are present, free or combined, in the air and in water, in much of the earth's crust, and in all forms of plant and animal life. Atoms of nitrogen, another gaseous element, make up four-fifths of our atmosphere and are also necessary components of all living matter.

Atoms of hydrogen, in chemical combination with those of oxygen, account for the oceans, lakes, and rivers of the earth's surface, and are likewise found in the molecules of all living matter. The element carbon is something of an exception. The presence of its atoms is characteristic of all living organisms and their products; and because carbon or its compounds are also found in the form of petroleum, coal, or limestone, these minerals are taken to be of ancient animal or plant origin.

A basic distinction between living and nonliving nature occurs on a higher level of organization. All living organisms are made up of cells, while lifeless matter is not. Cells constitute the basic structural units of all life. Even though most cells are too small to be seen without the aid of a microscope, they are nevertheless unbelievably complex. Incredible as it may seem, it is estimated that each human cell contains an amount of coded information which, if written out in words, would take up about nine sets of the *Encyclopaedia Britannica*. We shall return to this remarkable capacity of human body cells as we discuss modern genetics.

Even though cells differ considerably in size, shape, and function, they typically consist of two essential parts, the nucleus and the cytoplasm. The

All human body cells are made up of a nucleus and cytoplasm. The nucleus acts as the control center for the countless number of cell activities that are taking place at all times.

nucleus may be thought of as the control center for the busy life activity that is continuously taking place around it in the cell cytoplasm.

From the point of view of their chemical makeup, all living cells contain certain classes of compounds that are basic to the maintenance of life activities. Foremost among these compounds are the **proteins.** The protein makeup of cells differs considerably not only from one organism to another, but even within the same organism. Proteins are constructed from the countless possible arrangements of the molecules of some two dozen **amino acids,** commonly known as the "building blocks" of proteins. As many as a million atoms may be employed in the construction of a large protein molecule, and yet the variety of these atoms is surprisingly limited. All proteins contain atoms of carbon, hydrogen, nitrogen, and oxygen. Some proteins also contain atoms of other elements, often sulfur and phosphorus.

Among the other classes of compounds that characterize living organisms are carbohydrates, fats, and nucleic acids. **Nucleic acids,** found in the nuclei of cells, are the agents responsible for controlling many important cell activities. The molecules that compose fats and carbohydrates are made up of atoms of carbon, hydrogen, and oxygen. Nucleic acid molecules include atoms of these same elements, with the addition of atoms of nitrogen and phosphorus.

Table 1   Nature's Most Abundant Elements

NONLIVING NATURE			ELEMENT	LIVING NATURE		
Air	Oceans	Land		Amino Acids and Nucleic Acids	Carbo-hydrates and Fats	Water
			hydrogen			
			oxygen			
			nitrogen			
			carbon			
			sulfur	(sometimes)		
			phosphorus	(sometimes)		
			silicon			
			aluminum			
			iron			
			chlorine			
			calcium			
			sodium			

Table 1, "Nature's Most Abundant Elements," makes clear how relatively few elements make up the bulk of matter, both living and nonliving. One can only be impressed by the economy with which nature has achieved its endless variety.

Primeval Conditions on Earth

We have now reminded ourselves of what the basic chemical substances that constitute a living organism are. The problem before Oparin and his followers was to work out a realistic sequence of chemical reactions which, under the conditions existing on primitive earth, could have produced complex living materials from nonliving matter. What were the conditions of the earth's surface and its atmosphere when the original life substance was in the making?

It is generally supposed that among the most common gaseous materials enveloping the primitive earth were water vapor (H_2O), ammonia (NH_3), methane (CH_4), and hydrogen(H). Note that all these substances are composed of those very elements most essential to the makeup of all living organisms: carbon (C), nitrogen (N), oxygen (O), and hydrogen (H). An extra abundance of hydrogen in the early atmosphere allowed for its combination into many gaseous materials, while a portion of it still remained free. Interestingly enough, geochemists and astronomers have reason to suspect that there was no free oxygen in the atmosphere. All of the atmospheric oxygen would have combined with the overabundant hydrogen to form water molecules.

Environmental conditions on the primitive earth are believed to have been very extreme. Temperatures were very possibly near the boiling point of water. There was intense ultraviolet radiation from the sun. And there were frequent and violent electrical storms. Were these conditions, operating on the chemical materials thought to have been most common in the primitive atmosphere, favorable to the creation of those other compounds which are the essential constituents of living cells? In 1953, Stanley L. Miller, then a student under the American Nobel scientist Harold Urey, reported on a crucial experiment which suggested that they were.

Miller's Experiment

Miller introduced into a sealed glass apparatus the four gases mentioned above as being common in the primitive atmosphere—water vapor, ammonia, methane, and hydrogen. Then, in order to simulate conditions on the primitive earth, he circulated the gases over a faint glow produced by a continuous electrical discharge. At the end of a week, Miller analyzed the results of his experiment. He discovered in the water solution of his original mixture an appreciable yield of several amino acids, the building blocks of proteins. His experiment had produced some of the basic stuff of life. Since 1953, other scientists elaborating on Miller's pioneering research have been able to produce in laboratory experiments some of the fundamental components of nucleic acids.

The startling discovery that the very simple gases believed to have characterized the early atmosphere do, under

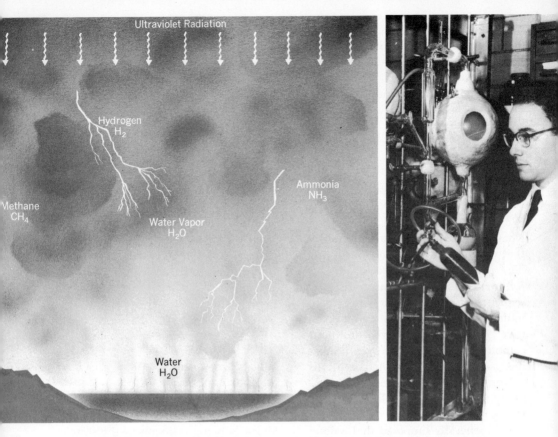

Fig. 1 The Origin of Life. The modern theory of life's origin holds that intense radiation and violent electrical storms acting upon the gaseous materials that composed the primitive atmosphere caused life to originate on earth. Working in the laboratory, the scientist Stanley Miller simulated the environment of the primitive earth and produced several amino acids.

certain conditions, combine into life-supporting compounds is very important. But research on this process is only at its beginning. The synthesis achieved by Miller and others still does not tell us *how* such extremely complex substances as proteins and nucleic acids came into being.

The Factor of Vast Numbers

One factor favors those scientists who support the modern theory of life's origin on primeval earth. This factor is the two billion years that preceded the appearance of life on earth. In such an enormous amount of time, scientists consider it quite possible for even the very complex molecules that make up nucleic acids to have formed by chance and to have accumulated to some extent.

Thinking of this kind is based on the mathematical study of the probability with which any particular event may be expected to occur—the event in this case being the combination of certain chemical substances into a simple, life-producing substance.

Probability is being used more and more to provide tentative answers to questions that defy more specific solution. Thus, to the question of whether or not life exists anywhere else in the universe, the mathematically oriented scientist is likely to consider it very probable. According to astronomers, so many celestial bodies not altogether unlike the earth exist in the universe that it is beyond our practical experience even to comprehend their number. There is mathematical likelihood that not only is there life on many of them but that in some cases it may closely resemble earthly life. Or, such life might be even more complex than life as we know it.

Seas as the Birthplace of Life

The rate at which the complex molecules crucial for the emergence of life accumulated must have been very slow. Moreover, had there been much free oxygen mixed with atmospheric gases or dissolved in the waters of primeval earth, oxidation of these life-producing molecules would have immediately destroyed their usefulness.

It is believed that the primitive seas may have provided a natural environment—a sort of "hot dilute soup"—suitable for the interaction of those basic organic molecules necessary to the formation of more complex ones. On the other hand, considering the seas as the birthplace of life has one major drawback. Under conditions of high temperatures, most of the essential materials needed for life would have dissolved in the warm seawater or dispersed before having had a chance to contact one another.

Where did life begin in this long and involved process of the development of life-generating organic molecules? It is not easy to say. Perhaps it was at the point when a single molecule assumed such a structure that it could draw actively on its environment in order to manufacture more of its own kind. This process, referred to in chemistry as **autocatalysis,** lies at the basis of a characteristic that all living organisms possess—the ability to reproduce.

The Bridge Between Living and Nonliving

Just as it is most unlikely that scientists will ever know exactly when and how life began, they can only guess at what form the first living substance may have taken. The oldest fossils reported to date bearing evidence of well-established life are simple one-celled microorganisms. These have been uncovered in rocks estimated to be well over two billion years old.

It is speculated that at some point in the course of organic development, living forms may not have been

This one-celled microorganism, discovered in rock estimated to be about two billion years old, is one of the earliest forms of life presently known to us.

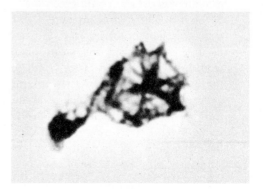

unlike the present-day viruses. **Viruses** are indeed remarkable; under certain conditions they appear to be lifeless crystals, yet under some circumstances they are capable of unlimited reproduction. Because they possess both these qualities, viruses are considered to be links between the world of minerals and living nature. In one important respect, however, the viruses known today cannot be used to illustrate the original boundary between lifeless and living matter. Viruses are **parasitic,** that is, they are dependent on other already existing organisms. But apart from this peculiarity, the protein makeup and the twofold nature of viruses places them at the very threshold of life.

What do scientists guess to be the stages in the development of life once the bridge from nonliving to living nature was crossed? We know that plant life requires the regular intake of carbon dioxide and animal life the intake of oxygen. It is likely that at an early stage of organic development, organisms were gaining energy by fermenting suitable organic molecules found around them. Eventually, sufficient amounts of the carbon dioxide gas needed by green plants became available for the first step in the complex process of photosynthesis. Not until an adequate supply of carbon dioxide was present could green plants develop to any significant extent. But once this had occurred, the addition of free oxygen to the atmosphere would have followed as a result of the output of oxygen by these plants.

We have just spanned a thousand million years of life-producing activity in several short paragraphs. What has been presented in terms of several crude leaps would in fact have been the result of uncountable small steps. With each step came substantial improvement in the chances that the materials of the earth's surface would ultimately build up the stuff of life. The step that has concerned us most is that first remarkable but little understood transition from nonliving matter to a simple one-celled organism. Yet even this step was no more wondrous than those leading from this one-celled organism ultimately to man himself.

SUMMARY

Several advances in our scientific understanding of the universe during recent centuries have led to a modern theory of life's origin. This theory assumes that the complicated chemical substances found today in all living organisms combined several billion years ago from simple, inorganic materials existing in the earth's seas. The atmospheric conditions prevailing at that time are believed to have aided the process by which life arose out of nonliving matter. Such conditions, simulated in the laboratory by Stanley Miller and other scientists, have resulted in the production of some of the fundamental components of living cells.

The process by which life arose on earth probably lasted well over a billion years. The first forms of life may have been viruslike. Our fossil evidence for the earliest forms of life begins with simple one-celled microorganisms. From life in the primeval seas to life on land was the next great step in the development of life on earth.

Chapter Review

Terms in Anthropology

amino acids   parasitic   spontaneous generation

autocatalysis   proteins   virus

nucleic acids

Questions for Review

1. What are the three major theories concerning the origin of life on earth? Which theory is of most importance in a scientific discussion?
2. Define "spontaneous generation." Briefly describe the history of the original theory of spontaneous generation. How was this theory refuted?
3. How does the modern theory of life's origin differ from the original theory of spontaneous generation?
4. What four chemical elements are most essential in the makeup of all living organisms? How important is each of these elements in the nonliving environment?
5. Describe the structure of a cell. What classes of compounds are found in all living cells?
6. What materials are thought to have been most common in the environment of the primitive earth?
7. What was the significance of Miller's experiment?
8. What is meant by "the factor of vast numbers"? What does it suggest about the possibility of life existing elsewhere in the universe?
9. What did the crucial step from organic materials to life-generating molecules involve?
10. Why are viruses considered a link between the worlds of nonliving and living nature? What characteristic of viruses known today rules them out as the original link between nonliving and living matter?

Chapter **5**

Nature's Progress
Toward Man

In 1831, the H.M.S. *Beagle* pulled out of an English port and set course for the distant coast of South America and the Pacific islands. On board ship was a young man named Charles Darwin, who had taken a job as the ship's naturalist on its long scientific voyage around the world. The ship made its way across the Atlantic and up the far coast of South America, where its naturalist took copious notes on the exotic forms of plant and animal life observed wherever the ship put ashore. But it was when the *Beagle* reached the Galápagos islands in the eastern Pacific that Darwin's interest was really kindled.

There, in what was actually a rather limited geographical area, Darwin made some observations about forms of life that were to be revolutionary in their implications. Although the Galápagos did not possess a large number of different animal species, Darwin saw that they were rich in the varieties of species in existence. From island to island, he observed different kinds of finches and

tortoises, each possessing only slight variations from the other. Totaling them up, Darwin counted in these islands thirteen different species of the finch and several more of the tortoise. Why should Darwin, and subsequently the whole scientific world, take such an interest in the varieties of life in the Galápagos? We will return to this question a little later in the chapter.

The Kingdoms of Nature

You learned in the last chapter what many scientists now consider a reasonable scientific explanation of life's origin. We can now carry our discussion of the development of life somewhat further. Once life-producing substances became established on the earth, a continuous process of change gave rise to an ever-increasing number of different organisms. A major distinction among all living organisms is that which separates plants from animals.

How are plants and animals distinguished from each other? Organisms in both the plant and animal kingdoms are fundamentally alike in several respects. Notably, both plants and animals are made up of similar structural and functional units—the cells. But plants and animals also differ in several conspicuous ways. In general, plants remain fixed in one place during their lifetime, while animals are capable of locomotion; plants manufacture food from raw materials, while animals obtain nourishment from other organisms in their environment; and plant bodies derive their support from the relatively firm wall of cellulose around their cells, while animal bodies receive support by other means—the skeleton, for example.

It is commonly accepted that primitive plants preceded the earliest forms of animal life. It is thought that the first forms of animal life may have derived from single-celled green algae, some of which they resemble in several ways. Scientists cannot yet account strictly for the leap from plant to animal life. *Euglena,* a one-celled organism whose mode of nutrition ranks it with plants but whose capacity for locomotion and absence of solid cell wall ranks it with animals, serves today as an example of what may have been the original bridge between the plant and animal kingdoms. Very likely the first animal forms were the flagellate protozoa, simple one-celled organisms that move with the aid of one or more long whiplike appendages called flagella.

Let us now consider man's place in the animal kingdom, of which he, a relative newcomer, has become undisputed king.

The Relationship of Man to Other Animals

The physical similarities between man and other members of the animal kingdom are far too numerous to ignore. The most obvious of these are **homologies,** or structural likenesses between parts of different organisms that are best accounted for by common origin. Man's arm, the frog's foreleg, the whale's flipper, and the bird's wing are homologous structures, even though they no longer serve identical functions. The circulatory and skeletal systems, and major portions of the nervous systems, also correspond so closely in higher animals as to leave no doubt that they represent specialized developments of the same basic blueprint.

Vestigial organs also serve to demonstrate the relationship between man and other animals. A **vestigial organ** is any part of an organism that no longer serves a useful function. A large group of related animals, including man, once shared use of the cecum and the appendix to aid plant digestion. But as the dietary habits of our prehuman ancestors changed, these structures became superfluous and in the course of time greatly diminished in size. In animals which continued feeding exclusively on plants, however, these structures remained large and fully functioning. In rabbits, the size of the cecum approximates the size of the stomach.

Still other evidence for the relationship between man and other animal species is the many similarities in the course of their embryonic developments. **Embryonic development** refers to the changes that occur during the early stages of a young organism's de-

Homologous Structures

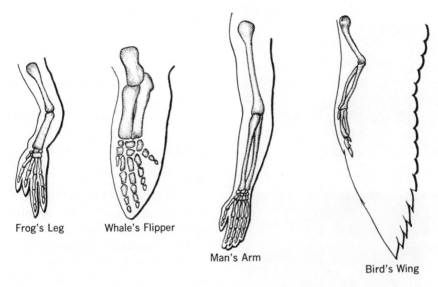

Frog's Leg Whale's Flipper

Man's Arm

Bird's Wing

Fig. 2 Homologous Structures. Man's arm, the frog's leg, the whale's flipper, and the bird's wing are similar enough in structure to suggest a common origin. What are their similarities?

velopment. Scientists also demonstrate the relationship between man and such close relatives as the chimpanzee by pointing out the basic similarity of their blood chemistry.

The Classification of Animals

If one considers the tremendous variety among animals—one need only think of the gulf that separates man from the amoeba—it is no wonder that scientists do not always agree in detail on the meaning of the similarities and differences between any two kinds of organisms. But there is substantial agreement among scientists on an overall classification of animals. Let us now review this classification

of the **animal kingdom** (the kingdom Animalia).

First, it is customary to contrast the **protozoans,** microscopic animals of single-celled bodies, with all of the more complex and multicelled animal forms—the **metazoans** (the subkingdom Metazoa). Among the metazoans are those animals which are symmetrical radially, that is, which develop uniformly around a central bodily axis, and those symmetrical bilaterally. The bilateral animals, which are by far the more common and include man, have two like sides with respect to a single median plane. Our main concern is with the **chordates** (the phylum Chordata), which are both the most complex and the most familiar bilateral forms. Among the

The three types of mammals are represented here by: the spiny anteater, whose young are hatched from eggs; the kangaroo, whose offspring complete their early development in the mother's pouch; and the horse, a member of the large subclass of placental mammals.

member species of this very large phylum is the human species, including both early and recent mankind.

The characteristic feature that all chordates share and from which they derive their name is the **notochord,** a flexible internal rodlike structure which supports their bodies during early development or throughout their lifetime. In a great many adult chordates, man among them, the notochord is replaced in part or in full by either a cartilaginous or a bony vertebral column. These chordates are grouped together as the **vertebrates** (the subphylum Vertebrata).

There are five well-known classes of vertebrates—the bony fishes, amphibians, reptiles, birds, and mammals. The **mammals** (the class Mammalia), with a few exceptions, have a body covering of hair and nourish their young with milk secreted from the mammary glands of the females. Furthermore, like the birds, they have evolved a mechanism that maintains constant body temperature regardless of changes in the environment. A few mammals, such as the spiny anteater and the duckbill platypus, are hatched from eggs; some others—the kangaroo and opossum among them—are born in an immature state and complete their early development in the external pouches of their mothers. But most mammals, man included, are **placental mammals** (the subclass Eutheria), whose offspring develop within the mother's womb.

The placental mammals subdivide into a number of orders, including insectivores, rodents, carnivores, and primates. The **primates** (the order Primates) are represented by so-called lower forms, such as the tree-dwelling lemurs, tarsiers, and tree shrews, and by more advanced forms, such as monkeys, apes, and man. The lower primates form the suborder of **prosimians** (the suborder Prosimii); the higher primates are referred to as the **anthropoids** (the suborder Anthropoidea).

We have now reached the point in the scheme of biological classification where man's relationship to other members of his division becomes more easily recognizable. Among the anthropoids, man and the apes—including certain fossil forms intermediate between the two—belong to a group termed **hominoids** (the superfamily Hominoidea). This group is distinguished from both the Old World and the New World monkeys.

Among the hominoids, both early man and recent man are classified as **hominids** (the family Hominidae). They are differentiated from all of the apes, or **pongids** (the family Pongidae). Since the distinction between man and the apes is of primary importance to physical anthropologists, a fuller discussion of the relationship between these two branches of hominoids will follow in Chapter 6, "The Precursors of Man." But before concluding our discussion of the place scientists have assigned man among the animals, we need to remind ourselves of the system of naming used in biology.

Each distinct group of organisms, whether animals or plants, bears in addition to its common name or names a scientific designation made up of two Latin words (customarily printed in italics). The first of these two words (always capitalized) is the name of the **genus,** or the grouping in biological classification that comes next below the family. The second word (written with a small initial letter) is the name of the particular species. The term **species** refers to any group of plants or animals whose members have the same structural characteristics and mate with each other to produce fertile offspring. A genus may include several distinct species. For example, the genus *Felis* (from Latin *felis* meaning "cat") includes among its different species the domestic cat (*Felis catus* or *Felis domestica*), the tiger (*Felis tigris*), the lion (*Felis leo*), and others.

Finally, it is sometimes convenient to recognize several **subspecies** ("varieties" or "races") of a species that differ from each other only slightly and are at least in part separated geographically. For instance, the species of blue jays includes subspecies of Florida blue jays, northern blue jays, and others. The different kinds of apples we eat, Baldwin, Delicious, Jonathan, and the like, represent some of the several thousand varieties of a single species.

Man is classified as belonging to the genus *Homo,* the sole surviving member genus of the family Hominidae. Although all of recent mankind belongs to the species *Homo sapiens* (from Latin *sapiens,* meaning "wise, intelligent"), there was at one time another species of the genus *Homo.* Both this extinct species and *Homo sapiens* are considered to include a number of subspecies of mankind, as we shall see in the chapters that follow.

We may now review this discussion by examining Table 2, "Man's Place in the Animal Kingdom," which appears on the following page.

Table 2 Man's Place in the Animal Kingdom

General Division	Scientific Designation	English Equivalent
kingdom	Animalia	animals
subkingdom	Metazoa	metazoans
phylum	Chordata	chordates
subphylum	Vertebrata	vertebrates
class	Mammalia	mammals
subclass	Eutheria	placental mammals
order	Primates	primates
suborder	Anthropoidea	anthropoids
superfamily	Hominoidea	hominoids
family	Hominidae	hominids
genus	*Homo*	man
species	*sapiens*	wise

Early Theories of Evolution

Two and a half thousand years ago the Greeks recognized that living forms vary tremendously in complexity and that some forms may eventually become extinct while other new ones arise gradually. Aristotle saw in man the peak of a progression extending from nonliving matter through a graded series of organisms. But not until the eighteenth century was serious thought again given to the origin and classification of living forms. Among those who newly pondered the source of nature's great richness of forms was the Frenchman Jean Baptiste de Lamarck (1744–1829), who offered what seemed a very reasonable explanation of the variety in nature.

According to Lamarck, organisms are always striving to adapt themselves better to their environments. When organisms make such adaptations, they transmit their newly acquired characteristics to succeeding generations by inheritance. Thus, according to Lamarck, modern giraffes are the descendants of generations of giraffes that were particularly successful in extending the length of their necks and forelegs as they sought nourishment from the leaves of tall trees. Those giraffes which were unable to make this adaptation eventually became extinct, Lamarck believed.

Plausible as Lamarck's explanation of the varieties in nature once seemed, overwhelming evidence has since shown his theory to be invalid. The physical characteristics that an individual organism acquires during its lifetime in an effort to adapt to the environment cannot be transmitted to its offspring. Lamarck's theory cannot be used to explain **evolution**—the process by which an organism, or group of organisms, develops such distinct characteristics as ·to form a new species.

Evolution by Natural Selection

For the fundamental features of the modern theory of evolution we are indebted to that ship's naturalist who was mentioned earlier, Charles Robert Darwin (1809–1882). Darwin's scientific career began in earnest when, at age twenty-two, he boarded the *Beagle* for its five-year scientific voyage around the world. During this time, Darwin collected innumerable natural specimens from both the seas and the lands he visited. He recorded his many observations in the notebooks that he kept meticulously throughout the entire voyage. When the *Beagle* returned to England, Darwin set to work evaluating the vast body of information he had collected. During this process of weighing and correlating his data, the theory of evolution by natural selection for which Darwin was to become famous some twenty years later began to take shape.

It is of historical interest that although the modern theory of evolution is inseparably bound with Darwin's name, it was arrived at independently at about the same time by another English naturalist, Alfred Russel Wallace. The ideas of both men were presented jointly at a meeting of the Linnaean Society in London in 1858. A year later, *The Origin of Species,* an abridged version of Darwin's extensive research, appeared in a first edition of 1250 copies and was sold out on the day of publication. With this and a subsequent publication, *The Descent of Man,* Darwin fathered an intellectual revolution whose echoes have not died out to the present day.

The theory of evolution arrived at by Darwin is dependent upon the concept of **natural selection.** The Darwinian theory of evolution by natural selection may be summarized as follows:

1. Upon careful examination, no two organisms of whatever kind, whether animal or plant, natural or domesticated, turn out to be exactly alike. The differences in the inborn characteristics of individual organisms, termed **variations,** are to be taken as a law of nature.
2. Plants and animals produce more offspring than can be provided for. There exist many natural checks to compensate for the **overproduction** of all living forms and to keep their numbers within reasonable bounds.
3. The most effective natural check upon overpopulation is the competition of organisms for space and food—the **struggle for existence.**
4. In the course of this constant competition, those organisms possessing variations that make them especially well adapted to the conditions under which they live have a decided advantage. The struggle for existence results in the **survival of the fittest.**
5. Those better-adapted organisms that manage to survive transmit the traits that contributed to their survival to their offspring through inheritance.
6. The inheritance of traits with high survival value furthers the process of natural selection and may in time give rise to a new species.

Darwin's reasoning was supported at every point by well-chosen examples drawn from his observation during the *Beagle*'s voyage, the high point of which had been the five weeks spent in the Galápagos islands. It was there that Darwin had been able to observe how many variations can take place in an animal population even within a very limited geographical area. The Galápagos have rightly been referred to as the "showcase for evolution."

In *The Descent of Man,* Darwin's theory of evolution was presented even more boldly. Darwin suggested that man himself was descended from a less highly organized form of animal life. Darwin recognized that there was a great gap to be bridged before man would understand fully his relationship to his closest apelike ancestors.

"Those regions which are the most likely to afford remains connecting man with some extinct ape-like creature have not as yet been searched," he wrote. Here, too, Darwin was able to see far ahead of his time.

Mendel's Laws of Inheritance

We have seen that Darwin's theory of evolution differed from the Lamarckian explanation in a very significant way. Darwin rejected the idea that traits acquired by an organism during its lifetime, however much they may contribute to its survival, can be transmitted to its offspring by inheritance. On the other hand, Darwin did believe that the variations observable in individual organisms are transmissible to offspring. However,

This engraving shows Charles Darwin as naturalist of the *Beagle,* testing the speed of a giant tortoise on an island in the Galápagos. Darwin was amazed to discover how many different species of tortoise inhabited this small island group. How did he explain this discovery?

Darwin himself did not account clearly either for the source of variation or for the mechanism of heredity.

A reasonable explanation of the source of variation did not appear until the beginning of this century. But, by a strange coincidence, the secret of heredity was being unraveled at the very time that Darwin was readying *The Origin of Species* for publication. For this story we need to shift our attention to a garden plot in an Augustinian monastery at Brno in what today is Czechoslovakia. There, a monk named Gregor Johann Mendel (1822–1884) was conducting experiments on heredity using pea plants of the common garden variety.

For his experiments, Mendel managed to obtain strains of pea plants that had been bred pure for certain sharply contrasting pairs of characteristics—for long or short stems, for smooth or wrinkled ripe seeds, and for green or yellow unripe pods. Mendel crossed the two parent varieties of each of the pairs, subsequently crossing their offspring for several more generations. During all this time, he kept a careful record of the regularities with which the contrasting traits of the parent plants occurred.

What did Mendel discover? He discovered that pure smooth-seeded and pure wrinkle-seeded plants when crossed produced a generation of plants with smooth seeds. But when next these smooth-seeded plants were crossed, the "hidden" character of wrinkledness began to show up again. Out of some 7,300 seeds derived from the original set, Mendel counted three fourths that were smooth, one fourth wrinkled. Not only this, but when Mendel crossed pure long and short-stemmed plants, and plants with other contrasting characteristics, he obtained a similar ratio in the traits observable in succeeding generations.

Mendel's observations were based on those traits of the pea plant that are outwardly visible. Scientists now term an observable biological characteristic of an organism a **phenotype.** What Mendel sought to account for was the internal constitution of an organism that controls its outward appearance. The internal mechanism that controls the inheritance of a specific trait by an organism is called a **genotype.** Twelve years of patient experimentation by Mendel brought about a significant breakthrough in our understanding of how biological inheritance works. In brief, the laws Mendel proposed to account for his interesting observations are as follows:

1. Heredity is based on the combination of many pairs of units, each pair being responsible for one trait in the biological makeup of an organism. (The units that determine the biological makeup of an organism are now termed **genes.**) Each parent furnishes one of the units in each pair held by an offspring.

2. Whenever parents furnish genes of contrasting character to an offspring, the offspring will be **hybrid;** that is, it will possess contrasting units for the particular characteristic. The characteristic that is observable in such an offspring is termed **dominant,** the one that tends to be hidden, **recessive.** Thus, if one parent contributes the unit for tallness, T, and the other parent the unit for shortness, t, the result will be a hybrid, Tt. Outwardly this individual will be tall, since the gene for tallness, T, is

Mendel's Laws of Inheritance

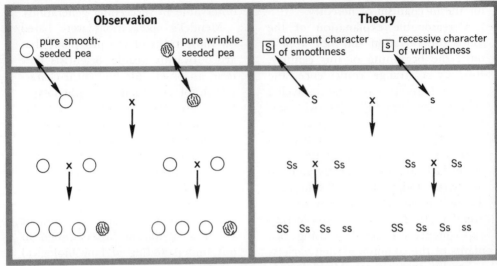

Fig. 3 Mendel's Laws of Inheritance. These diagrams summarize what Mendel's experiments revealed about the nature of heredity. The diagram at left shows what Mendel observed in the offspring of pea plants bred pure for contrasting traits. The diagram at right shows how Mendel accounted for the 3:1 ratio of smooth- to wrinkle-seeded offspring.

dominant and the gene for shortness, *t,* recessive. (Should both parents endow their offspring with a unit of the dominant character, *T,* the individual will be pure for tallness, *TT,* and will so appear. If both parents furnish units of the recessive character, shortness, the offspring will be pure for shortness, *tt,* and will so appear.)

3. For each characteristic transmitted to an offspring, a parent furnishes only one of the two genes in his possession for that trait. The parental genes in each pair separate, but the individual genes remain unaltered.

4. Genes assort randomly, but in a predictable ratio, from generation to generation.

Even though Mendel's conclusions

were published during his lifetime (in 1866), he did not live to see the results of his experiments properly appreciated. It was more than a generation later, when three scientists working independently arrived at similar conclusions, that the importance of Mendel's original discovery was recognized. Mendel's laws have undergone many subsequent elaborations, but his achievement still constitutes one of the greatest single discoveries in the history of the science of life.

Modern Genetics

One of the three biologists who rediscovered the principles of heredity first formulated by Mendel was Hugo De Vries, who is known primarily for his study of the source of variation. According to De Vries, variations arise from **mutations,** or sudden changes in the genetic makeup of an organism. De Vries's explanation of the source of variation was correct, as far as it went. But for many scientists of the early twentieth century, it simply did not go far enough.

In the field of biology, the first half of this century was characterized by attempts to understand more fully the mechanism of heredity. Scientists recognized the fundamental units of biological inheritance, the genes, to be those tiny beadlike structures located on chromosomes in the nuclei of cells. They observed that during the process of reproduction, the normal, full number of chromosomes in a cell nucleus is halved, and that the combination of two such cells, each possessing half the usual number of chromosomes, results in the production of a new organism.

But students of genetics were still puzzled about many things. They were puzzled about **linkage,** the tendency of certain biological traits to be inherited together. When they understood this to be the result of the location of certain genes on the same chromosome, they were even more puzzled about what caused the occasional exchange of corresponding segments of paired chromosomes, known as **crossing-over.** Most of all, they continued to wonder about the nature of mutation and the circumstances under which mutations in hereditary material were likely to occur.

Most revolutionary in the modern study of genetics have been the recent advances in our understanding of the chemical basis of life and the evolution of its forms. What is the nature of the hereditary material in the nuclei of all living cells? Chemical studies have revealed that chromosomes are composed largely of proteins and deoxyribonucleic acid, better known as **DNA.** The fact that DNA is found primarily in cell nuclei, that the amount of DNA appears to be different for different kinds of organisms but constant for the different kinds of cells in any one type of organism, and that egg and sperm cells contain only half of the normal amount of DNA suggested to some scientists that it might be the basic hereditary mate-

Fig. 4 **The Structure of a DNA Molecule. (a) The DNA molecule is a double helix held together by weak chemical bonds. (b) It reproduces itself by "unzipping" along the middle of its rungs, each half then forming a new complete molecule of DNA.**

The Structure of a DNA Molecule

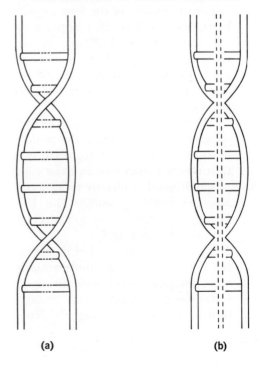

(a)　　　　　　　　　　　(b)

rial. Several different experiments with bacteria and viruses confirmed this to be so.

In 1953, three scientists, among them the American James Dewey Watson, succeeded in describing the structure of the DNA molecule in surprising detail. Their research, for which they received the coveted Nobel prize in 1962, culminated in one of the most significant developments in biochemistry of this century. As a result of their work, it is now generally accepted that the DNA molecule is a double helix, in appearance not unlike a twisted rope ladder (see Figure 4a on the preceding page). Its sidepieces are made up of certain chemical substances, while its rungs are composed of four different organic bases. Each rung consists of two unlike bases held together by relatively weak chemical bonds, dividing the ladder into two parallel halves. A half-rung may consist of any one of the four organic bases, but the base that appears on the corresponding half-rung is not chosen at random. The sequence of the bases along one half of the ladder determines the order of the bases on the other half.

In cell division, the ladderlike DNA molecule "unzips" along the middle of its rungs (see Figure 4b). Each side then rebuilds itself into an exact copy of the original ladder by using available free building blocks. This biological reproduction at a molecular level is called **replication.**

Regardless of the kind of organism, DNA molecules are fundamentally alike, except for one important aspect —the specific sequence of arrangements in which the organic bases occur along the molecular ladder. It is precisely this sequence that is believed to constitute the "coded message" in which "instructions" are "communicated" for the many intricate chemical reactions that govern cell life. In this view, mutations are simply occasional mistakes that occur as DNA molecules replicate.

SUMMARY

Three scientific theories formulated during the nineteenth century greatly contributed to man's understanding of his place in the world of living nature. The Darwinian theory of evolution by natural selection suggested how an organism as complex as man himself could have evolved, over hundreds of millions of years, from the simple one-celled microorganisms that formed the original bridge between lifeless and living matter.

While Darwin made plausible belief in a steady progression from simple to complex forms of life, he was not able to acount scientifically for the variations that brought about the rise of new species. The basis for understanding this process was laid by Gregor Mendel, who through experiments with common garden peas worked out the fundamental laws governing heredity, and by Hugo De Vries, who explained variation as the result of mutation—sudden change in the genetic makeup of an organism. Modern genetic theory attributes mutation to the action of DNA molecules in cell nuclei during the process of cell reproduction.

Chapter Review

Terms in Anthropology

animal kingdom	*Homo*	pongid
anthropoid	homology	primate
chordate	*Homo sapiens*	prosimian
crossing-over	hybrid	protozoan
DNA	linkage	recessive
dominant	mammal	replication
embryonic development	metazoan	species (pl. species)
evolution	mutation	struggle for existence
gene	natural selection	subspecies
genotype	notochord	survival of the fittest
genus (pl. genera)	overproduction	variation
hominid	phenotype	vertebrate
hominoid	placental mammal	vestigial organ

Questions for Review

1. How are plants and animals distinguished from each other? Why is *Euglena* considered a bridge between the plant and animal kingdoms?
2. What are some of the types of evidence for man's relationship to other animal species?
3. List all of the divisions in the scheme of animal classification. To what animal group does man belong at each level of classification?
4. What animal groups are included among the order Primates? the suborder Anthropoidea? the superfamily Hominoidea? the family Hominidae?
5. What is meant by "evolution"? How did Lamarck account for the tremendous variation in living forms? Why has Lamarck's theory of evolution been discredited?
6. What are the main points in the Darwinian theory of evolution? List these points in logical order.
7. What is the difference between a phenotype and a genotype?
8. How did Mendel account for the mechanism of heredity?
9. Define "mutation." Of what importance are mutations in the evolution of animal species?
10. What discovery in modern genetics helps to explain the source of variation in nature?

Chapter **6**

The Precursors of Man

When Darwin suggested that fossil remains linking man with an "extinct ape-like creature" might someday be found, he most certainly did not expect that fifty years later one of his countrymen would go to the length of fabricating such a fossil.

Between the years 1911 and 1915, an amateur prehistorian named Charles Dawson reported finding several fossilized fragments of a human skull in a gravel pit at Piltdown in Sussex, England. The skull that was subsequently reconstructed from these fragments turned out to be most unusual and puzzled even the most eminent scholars. The peculiarity of the skull lay in its combination of a large braincase, approximating in capacity that of modern man, with a primitive, apelike jaw. Evaluating this fossil, which came to be known as **Piltdown man,** proved exceedingly difficult. It is probably fair to say that scholars were about equally divided on the problem. There were those who believed in the authenticity of Piltdown man and those who doubted the likelihood that such a creature could ever have existed.

Not until 1953 was the community of anthropologists relieved of its nearly forty years of speculation. In that year, three British scientists announced their findings upon completion of a thorough reexamination of the Piltdown bones. One of the crucial tests they had employed was the newly developed **fluorine test.** This test of skeletal age is based upon the fact that the fluorine content of bones buried in earth tends to increase through time at a rate particular to a given locality. The fluorine test had proved conclusively that the Piltdown bones were of no great antiquity, dating back only to a time when modern man had long been established. Other tests revealed that while the upper skull fragments were those of a recent human, the companion jaw was that of a modern ape! The perpetrator of this fantastic hoax had planed down the teeth and doctored the jaw with chemical substances. The celebrated Piltdown man, far from being the long-sought "missing link" between some ancient ape and man, was nothing more than an elaborate fraud.

If such a forgery as Piltdown man were to be attempted today, it is highly unlikely that scientists would be taken in by it even briefly. Not only have several new methods of dating been developed since World War II, but new fossil discoveries have greatly increased our understanding of human evolution and the stages immediately preceding it. In this chapter, we will examine some of the most important evidence bearing on man's early development.

The Geologic Time Scale

Before focusing our attention on the emergence of man during the last two million years, it is important that we consider the primary means by which scientists have established the sequence of life on earth. This has been done by study of the earth itself.

Geologists have established a time scale of the earth's history, based upon observation of the layers of sediment in the earth's upper crust. The depositing of sediment on the earth's surface by wind and by water is a continuing geologic process. As more and more sediment is deposited, older layers of sediment shift farther and farther below the earth's surface, eventually hardening into rock because of the pressure from above. Geologists can therefore assume that lower layers of sediment are older, except in cases where there has been a major disturbance in the earth's crust. By matching layers of sediment ending in one locality with similar layers extending upward in another region, geologists have established a time scale of the earth's history. This time scale is of great importance in determining the sequence of life on earth, since the fossils found in older layers of sediment can be assumed to predate those of younger layers.

Geologists have divided the entire length of earth's history into six major **eras.** These eras are further subdivided into **periods,** and the periods into **epochs.** The geologic eras, along with the dominant forms of life that characterized them, are summarized in Table 3, "The Geologic Time Scale."

The Cenozoic Era

Our concern in tracing man's immediate ancestry is with what happened during the most recent geologic era, the **Cenozoic.** The early part of this era was marked by the formation of recent mountain systems such as the Alps, the Himalayas, and the Rockies, and by the establishment of climatic belts. As these profound changes were being wrought on the earth's surface, both mammals and birds were evolving from two different reptilian stocks.

Geologists distinguish two periods during the Cenozoic, the Tertiary and the Quaternary, and further subdivide each period into a number of epochs. These divisions are summarized in Table 4, "Timetable of the Cenozoic," on page 64.

Of particular interest to anthropologists is the **Pleistocene** epoch, which extended throughout most of the Quaternary period. The Pleistocene gave way to the **Holocene,** or Recent, epoch only between ten and fifteen thousand years ago. The Pleistocene takes its English designation, Glacial epoch, from a succession of glaciations that advanced from both poles toward the equator during the epoch. Each glacial stage was followed by a pe-

Table 3 The Geologic Time Scale

Geologic Era	Approximate Date of Beginning	Dominant Forms of Animal Life
Cenozoic (Era of Recent Life)	70 million years ago	Man Mammals Birds
Mesozoic (Era of Intermediate Life)	225 million years ago	Reptiles
Paleozoic (Era of Ancient Life)	600 million years ago	Insects Fishes Amphibians
Proterozoic (Era of Earlier Life)	1 billion years ago or earlier	Marine invertebrates
Archeozoic (Era of Primitive Life)	1.5 billion years ago or earlier	Single-celled marine forms
Azoic (Era of No Life)	5 billion years ago or earlier	None

riod of warm weather and melting. The northern half of North America, northwestern Europe, and parts of Asia were particularly affected by these glacial advances, four of which are recognized for both the New and the Old World. The drastic climatic changes they entailed exerted considerable influence on the earth's environment, having their share of effect on human evolution. In fact, it was during the Pleistocene epoch that nature was putting the finishing touches on its latest development, man.

The reasons for the climatic changes during the Pleistocene are not fully understood. Nor are scholars in complete agreement on the chronology of the epoch. On the basis of geological and paleontological evidence, it has been customary to distinguish three time divisions within the Pleistocene: the Lower, the Middle, and the Upper. The Lower Pleistocene is taken by many scholars to have extended up until the onset of the second glacial stage, some half a million years ago. In this view, the Middle Pleistocene would have encompassed the second and third wave of glacial advances together with a long intervening second interglacial phase. The Upper Pleistocene would then include the third interglacial phase and the fourth glacial stage—most of the hundred and fifty or two hundred thousand years before the present.

We are now ready to examine some of the changes in mammalian development that occurred within the various stages of the Pleistocene. Our particular concern is with developments among that order of mammals whose membership includes the immediate precursors of man—the primates.

The Primate Pattern

Judging from the fossil record, some of the early mammals that were ancestral to the primates were shrewlike insectivores, approximating squirrels in size and spending some of their time in trees. During the Paleocene epoch, between seventy and sixty million years ago, these undistinguished mammals were to become the starting point for primate evolution. It was probably not until the second epoch of the Tertiary period, the Eocene, that the primates became established as a distinct group. There is abundant evidence to show that this epoch saw a great proliferation and a wide distribution of prosimian forms, the ancestors of today's tree shrews, tarsiers, and lemurs.

There is no doubt that the primates have developed into a very successful group of mammals. They have displayed in the course of their evolution an unusual degree of adaptability to a wide range of environments, thus be-

Table 4   Timetable of the Cenozoic

Period and Epoch		Approximate Date of Beginning	Stages in Primate Evolution
QUATERNARY	Holocene (Recent)	15 thousand years ago	Modern man dominant
	Pleistocene (Glacial)	2 million years ago	Modern man evolving Hominids firmly established
TERTIARY	Pliocene	13 million years ago	Primate evolution foreshadows human forms
	Miocene	25 million years ago	Development of manlike apes
	Oligocene	40 million years ago	Establishment of the hominoids
	Eocene	60 million years ago	Division of Old and New World monkeys Wide distribution of prosimians
	Paleocene	70 million years ago	Shrewlike insectivores

coming relatively unspecialized members of the mammalian class. Among the most important trends in primate evolution are the following:

increasing flexibility of the forelimbs, particularly at the joints;

increasing refinement and mobility of the hands and feet, including the replacement of sharp claws by flattened nails and the development of sensitive tactile pads on hairless toes and fingers;

the development of **binocular vision,** meaning vision through both eyes resulting in depth perception;

increasing **cranial capacity,** or capacity of the braincase (measured in cubic centimeters);

remarkable expansion and differentiation of the cerebral cortex as part of the overall development of the brain;

a decreasing number of young produced at one time;

lengthening of the period of embryonic development and of the period of dependence for the young;

an increasing life span in comparison with other mammals of equal size; and

a growing amount and complexity of social behavior.

Man, who has derived immense benefit from the possession of all of these and still other primate characteristics, does not always realize that his good fortune began at the time when his primitive primate ancestors began to adapt to life in trees.

While the members of the suborder of prosimians were thriving, the other suborder of the primates—that of the anthropoids—was in nature's making. The earliest evidence of separate branches of the two suborders comes

The tarsier belongs to the group of prosimians whose ancestors were so widely spread during the Eocene epoch. This tiny primate possesses the binocular vision that makes it possible to perceive depth. It really "looks before it leaps" from tree to tree in its wooded habitat.

from the late Eocene. Not long after, an interesting splitting occurred on the anthropoid branch. The ancestors of today's monkeys split into two groups, the Old World and the New World monkeys. However, despite the separation of the monkeys in two hemispheres, their development in some respects was remarkably parallel. Unfortunately for our story of primate evolution, fossil forms from the next epoch, the Oligocene, are relatively rare. We can only assume that a third anthropoid stock including the ancestral hominoid forms leading to man and the apes became definitely established during this epoch.

About twenty-five million years ago, the ancestors of man and of the modern great apes probably began evolving along at least two distinct lines. One of the major factors in their subsequent differentiation was the adaptation to two different modes of life and locomotion. For the apes, it was living a large part of the time in trees, moving about from branch to branch swinging by their arms. For certain prehuman forms, it was living at ground level and moving about on two feet.

From Apes to Men

One of the questions commonly put to anthropologists concerns the precise boundary line between human forms and the prehuman forms that led to them. To draw such a line is no less difficult than to attempt to pinpoint when childhood ends and adolescence begins or when adolescence gives way to adulthood. Such criteria as the use of tools are not as helpful as one might suppose. For example, chimpanzees in the wild have been observed making a careful selection of twigs for use in catching termites and fashioning them to fit the holes of a termite nest. Chimpanzees are also well known for their ability to learn to solve a variety of problems, to express and, even more surprisingly, to control emotions, and to walk upright on the ground.

Thus, it is primarily on the evidence of skeletal remains that the distinction between prehuman and human forms is made. For the specialist, the criteria are numerous and sometimes very subtle. But the principal differences between man and the apes or apelike forms are to be found in the brain, the jaws, and the limbs. In man, as opposed to the apes:

cranial capacity and the development of specialized areas in the brain increased markedly and rapidly;

the jaws diminished in size, forming evenly rounded arches in contrast to the larger U-shaped jaws of apes;

the canine teeth also decreased in size, becoming more spadelike in shape and practically indistinguishable between the sexes;

the molars tended to decrease in size, particularly in the later stages of human development; and

the lower limbs became relatively longer, at the same time that other changes in the bones of the foot, leg, and pelvis were aiding in the assumption of erect posture.

We shall have more to say about the relationships between these skeletal changes later in the chapter.

It is important to realize that the fossil record, fragmentary as it is, provides for the most part only indirect clues as to the appearance and behavior of man's immediate ancestors. Since World War II, however, a number of finds of great importance have added to our knowledge of these ancestral forms. Scientists are now rethinking and rewriting the evolutionary history of the Miocene and Pliocene primates. Three groups of fossil specimens are of special importance as we consider this late stage of primate evolution. They are designated by the generic names *Dryopithecus, Oreopithecus,* and *Ramapithecus.* Use of the Greek *pithēkos,* meaning "ape," in naming them suggests that these forms are considered basically apelike rather than manlike.

The family of apes consists of four members. The chimpanzee (upper l.) and the gorilla (upper r.), both native to Africa, are capable of locomotion in the trees but are also partially adapted to ground dwelling. The gibbon (lower l.) and the orangutan (lower r.) are Asiatic primates who are completely adapted to life in the trees. The gibbon's small body and very long forelimbs make it capable of impressive feats of acrobatics. The most intelligent of the apes is the chimpanzee, who can solve a variety of simple problems.

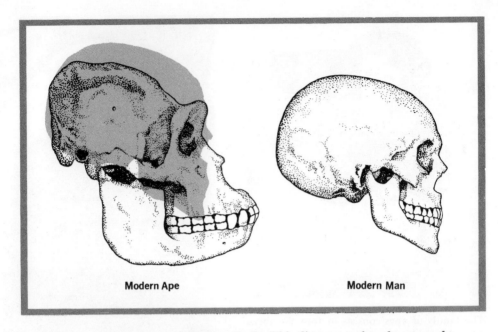

Fig. 5   **Modern Ape and Human Skulls. This diagram makes clear how the skulls of the largest ape—the gorilla—and of modern man differ. Man's jaw is smaller and less ruggedly equipped than the gorilla's. The ridge above the eye socket so prominent in the gorilla's skull is barely noticeable in man's skull. And, as this comparison indicates, the gorilla's skull—while larger overall—slopes backward and contains a much smaller braincase.**

Specimens of **Dryopithecus,** found over the last hundred years in Europe, Africa, and Asia, are restricted largely to teeth and jaw fragments. The ancient apes they represent are closely related to the more familiar group of **Proconsul** fossils. *Proconsul,* named after "Consul," a favorite chimpanzee in the London zoo, existed in several varieties. Some of its features suggest that it may have been ancestral to the modern chimpanzees and gorillas. Both *Proconsul* and *Dryopithecus* exhibit apelike jaws and teeth. However, certain features of their dentition suggest progress in a manlike direction. All the forms of *Dryopithecus* have been assigned to late in the Miocene epoch.

Fossil remains of **Oreopithecus** were first discovered about a century ago in brown coal deposits in central Italy. A jawbone and some teeth were turned up at that time. Subsequently, partial remains of a number of individuals have been recovered, including an almost complete skeleton discovered about a decade ago. *Oreopithecus* dates back about thirteen million years, being placed in the late Miocene or early Pliocene epoch. This form had certainly developed **brachiation,** meaning the ability to move about in trees by swinging from branch to branch, a characteristic of apes. Although interpretation of this form has elicited much controversy, *Oreopithecus* may best be characterized as an ape which in some respects evolved in a manlike direction. However, *Oreopithecus* may be a "dead end" fossil. Apparently the form became extinct, thus representing a dead side branch on the stem of primate evolution leading toward man.

The last, and from our point of view the most important, group of fossils belong to **Ramapithecus.** These fossils, found over the last thirty years in India and in East Africa (in a variety called *Kenyapithecus*), are judged to be at least thirteen million years old. *Ramapithecus* is generally considered to be ancestral to man, even though

the evidence is limited to fragments of upper and lower jaws and several teeth. Among the characteristics that make these specimens resemble man are the small size of their front teeth, an arched upper palate, and an evenly curved jaw that causes the distance between opposite molars to widen toward the back of the mouth. The reduction in the size of the front teeth of *Ramapithecus* suggests that these "man apes" may have had to use their forelimbs to grasp and tear their vegetable food before it reached their less ruggedly equipped mouths. If indeed this was so, their forelimbs would

Fig. 6 Modern Ape and Human Dentition. The jaw of a gorilla is large and U-shaped, while man's jaw is smaller and forms an evenly rounded arch. Notice the shape of man's canine teeth; the gorilla's larger, sharper canines are good equipment for tearing food.

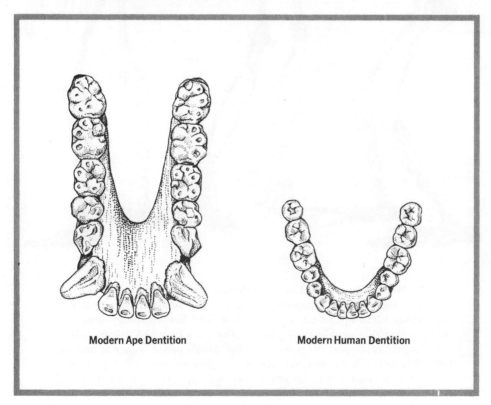

Modern Ape Dentition   Modern Human Dentition

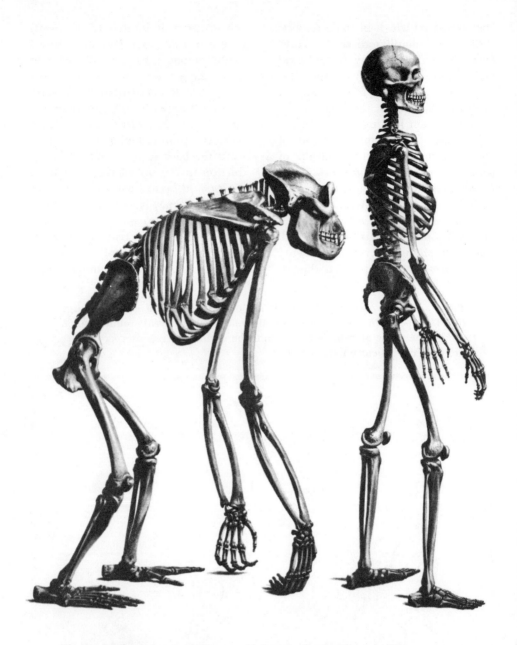

Fig. 7 Modern Ape and Human Skeletons. Ape and man differ at many points in their skeletal structures. (The gorilla has again been chosen for comparison.) The ape's backbone is arched. The human spine forms an S-shaped curve that permits erect posture. The ape's long and narrow pelvis is used mainly to support his powerful torso. Man's pelvic bone not only supports his upper body, but has muscle attachments that aid him to walk. Man's legs are longer than his arms, while the opposite is true of the gorilla, whose extended forelimbs aid locomotion on the ground and in trees.

have become less available for locomotion, which would in turn indicate the beginning of greater reliance on legs for movement. Unfortunately, we do not have a pelvic bone of *Ramapithecus*. We do not know whether he attained habitually erect posture and locomotion on two feet, referred to as **bipedalism**. But as we shall see, these revolutionary adaptations may well have been in the making.

Before continuing with our account of man's entrance upon the world stage, we should note two things about the relevant fossil evidence: this evidence is restricted to the Old World, and the Old World is also the original home of the great apes. It may come as a surprise that for the next traces of our human ancestors we must move forward more than ten million years.

Human Evolution During the Lower Pleistocene

Just as the interpretation of the pre-Pleistocene primate fossils is far from uniform, so is the reading of the fossil record now available for the last two million years of human evolution. The simplified account offered here must therefore be viewed as tentative and subject to revision as new fossil finds are uncovered, analyzed, and classified.

Most physical anthropologists today are in agreement about at least one thing: too many different names have been given to the various human and prehuman fossils of the Pleistocene epoch. A majority of anthropologists now recognize all of these fossils as belonging to only two genera, the genus *Australopithecus* and the genus *Homo*. The designation *Au-*

stralopithecus is derived from the Latin *australis,* meaning "southern," and the Greek *pithēkos,* "ape." Despite the name, however, members of the genus *Australopithecus* are considered hominids. The genus *Homo* includes two recognized species of mankind—an extinct species and *Homo sapiens.* They will be discussed in Chapter 7, "The Evolution of Man."

The australopithecine fossils, so named because their best-known specimens were discovered in southern Africa, may be said to represent two different species—*Australopithecus africanus* and *Australopithecus robustus.* The individuals of the first type appear to have been rather small and slender. They may have stood four feet tall, and probably weighed no more than sixty or seventy pounds. *Australopithecus africanus* was further characterized by a narrow face,

Fig. 8 Australopithecus africanus. **The skull of *Australopithecus africanus* exhibits both hominid and apelike features. Observe how it compares with the skull of modern man (in gray). Now compare it with the ape skull on page 68.**

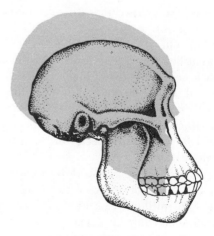

Australopithecus africanus

an arched forehead, near-human dentition, and a braincase about one third the capacity of modern man's, or about 500 cc. (cubic centimeters). More significantly, his pelvic structure leaves no doubt that *Australopithecus africanus* moved about on two limbs habitually and efficiently. He doubtless also made use of simple weapons, quite possibly antelope thighbones, as he went about supplementing his vegetable diet with an occasional fea of meat.

Australopithecus robustus (also termed *Paranthropus*) was by comparison considerably bigger and more rugged. His forehead was more sloping and the top of his skull projected into a bony ridge, which in the modern gorilla anchors the sturdy muscles that aid in chewing food. This australopithecine's teeth suggest that he was still a typical vegetarian primate, though he was fairly upright in gait.

Another famous fossil skull from the Lower Pleistocene was discovered in Tanzania (then Tanganyika) in 1959. Its discoverers, Dr. L. S. B. and Mary Leakey, have made many other widely publicized finds in the fossil-rich Olduvai Gorge in Tanzania. (Dr. Leakey was also the discoverer of the first *Proconsul* fossil in Kenya in 1930.) The skull turned up in 1959 was at first thought to represent a distinct genus of early man and was named **Zinjanthropus**. However, this fossil is now generally considered to be either a variety of *Australopithecus robustus* or a third species of the australopithecines.

What were these australopithecines, in existence for at least the first of the two million years of the Pleistocene? Were they apes, man apes, apemen, or very primitive humans? It is difficult to say, especially when we do not even know whether all of the important evidence is in yet. But we may say with assurance that the australopithecines were certainly closer to evolving into man than into just another kind of great ape.

Biocultural Interaction

In a later chapter we shall be concerned with the cultural origins of mankind. We shall note particularly the early development of tools, which marked man's first purposeful attempt to adapt to his environment. But it would be a serious error to think that man's biological and cultural evolution are two separate and unrelated processes. Modern anthropologists are well aware of the many and intricate instances of biological and cultural interaction in human evolution. We shall henceforth refer to the process by which trends in biological and cultural evolution mutually affect and advance each other as **biocultural interaction.**

What are some examples of biocultural interaction? To begin with, it was not until man became efficiently bipedal that he could employ his forelimbs—his arms and hands—to use and make tools. Once man's survival became dependent upon tools, an erect posture and bipedalism were absolutely essential. Moreover, since toolmaking required learning, a larger and better-developed brain acquired special survival value. We can assume that natural selection favored those individuals who were so equipped.

Greater complexity of the brain made possible even more learning and consequently more extensive use of more complicated tools, which in turn furthered the selection of an even larger brain with a more differentiated cerebral cortex. Then, too, at some point in the early evolution of man, the beginnings of human speech must have been laid. By aiding communication among its users, language promoted the manufacture of more elaborate tools. These changes in turn favored the long-range success of those individuals having brains with still greater capacity, who then passed on this desirable trait to their offspring.

One could set up many other such chains of biocultural interaction. Man's handgrip, which is characterized not only by strength but by precision as well, is the result of two major developments. The first was the selection early in primate evolution of an opposable thumb adapted to grasping branches. The second occurred much later, at the time when bipedalism was freeing the forelimbs for their newly emerging function of manipulating tools. During this stage of development, the fingers became fully straight and the thumb became much strengthened. The result was the human hand, admirably suited to toolmaking and artistry. Assisted by another primate specialization, a highly developed visual sense, the hand became an indispensable organ of infinite usefulness.

Let us now review the process of biocultural interaction, using as our example the development of the brain and the growing complexity of man's learned behavior. Note that this example encompasses two of the processes of biocultural interaction described above: the relation of brain development to advances in toolmaking and to the growth of language.

Increasing brain development made possible more complex learned behavior, which in turn favored even greater development of the brain. The partial return of the effects of a process back to its original source is referred to as **feedback.** Our understanding of human evolution would be incomplete without a full appreciation of the importance of feedback in advancing many evolutionary processes.

SUMMARY

Although the search for man's origins is by no means complete, many fossil discoveries of the recent past have shed considerable light on the matter. Man as a primate shares important features in common with the lowest prosimians as well as with the higher primates. However, natural selection has favored certain developments of the brain, jaws, and limbs that have put an apparently unbridgeable distance between man and even the great apes.

It is thought that man began evolving along a line distinct from the great apes about twenty-five million years ago. A number of fossil specimens of the Miocene and Pliocene epochs are candidates for the title of "missing link" between ape and man. *Ramapithecus* has been described as "man ape," the australopithecines as "ape-men." Perhaps scholars never will determine the precise boundary line between the two forms. But with the discovery of the fossils of *Australopithecus,* scholars can point to at least one form who, being erect and bipedal, turned his attention purposefully to how to make the best of his environment.

Chapter Review

Terms in Anthropology

Australopithecus	cranial capacity	*Oreopithecus*
Australopithecus africanus	*Dryopithecus*	period (geologic)
Australopithecus robustus	epoch (geologic)	Piltdown man
binocular vision	era (geologic)	Pleistocene
biocultural interaction	feedback	*Proconsul*
bipedalism	fluorine test	*Ramapithecus*
brachiation	Holocene	*Zinjanthropus*
Cenozoic		

Questions for Review

1. Recount the history of the Piltdown man, who was once so puzzling to students of human evolution. Why would it be difficult to perpetrate a similar hoax today?
2. On what basis have geologists devised a time scale of the earth's history? What are the major divisions of time on the geologic time scale?
3. How is the Cenozoic era subdivided? What happened with respect to primate evolution during the first five epochs of the Cenozoic?
4. Describe the most important trends in primate evolution.
5. The principal differences between man and the great apes are indicated by what parts of the skeleton?
6. What features of *Ramapithecus* suggest that it may have been ancestral to man?
7. During what division of the Pleistocene epoch did the australopithecines make their appearance? How long are they thought to have existed?
8. How did the two species of australopithecines differ from each other? Which of the two species seems to have exhibited the more human features?
9. How does the Darwinian theory of evolution help to explain the relationship between erect posture and increasing cranial capacity?
10. Of what importance is the concept of biocultural interaction in explaining the evolutionary transition from ape to man?

Chapter **7**

The Evolution of Man

It's not a long trip by air from Tanzania's modern capital, Dar es Salaam, to the city of Djakarta in Indonesia. A short flight to Nairobi, eight hours on to a stopover in Bombay, brief set-downs in Rangoon and Singapore, and one has arrived in Djakarta—island of Java. True, the trip takes more than a full day, but there are pleasant meals served on the planes, soft music or first-run movies to lull away the time, and exotic shopping in the airports where one puts down.

Travel by sea from eastern Africa to Indonesia is not quite so convenient. Most passenger ships passing through the Suez Canal and down the Red Sea then strike out across the Indian Ocean, ignoring the ports of east-coast Africa. One might travel overland to South Africa and catch a tramp steamer out of Capetown to points east. This is not an elegant way to travel, but one has a berth and does not have to paddle.

It is eight thousand miles overland

from Tanzania to the tip of the Malay peninsula. Continuing down the Indonesian archipelago to the island of Java requires travel over two short stretches of water. The entire journey requires something of the adventurer's blood. Beyond hilly Tanzania, one may plot one's automobile route across Sudanese grasslands and down the Nile Valley to Cairo. From there, the driving becomes even more difficult. Beyond the Arabian peninsula stretch the dry plateaus of Iran and Pakistan, and beyond them the towering peaks of the Himalayas. Through Burma and down the Malay peninsula may be the easiest lap of the journey—that is, if one avoids the monsoon season.

Still, the overland journey is within the capacity of modern man. But imagine beginning this trip on foot, clothed—if at all—in the coarsest of animal skins, equipped with a few crudely chipped stones or an antelope thighbone, and traveling in the companionship of ten or twelve of your kind. You have no maps to guide you,

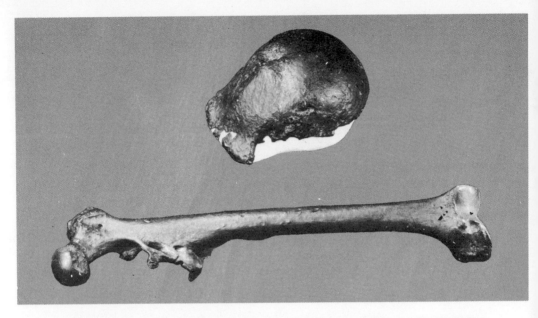

Pictured here are the fossil skullcap and thighbone discovered by Dubois on the island of Java. Dubois contended that the shape of the thighbone clearly indicated that its owner had walked upright.

no compass to distinguish north from south, and perhaps no conception whatsoever of direction. Yet you —or others of your kind—will appear on the island of Java perhaps fifty, five hundred, or five hundred thousand years later. This, at least, is one theory of the relationship between the earliest men in Africa and a more advanced being whose traces have been discovered on Java and elsewhere in the Far East.

A Discovery in Java

Twenty years before the first discovery of *Australopithecus* in South Africa, a young Dutch physician working on the island of Java announced his discovery of some fossil bones that he described as belonging to an ape-man who was both erect and a walking

creature. It was no accident that led Dr. Eugene Dubois to certain fossil-rich volcanic deposits on the banks of the Solo River in Java. He had attached himself to the Dutch army in Indonesia with the specific purpose in mind of performing some amateur investigations in anthropology. Dubois guessed this area of the world to be a likely place for tracing at least part of the story of human evolution. It was the only surviving habitat of an important group of the great apes, the orangutans. And at the time, conveniently for Dubois, the Dutch were ruling Indonesia.

Dubois's earliest finds were a hominid skullcap, discovered in 1891, and a human thighbone uncovered nearby about a year later. In 1894, Dubois announced his discovery of the fossil bones in a widely circulated pamphlet. He designated the creature to whom they belonged *Pithecanthropus erectus* (Greek *pithēkos,* "ape," and *anthropōs,* "man," and Latin *erectus,* "upright, erect"). Before long, his fossil specimen had been dubbed, somewhat less scientifically, **Java man.**

Dubois's fossils presented a puzzle to scientists for several decades after their discovery. From so little, how much could with certainty be stated about the creature termed *Pithecanthropus erectus?* The skullcap discovered was small and relatively flattened and projected into a heavy ridge above the eye sockets that is characteristic of apes. Dubois contended that the shape of the thighbone clearly indicated that its owner had attained erect posture.

Subsequently, the discovery of more skulls of Java man led scholars to venture that this form most certainly was erect and bipedal; he probably had the manipulative ability to fashion simple tools (but to date, no tools have been found in direct association with his remains); and he quite possibly had mastered the rudiments of human speech. Java man, in other words, had attained to at least some degree of human respectability!

The search for traces of Java man was abandoned for several decades after Dubois made his original discoveries. This picture shows the site of discovery of "Pithecanthropus III" in 1938. The new find consisted of several fragments of a child's skull.

Fossil Finds Near Peking

Even more startling than the Java finds were a series of discoveries at Choukoutien, twenty-five miles southwest of Peking, beginning in the 1920's. In cave deposits at Choukoutien, anthropologists uncovered not only very ancient hominid skulls, jaws, teeth, and limb bones; but in association with these skeletal remains they found crude tools fashioned from coarse-grained quartz and greenstone, minerals not common to the region.

A wealth of human and animal fossils was discovered in this deep cave pit at Choukoutien, near Peking, China. Simple stone tools and charcoal remains found among the bones suggest that Peking man was a toolmaker who knew at least the use of fire.

Some sites at Choukoutien were uncovered to reveal the bones of numerous large mammals, on which the cave dwellers had apparently feasted. Ash heaps and pieces of charcoal found among these bones indicate that the cave dwellers made deliberate use of fire.

A new member was added to the list of known fossil men. *Sinanthropus pekinensis*, or **Peking man** as he came to be known, was soon the subject of lively debates among scientists all over the world. The debates, as might be expected, focused on the relationship of the Peking hominid fossils to the more familiar Java fossils. Peking man had a greater brain capacity than Java man (about 1,050 cc., as compared with about 900 cc. for Java man). This fact, coupled with the definite indications that Peking man employed tools and made use of fire, resulted in his being judged the more advanced of the two.

Both Java man and Peking man lived during the Middle Pleistocene. The Choukoutien site is dated at about 400,000 years before the present, but the thickness of the deposited materials in these caves suggests that they must have been occupied for many thousands of years. The age of Java man is even greater. He appears to have overlapped in time with *Australopithecus robustus* and may date back 700,000 years or more, having first appeared during the Lower Pleistocene.

The Varieties of Homo erectus

Scholars early recognized the great similarities between Java man and Peking man. But for many years they continued to refer to each by his original scientific designation, *Pithecan-thropus erectus* and *Sinanthropus pekinensis,* respectively. In recent years, scientists have drastically reduced the number of names given to fossil men by their discoverers. Java man, Peking man, and certain other fossil hominids that appear similar are now referred to by the single designation **Homo erectus.** Java man, the earliest discovered, is referred to as the subspecies *Homo erectus erectus;* Peking man as *Homo erectus pekinensis.*

Our knowledge of *Homo erectus* is supported by many more fossils than are available for the australopithecines. In summary, he stood at least five feet fully erect. His skull, with a sloping forehead, was noticeably thicker than that of modern man. A small chin and a broad flat nose were balanced by massive jaws and a prominent browridge. He had an average cranial capacity of about 1,000 cubic centimeters, as compared with the smaller brain of a gorilla (*ca.* 500 cc.) and the larger brain of modern man (*ca.* 1,400 cc.).

Homo erectus was probably in all cases a toolmaker, although this cannot be proven. At least one of his varieties made purposeful use of fire. There is no question that *Homo erectus* was a most accomplished walker. Judging from the many and widespread sites where his remains have been found, he managed to cover about as much distance walking as the Old World continents permit.

Claims have been made for the existence of *Homo erectus* in several parts of the Old World. In addition to the Java and Peking fossils, fossils discovered in South Africa, in Algeria, in Germany, and very recently in China's Shensi province and

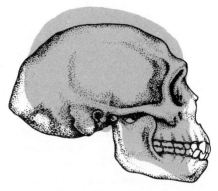

Homo erectus

Fig. 9 **Homo erectus. This skull belongs to the variety of *Homo erectus* discovered near Peking. Notice especially the heavy jaw, prominent browridge, and sloping forehead. Peking man's cranial capacity was about two-thirds that of modern man (in gray).**

in Hungary, all have supporters who maintain they are varieties of *Homo erectus.* Two jaws and a facial fragment uncovered at Swartkrans, South Africa, in 1949 have particularly excited anthropologists. Swartkrans is the site of many australopithecine remains, and the so-called *Homo erectus* of Swartkrans was found in a fossil bed with australopithecines. Could these fossils really be contemporary? Did two different species of hominid share this habitat during some period of the Lower or Middle Pleistocene? This is a matter of some controversy, but the general consensus among anthropologists is that they did.

The Evidence of the Olduvai Gorge

The fact that two species of hominid appear to have existed at the same time in South Africa presents a problem to some anthropologists. The discovery of *Australopithecus* was originally welcomed as bridging the gap between the apes and the most primitive members of the genus *Homo*. Some anthropologists now doubt the validity of this theory. If *Homo erectus* was really descended from the australopithecines, they think it unlikely that the two could have shared one environment for very long. The more advanced form would have been likely to take over this environment.

This puzzle also involves the proper interpretation of the fossil sequence extending upward through the rock layers of the Olduvai Gorge in Tanzania. This sequence has been carefully recorded by the Leakeys. It begins with australopithecine fossils (*Zinjanthropus* and others) discovered in the lowest of five fossil beds, Bed I. It is with the evidence in Beds I and II that anthropologists are particularly concerned.

Within the last several years, Leakey has announced the discovery of fossils belonging to still another kind of hominid in Bed I and lower Bed II at Olduvai. This group of fossils includes several skull fragments, jaws, and a large number of teeth. Found in association with these skeletal remains were a number of simple tools made out of pebbles. No larger than *Australopithecus africanus,* this new form is described as possessing a somewhat larger cranial capacity (*ca.* 680 cc.) and more manlike teeth. And, like *Australopithecus africanus,* he is thought to have been a flesh eater.

Leakey has gone so far as to give an entirely new designation to this discovery: **Homo habilis** (Latin *habilis,* "skillful"). The designation sets this form apart from both the australopithecines and the two established species of the genus *Homo*. Leakey considers this form, and not *Australopithecus,* to have given rise to the later forms of mankind. He postulates for both the australopithecines and *Homo habilis* a common ancestor in the even more remote past.

Leakey's designation of a new species within the genus *Homo* has truly sparked a controversy! His dissenters argue against the naming of *Homo habilis* as a separate species, contending that some of his fossils belong to *Australopithecus* and some to *Homo erectus*. Moreover, while certain anthropologists recognize a problem in the contemporary existence of *Australopithecus* and *Homo erectus,* others see no reason why the former could not have been ancestral to the latter. As in so many other cases, solution of this controversy seems to await the discovery of still more fossil evidence.

Early Varieties of *Homo sapiens*

Whatever anthropologists may eventually decide about the sequence of human evolution, it is certain that they will have to take this into account: much of the earliest evidence for *Homo sapiens* comes from Europe. In 1933, the community of anthropologists learned of the discovery of a skull at Steinheim in Germany. The dates assigned to **Steinheim man** vary, but a good estimate is near the end of the Middle Pleistocene, about 300,000 years ago at the earliest. The cranial capacity of Steinheim man measures about 1,125 cc., already at the lower end of the range for modern man.

But the Steinheim skull exhibits some rather primitive features, including heavy browridges and a low forehead.

Thought to be nearly contemporary with the Steinheim fossil are three fragments of a skull found at Swanscombe in Kent, England, in 1935. The skull of this hominid is estimated to have held a brain of at least 1,300 cc., clearly within the range for modern man. Unfortunately, the forehead and facial portion of the skull are missing, so that meaningful comparisons with other fossils are limited. The remains of **Swanscombe man** are noteworthy, however, because found in association with them were numerous stone axes and other primitive tools.

Best-known of all the early varieties of *Homo sapiens* is the **Neanderthal man** (*Homo sapiens neanderthalensis*), specimens of which have been found in Europe, Asia, Africa, and the Middle East. His name derives from a partially preserved skeleton discovered more than a century ago in the Neandertal gorge, several miles east of Düsseldorf in the Rhine Valley in Germany. So many fossils of the Neanderthal type have been located during the last hundred years that we are able to reconstruct with some assurance the typical appearance of a "classic" European Neanderthal.

The "classic" Neanderthal of Europe was powerfully built, with a sturdy trunk placed upon relatively short legs. His compact and rugged body build, as compared with other Neanderthals as well as with other varieties of *Homo sapiens,* probably represents an adaptation to extremely cold temperatures. He lived between about 50,000 and 30,000 years ago, during the fourth and last Pleistocene glaciation, which hit particularly hard at western Europe and northern Asia. His skull was characterized by a retreating forehead, beetle brows, large cheek areas, a broad nose, and a receding chin. His cranial capacity was large, ranging between 1,300 and 1,600 cubic centimeters. There are scholars who claim that his forebrain, the area primarily concerned with thinking, was less highly developed than that of modern *Homo sapiens.* Yet, considering the large capacity of his braincase, we have every reason to believe that we are dealing with a prehistoric man of good mental capacity.

Moreover, Neanderthal man in Europe has left convincing evidence of his capacity for culture. Delicately finished stone tools found among his fossil remains attest to skillful use of

Fig. 10 Neanderthal man. The Neanderthal skull shows more primitive features than the skull of modern man (in gray). How do the skulls of these two *Homo sapiens* compare in cranial capacity?

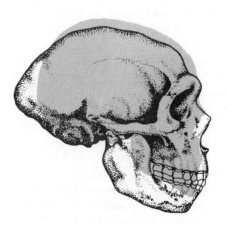

Neanderthal man

look for evidence of further transition into a race of completely modern men.

Modern *Homo sapiens*

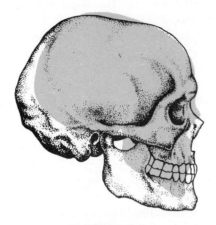

Cro-Magnon man

Fig. 11 Cro-Magnon man. The Cro-Magnon's skull was somewhat larger than that of modern man (in gray). Otherwise, it is almost impossible to distinguish between the skulls of these two varieties of *Homo sapiens.*

the hands. He knew how to use and how to make fire. The burial sites he left behind point to an awakening religious consciousness. A more lengthy discussion of the Neanderthal culture in Europe will follow in Chapter 10, "The Cultural Prehistory of the Old World."

The Neanderthal people—relatives of this European Neanderthal—roamed many parts of the Old World during Upper Pleistocene times. Neanderthal sites have been discovered in what formerly was Palestine, in Iraq, throughout Africa, and in parts of Asia. A Neanderthal group in Turkestan is thought to have developed a religious cult that centered around worship of the bear. Some scholars think that it is to the Neanderthals in Palestine that we should

Most scholars today do not credit the idea that Neanderthal man evolved in an uninterrupted line into any of the races of modern mankind. At least 35,000 years ago, a new people appeared in Europe who are thought to have either replaced or absorbed the Neanderthals who preceded them. Where this new people came from is not known. They are named after the site of their discovery just about a century ago, in 1868: the Cro-Magnon rock shelter, near Les Eyzies in the Dordogne region of southern France.

Cro-Magnon man (*Homo sapiens sapiens*) was fully modern in the biological sense. In appearance, he could not be distinguished from modern man, except perhaps by size: Cro-Magnon man was on the average somewhat larger and possessed a correspondingly larger cranial capacity (average 1,600 cc.). From a cultural point of view, Cro-Magnon man was a highly skilled toolmaker and a firemaker. He buried his dead with care and in other ways demonstrated a growing religious awareness. He left beautiful paintings for us to admire on the walls of his caves in southern France and northern Spain. All these aspects of Cro-Magnon culture will be discussed in more detail in Chapter 10.

Europe was not the only area where modern varieties of *Homo sapiens* were becoming established during late Pleistocene times. Fossil evidence bespeaks their presence in many other parts of the Old World. And about this time, a wanderer as he had been from his earliest days, man began migrating into the New World as well.

Northeast Asia was connected with present-day Alaska several times during the earth's history. The final land bridge was available to animal migrations toward the very end of the Pleistocene, during much of the last hundred thousand years. The best available estimate puts the first peopling of the New World at about 30,000 years ago. Small bands of *Homo sapiens sapiens* began arriving across what is now the Bering Strait and then slowly making their way south along an ice-free corridor east of the Rocky Mountains. Skeletal remains and stone objects of human manufacture that can be fairly reliably dated suggest that by about ten thousand years ago, ancestors of the American Indians had penetrated throughout most of North and South America. The peopling of the major land masses of the world by modern *Homo sapiens* was now fairly well completed.

The Unfinished Quest for Man's Origins

By now you are well aware of how many questions about man's origins and evolution remain shrouded in mystery or surrounded by controversy. Was it an australopithecine who traveled from his African homeland east to Java and Peking, evolving along the way and over hundreds of thousands of years into *Homo erectus?* Or did *Homo erectus* make the journey himself? Or do man's earliest hominid ancestors still await discovery in the Far East, having traveled from there

to Africa? Or did man originate in both places?

Who was *Homo habilis?* Was he really a species apart? Where did the first *Homo sapiens* in Europe come from? Where did they go? Are they, as one theory suggests, ancestral to the Cro-Magnon people, having wandered out of Europe and returned late in the Pleistocene? What happened to the European Neanderthals? Did they die out before the arrival of the Cro-Magnon people? Or was their culture destroyed, and were they driven off by modern *Homo sapiens?* Or did they perhaps interbreed with the Cro-Magnons, thus contributing some of their own characteristics to modern mankind?

The many new finds of human fossil remains and the improvements in methods of dating them since World War II have brought about vigorous activity in the study of early man. Much that was formerly puzzling to anthropologists is now better understood. But this is not to say that the new fossil discoveries have created no puzzles in themselves. Assuredly, they have done just that.

Table 5, "Milestones in Human Evolution," summarizes the discussion in this and the preceding chapter. It is important to recognize that we have merely sampled the important fossil discoveries bearing upon mankind's evolutionary development. Moreover, the fact that this account has been presented chronologically is not meant to imply a straightforward progression from one hominid form to the next. Many more fossil finds are needed before the anthropologist can construct a family tree of mankind—if indeed this should ever be possible.

Table 5   Milestones

Popular or Traditional Designation	Scientific Designation	Geologic Epoch	Approximate Age (in years before the present)
Cro-Magnon people	Homo sapiens sapiens	Upper Pleistocene–Holocene	40,000–12,000
Cro-Magnon man	Homo sapiens sapiens	Upper Pleistocene	40,000–30,000
Neanderthal man in Europe	Homo sapiens neanderthalensis	Upper Pleistocene	50,000 (?)–30,000
Neanderthal people	Homo sapiens neanderthalensis	Upper Pleistocene	120,000–30,000
Swanscombe man	Homo sapiens steinheimensis	late Middle Pleistocene	300,000–250,000
Steinheim man	Homo sapiens steinheimensis	late Middle Pleistocene	300,000–250,000
Peking man or Sinanthropus	Homo erectus pekinensis	Middle Pleistocene	400,000–375,000
Java man or Pithecanthropus	Homo erectus erectus	late Lower Pleistocene to early Middle Pleistocene	700,000–500,000
"Ape-man"	Australopithecus robustus	Lower Pleistocene to early Middle Pleistocene	1,500,000–600,000
Homo habilis (?)	Homo habilis (?)	Lower Pleistocene	1,800,000–1,000,000
"Ape-man"	Australopithecus africanus	Lower Pleistocene	1,800,000–1,000,000
Ramapithecus (also Kenyapithecus)	Ramapithecus punjabicus	Miocene–Pliocene boundary	13,000,000
Oreopithecus	Oreopithecus	Miocene–Pliocene boundary	13,000,000
Dryopithecus	Dryopithecus	late Miocene	15,000,000

in Human Evolution

Posture and Locomotion	Type of Diet	Employment of Basic Skills	Approximate Average Cranial Capacity	Site(s) of Discovery
erect and bipedal	omnivorous	toolmaking and fire-making	1,600 cc.	Europe
erect and bipedal	omnivorous	toolmaking and fire-making	1,600 cc.	Cro-Magnon, near Les Eyzies, France
erect and bipedal	omnivorous	toolmaking and fire-making	1,450 cc.	Neandertal, near Düsseldorf, Germany
erect and bipedal	omnivorous	toolmaking and fire-making	1,550 cc.	Europe, the Near East, Asia, and Africa
erect and bipedal	omnivorous	toolmaking and fire-using	1,300 cc.	Swanscombe, in Kent, England
erect and bipedal	omnivorous	toolmaking and fire-using	1,125 cc.	Steinheim, Germany
erect and bipedal	omnivorous	toolmaking and fire-using	1,050 cc.	Choukoutien, near Peking, China
erect and bipedal	omnivorous	toolmaking	900 cc.	Solo River valley, central Java, Indonesia
partially erect and bipedal	vegetarian	tool-using	650 cc. (?)	southern and eastern Africa
erect and bipedal	omnivorous	toolmaking	680 cc.	Olduvai Gorge, Tanzania
erect and bipedal	omnivorous	toolmaking	530 cc.	southern and eastern Africa
partially bipedal	vegetarian		unknown	Siwalik Hills, Punjab, India, and Kenya, Africa
quadruped and brachiating	vegetarian		275–530 cc.	Italy
quadruped	vegetarian		unknown	Europe, Asia, Africa

SUMMARY

Most students of human evolution today recognize two main species within the genus *Homo.* They are the species *Homo erectus,* which includes Java man, Peking man, and other Old World hominids, and the species *Homo sapiens,* which includes certain extinct varieties of man as well as all of recent mankind. Dr. L. S. B. Leakey has suggested the existence of a third species, *Homo habilis,* whom he considers of critical importance in the sequence of human evolution.

Homo erectus, an erect and bipedal hominid, retained certain apelike characteristics in his skeletal formation. Probably in all cases a toolmaker, in at least one variety he was a fire–user. *Homo erectus* had an average cranial capacity of about 1,050 cc., just about midway between that of a gorilla and modern man.

Homo sapiens is known in a number of varieties. All possessed a cranial capacity within the range of modern man's. The Neanderthal's brain was large but perhaps not yet fully developed; Cro-Magnon man's was fully modern in the biological sense. Both Neanderthal man and Cro-Magnon man created distinctive cultures, the Neanderthal culture in Europe having disappeared at about the time of the Cro-Magnons' arrival. Evidence of both Neanderthal man and modern *Homo sapiens* has been found in Europe, Asia, and Africa. And some varieties of modern man migrated into the New World as well.

Many recent fossil finds have increased our knowledge of early man. But the whole story of human evolution still remains a puzzle to us. Its solution must await the discovery of additional fossil evidence. Yet it does seem today that mankind is well on the way toward unraveling the mysteries of its far distant past.

Chapter Review

Terms in Anthropology

Cro-Magnon man	Java man	Steinheim man
Homo erectus	Neanderthal man	Swanscombe man
Homo habilis	Peking man	

Questions for Review

1. How did Dubois characterize the fossil hominid that he discovered in Java in 1891–92? What led Dubois to seek traces of early man in this area of the world?
2. Describe the discoveries made at Choukoutien. In what ways was Peking man more advanced than Java man?
3. Summarize the important characteristics of *Homo erectus*. What are the significant differences between this species of hominid and the australopithecines?
4. Describe the fossil sequence extending upward in the Olduvai Gorge. What controversy surrounds the interpretation of the Olduvai fossils?
5. How much can be deduced about early *Homo sapiens* from the fossils discovered at Steinheim, Germany, and at Swanscombe, England? How old are these fossil men estimated to be?
6. Describe the characteristics of the "classic" Neanderthal of Europe.
7. What evidences do we have of a Neanderthal culture in Europe? of a Cro-Magnon culture in Europe?
8. What was the geographical distribution of the Neanderthal peoples? of the Cro-Magnon peoples? of other modern *Homo sapiens*?
9. What are the significant differences between members of the species *Homo erectus* and the species *Homo sapiens?*
10. Where do each of the early men described in this chapter belong on a timeline of the Pleistocene? Why would it be wrong to consider this chronological progression an accurate representation of human evolutionary development?

Chapter **8**

The Races of Mankind

Have you ever had occasion to study carefully the faces of the people around you? Perhaps you were waiting in line for tickets to a movie or a baseball game and found yourself with plenty of time to observe the features and behavior of others. Most people, when they do begin to observe others carefully, become conscious of the many differences that distinguish one individual from another. Suppose you were to concentrate on the mouth alone. You would probably discover not only that no two mouths are alike, but that most mouths have a distinctive shape and appearance that would identify the owner almost as reliably as his signature. Yet the relativity of this viewpoint should quickly become apparent if you can imagine yourself in the following situation: you are standing in line and suddenly bump up against a version of *Australopithecus* or against *Homo erectus* in one of his varieties. You are not only surprised. It is a safe bet that you and others eyeing this fellow (with a certain amount of apprehension, if not terror, we might add) will be so aware of his differences that the rest of

the crowd will suddenly appear very much alike. Considered from such a perspective, the differences among modern men do become relatively minor. This is an important point to keep in mind in our discussion of "race" throughout this chapter.

The Traditional Classifications of Mankind

Man is an inveterate collector and classifier. Just as anthropologists study the cultures of the world and assign them to different culture areas, so have they attempted to classify mankind into groups or races according to biological characteristics. Because the species *Homo sapiens* is **polytypic**, that is, consists of many different types, schemes for classifying modern men have differed very widely. But in general, we can say that the criteria used thus far in classifying mankind have been phenotypic in nature; that is, they have dealt with directly observable traits of individuals, such as skull shape, eye color, or the texture of hair.

Different types of body-build may represent long-range adaptations to particular environmental conditions. The elongated torsos of the East African Watusi people have large surface areas that allow for rapid evaporation and loss of body heat. The short, stocky bodies of the Arctic Eskimos are better able to retain heat, a great advantage in a cold climate.

While the classification of mankind based on such phenotypic traits as these has been traditional, it has at least two major drawbacks. Classifications based on phenotypes, rather than on true genetic constitutions, are based on man's detectable characteristics only. Furthermore, most phenotypic traits tend to occur in continuous ranges. Skin color, for example, may range from off-white or light pink through olive, yellow, or copper red to chocolate brown or gray-black. This does not even take into account the temporary effects of tanning. Classifications of modern man based upon traits ranging so broadly and gradually can hardly be very precise.

These drawbacks have to an extent been overcome in recent classifications based on the distribution of major blood group systems throughout the world. Blood types—and we will refer here only to the best-known ABO system—are individually distinct. A person may display one of four major blood types: O, A, B, or AB. Studies of various populations have shown different percentage frequencies for the occurrence of these blood types among the people. For example, American Indian groups show a very high frequency of type O, a moderate or small percentage of type A, and almost no occurrence of B or AB types. By contrast, among the Pygmies of the Congo the O, A, and B types occur with about equal frequency.

Some Traditional Racial Criteria

Because genetic knowledge of man is as yet very incomplete, racial classifications continue to be based on phenotypes. We said that the criteria used in classifying mankind have been various physical characteristics, such as the texture of hair, the color of skin, hair, and eyes, and the form of nose and lips. In the past, these physical characteristics were considered to be the result of inheritance rather than of environmental influences. However, it is now generally accepted that some of these traits may have been selected over long periods of time as particularly well adapted to the conditions of a given environment. It may not be a matter of chance, for example, that among those people who inhabit the tropical regions of the world, dark skin predominates. The narrow nostrils and heavy body-build of the Eskimos are frequently cited as examples of adaptation to a cold climate. Narrow nasal passages are more efficient for warming the air before it reaches the lungs, and short and stocky bodies are better able to prevent the loss of body heat.

Among the most commonly applied racial criteria are the following:

1. The **cephalic index,** or the ratio of maximum head width to maximum head length. Long-headed (or narrow-headed) people are those who have relatively long and narrow heads, while short-headed (or broad-headed) people have relatively short and broad heads. Heads ranging between the two extremes are termed intermediate.
2. The **nasal index,** which similarly classifies noses according to their maximum width and length into narrow, intermediate, and wide.
3. The texture and form of hair. Hair may be fine or coarse in texture. In form, hair may range from straight through wavy, curly, and kinky to woolly. Straight hair derives its form from a circular cross section, while woolly hair shows a flattened oval cross section. The five forms of human hair are shown in Figure 12.
4. The form of the eye. Eye form varies according to the arrangement of the small fold of skin above the upper eyelid. In Asian peoples, this fold of skin may overhang and conceal completely the margin of the eyelid (complete fold), or it may cover only the inside corner of the eyelid (internal fold). In non-Asian peoples,

The Forms of Hair

Fig. 12 The Forms of Hair. Straight hair is found most commonly among Asian peoples, kinky or woolly hair among the peoples of sub-Saharan Africa. Most European populations have hair ranging between straight and curly.

this fold of skin generally runs parallel to the edge of the eyelid (described as "no fold"). The forms of the eye are shown in Figure 13.

5. The color of skin, hair, and eyes. We have already mentioned the wide range of skin color men exhibit the world over. The most common color of hair is dark brown or black. The occurrence of lighter shades of hair—from flaxen through golden to light brown or red—is largely restricted to some European populations and their descendants elsewhere. The iris, the colored portion of the eye, may vary from blue through light brown, green, or gray to dark brown or black. Dark shades are by far the most prevalent.

As you can see, a careful comparison of body measurements, whether taken on living people or on skeletal remains, is indispensable for the study of both man's biological evolution and the present distribution of his racial varieties. The technique of obtaining the necessary measurements is called **anthropometry.** Aside from an accurate scale and a measuring tape, the instruments most commonly used in anthropometry are the sliding caliper and the spreading caliper. The former measures short diameters, such as nose width and length, ear height, and other dimensions; the spreading caliper serves to determine the length and breadth of the head.

Using a variety of bodily criteria, anthropologists have traditionally distinguished at least three major "racial stocks." These are the Caucasoid, or white, stock; the Negroid stock; and the Mongoloid stock. Anthropologists have further subdivided these stocks into varying numbers of "races." Clas-

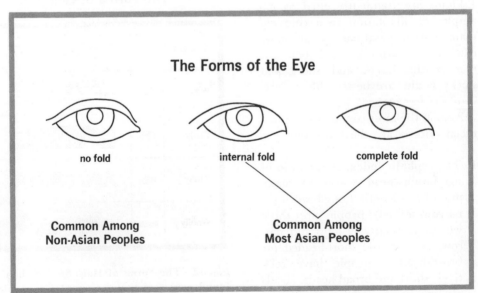

The Forms of the Eye

no fold   internal fold   complete fold

**Common Among
Non-Asian Peoples**

**Common Among
Most Asian Peoples**

Fig. 13 **The Forms of the Eye. Eye form is determined by the arrangement of the small fold of skin that adjoins the upper eyelid. Non-Asian peoples have "no fold." Asian peoples have either an internal or a complete fold.**

sifications of the races of the Caucasoid stock, for example, have customarily included the Nordic, Alpine, Dinaric, Polynesian, and other races. The American Indians have been classified as a subdivision of the Mongoloid stock. However, divisions such as these are now rapidly giving way to new classifications.

What Is "Race"?

We discussed the concept of "race" at the outset of this book. "Race" has been used by anthropologists traditionally to refer to a subdivision of mankind that is distinguishable from other population groups by reason of common physical inheritance. Quite recently, we noted, there has been a significant shift in the method of racial classification. Rather than classifying human types according to observable physical traits, anthropologists are moving toward a conception of "races" as breeding populations more or less isolated from each other genetically. This concept of race is based on the fact that any population sharing a particular environment and a common history and culture tends to breed within rather than outside its boundaries. It follows logically that such populations tend to maintain a common genetic heritage. One extreme example of this phenomenon is the Australian aboriginal population, which has been isolated for such a long period of time that it has become very inbred. The modern native Hawaiian population, on the other hand, demonstrates both recent and considerable racial mixture—in this case, of Polynesian, European, and Asian strains. Yet regardless of the many racial components that formed

these and other populations, they still represent distinct breeding populations. Accordingly, we may define the term "race" as follows: a **race** is a human population whose members breed among themselves and have become distinct from other populations by sharing a number of inherited physical traits.

A Modern Classification of Races

Following the recent classification of races by Stanley M. Garn, a noted American physical anthropologist, we may distinguish three different categories of human populations according to size. These are the geographical race, the local race, and the microrace. A **geographical race** refers to a collection of populations separated from other such collections by major geographical barriers, such as oceans or high mountain ranges. Native Africans south of the Sahara, for example, form a geographical race. So do the peoples of Asia who live roughly north and east of the Himalaya mountain barrier and on the islands near to the Chinese mainland. A **local race** refers to an actual breeding population maintained by either natural or social barriers. Thus, the native Dravidian population of southern India has a separate racial identity from the Indic population of the rest of the subcontinent—the two representing local races. A **microrace** is a highly localized population which, though not geographically isolated, tends to be tightly inbred and subtly distinct. Here we might include, for example, small fishing villages or backwoods communities whose populations fluctuate very little, if at all.

The following listing of nine geo-

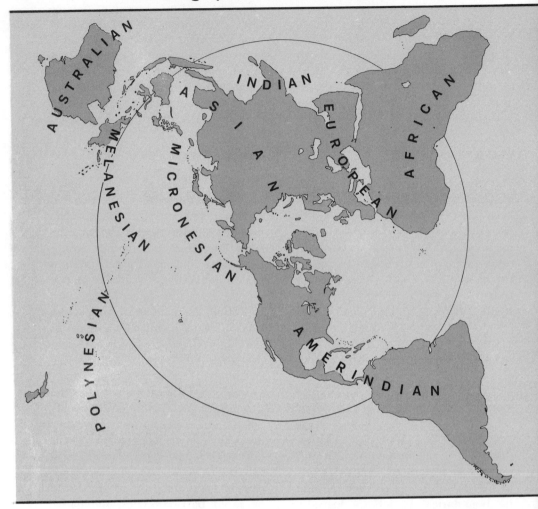

graphical races (those designated by Roman numerals) follows closely Garn's classification of races. Some of the local races included in each of the geographical races are also listed (designated by arabic numerals).

I. European
1. Northwest European
2. Northeast European (population of the eastern Baltic region and most of the European portion of the Soviet Union)
3. Alpine (population of central France, southern Germany, Switzerland, northern Italy, and regions extending eastward to the Black Sea)
4. Mediterranean (population of the regions surrounding the Mediterranean and of

the Arabian peninsula)

5. Iranian (population of Turkey, Iran, and the surrounding areas)

II. Indian
1. Dravidian (native population of southern India)
2. Indic (population of the rest of India, Pakistan, and Ceylon)

III. Asian
1. Extreme Mongoloid (population of Siberia, Mongolia, Korea, and Japan)
2. North Chinese (population of northern China)
3. Tibetan
4. Southeast Asian (population of southern China through Thailand, Burma, Malaysia, Indonesia, and the Philippines)
5. Turkic (population of western China and Turkestan)
and others

IV. Micronesian (no subdivisions)

V. Melanesian-Papuan (population of New Guinea and most of Melanesia)

VI. Polynesian
1. Polynesian (native population)
2. Modern Hawaiian

VII. Amerindian (American Indian)
1. North American
2. Central American
3. South American
and others

VIII. African
1. East African (population of East Africa to the Sudan)
2. Forest Negro (population of West Africa and most of the Congo)
3. Bantu (population of South Africa and adjacent parts of East Africa)

4. Bushmen and Hottentots (aboriginal inhabitants of South Africa)
5. Pygmy (small-statured population of the equatorial rain forest)
6. South African Colored (a racial blend found in South Africa)
and others

IX. Australian (two local races of aboriginal hunting populations)

While some local races have been isolated for a long time—the Bushmen and Hottentots of South Africa, for example—others have resulted from race mixture in recent centuries. The Modern Hawaiian and South African Colored races, listed above, are examples of local races resulting from such fairly recent race mixtures. The Northern American Colored (American Negro) race is another example. This race is the product of limited mixing, primarily of Northwest European and several African races, during the last three centuries.

A brief comparison of the Northwest European and the Mediterranean local races (see Table 6, page 97) will serve to indicate the nature of their genetic differences. But it must be emphatically pointed out that the characteristics shown in this table are *not* found in every member of these local races. The table is introduced to illustrate only the high frequency with which certain characteristics appear in each of these populations.

What "Race" Is Not

To the anthropologist, "race" does not mean a population based on a common language, religion, or any

Members of six local races classified within the Asian geographical race are pictured here. The local races represented are: (upper l. and r.), North Chinese and Tibetan; (middle l. and r.), Southeast Asian and Extreme Mongoloid; (lower l. and r.), Eskimo and Turkic. What physical characteristics do the members of these local races appear to have in common?

other cultural characteristic. When the word "race" is used in such a manner, then it becomes at best meaningless and at worst dangerously misleading. For this reason, anthropologists strongly disapprove of such wide-ranging usage of the term "race" as is indicated by the commonly employed expressions "the French race," "the Jewish race," "the Slavic race," or "the Spanish race." In these examples, the word is used to denote a large group of people bound together by a common cultural tie, whether historical, religious, or linguistic. From the point of view of the physical anthropologist, most Frenchmen belong to one of three European local races: the Northwest (in France represented primarily in the north), the Alpine (in central France), and the Mediterranean (in southern France). On the other hand, from the same point of view, Spaniards are not a local race distinct from the Portuguese, since both these groups belong to the Mediterranean local race.

The Myth of "Pure" Race

What of the myth of "pure" race, a doctrine that figured prominently in the ideology of Nazism and was used to justify the extermination of millions of innocent people? The concept of "pure" or "uncorrupted" race is a complete fiction. Yet it stubbornly persists because of the strong belief by many that racial mixture is genetically harmful and therefore undesirable.

To begin with, most of the present races of mankind have been evolving for many thousands of years. During this time, repeated contacts and genetic interchange have taken place among migrating populations. This intermingling has served as a dynamic agent throughout the entire period of man's development. Even in recent times, with the frequency and extent of migrations greatly increased, a number of new physical types have come into being. One such type, the local race of the North American

Table 6   A Comparison of Two European Local Races

PHYSICAL TRAIT	LOCAL RACE	
	Northwest European	Mediterranean
cephalic index	intermediate range	long-headed range
nasal index	narrow range	very narrow range
nasal profile	straight	straight or concave
lips	thin	medium
eye color	blue, gray, or hazel	brown
hair color	blond or light brown	dark brown to black
hair form	straight or wavy	wavy or curly
skin color	"white" or ruddy	olive to light brown
body-build	fairly tall, owing to long legs	relatively short

Colored, has already been mentioned. Representatives of another physical type of fairly recent origin may be found in Latin America. These are the Latin-American **mestizos**, persons primarily of mixed European and American Indian ancestry. This mixed local race, also referred to as "Ladino," exists in many different subtypes and makes up a majority of the Mexican and other Latin-American populations.

There are no "pure" races anywhere in the world, though there are some local races which until the present were isolated from other breeding populations for thousands of years. We have already mentioned the Bushmen and Hottentots and the Australian aborigines. Another race that must have lived in long isolation is the "hairy" Ainu people of northern Japan, who in all likelihood preceded the ancestors of the present Japanese. But even these highly inbred races must have been subject to hybridization prior to their isolation.

Race Mixture

Even today, the belief persists that the mixing of different races results in individuals who are indolent, unreliable, and of substandard mental capacity. There is not a single shred of scientific evidence to support this belief. Evidence from controlled experiments with plants and domestic animals suggests that hybrids may be expected to be more vigorous than either one of their parents. Such crosses as hybrid corn and hybrid tomatoes are characterized by superior growth and fertility and increased re-

sistance to diseases. Scientists refer to this as **hybrid vigor**

It would be extremely difficult to apply rigorous experimental controls to human beings and to attest to the occurrence of hybrid vigor in mixed human races. However, it is possible to argue—on theoretical grounds—that genetic crossing may have real biological merit. If we assume that any established population represents a time-tested selection of particularly well-adapted individuals, then the crossing of two such populations may well increase the fitness of the resulting generation; that is, provided that the particular circumstances under which the hybrid population is to live are compatible with its genetic constitution. To put it differently, extended and consistent inbreeding may in time reduce the genetic variability of a population, lessening both its ability to adapt to a changing environment and its opportunity for evolution.

Race and Mental Endowment

Another question which has been receiving a great deal of attention of late concerns the comparative mental capacity of human races. Is there evidence to show that members of some races are superior in "inborn intelligence" to members of other races?

The general mental ability of individuals is commonly measured by "intelligence tests." Up to a certain age, an individual's **IQ**, or **intelligence quotient**, is computed by dividing his mental age (as determined from such a test) by his chronological age (his actual age) and multiplying by 100.

An IQ of 100 might accordingly represent a mental age of ten in a ten-year-old child, an IQ of 120 a mental age of twelve in a ten-year-old, and so on. It is generally agreed by psychologists and anthropologists alike that no test currently employed does in fact test "innate intelligence" and that it is quite unlikely that such a test could ever be constructed. What any general mental ability test necessarily measures is how consistently an individual responds in a manner considered appropriate to a particular cultural setting.

For example, nearly all Americans of a certain background, if asked to supply the missing word in the incomplete sentence ". . . should prevail in churches," would without much hesitation choose the word "silence." As a result of their upbringing, these individuals expect to be respectfully silent during church services unless they are specifically invited to participate in group prayer or singing. But it would be a mistake to expect the same response to this question from Americans with a different background. For example, most southern Negroes have been taught quite a different attitude about participation in church services. A more active and audible role is expected of these worshipers, and frequent or extended periods of silence during a service would indicate a lack of involvement, if not complete unconcern on their part.

The test which could reliably compare the innate mental capacity of populations of partly or wholly different cultural backgrounds would have to be free of any cultural bias. To date no one has yet succeeded in constructing such a **culture-free test.** But,

The modern Hawaiian local race is a mixture of Polynesian, Asian, and European strains. What features of this Hawaiian girl suggest a racially mixed ancestry?

some will remark, are the cultural differences among people who were born and brought up in one country —the United States, for example—significant enough to put in doubt the validity of intelligence tests? The answer is an unqualified "yes."

A number of different studies have shown that overall results of standard intelligence tests are clearly affected by the educational background of the subjects tested, regardless of their race. It must be quite evident to any objective observer that growing up in an economically secure family offers the average child far greater opportunity for stimulating learning experiences. Such a child is motivated to achieve at least a comparable status as an adult. Schools serving neighborhoods that are better situated economically tend to be more adequately equipped and staffed and to have a generally lower student-teacher ratio than schools serving districts where poverty is widespread. What the differences in IQ ratings reflect, then, are a variety of factors commonly lumped together under the term "environment" rather than inborn differences in mental capacity among different human groups. These findings are not intended to obscure the fact that individuals vary in ability and performance. They do, of course; but these individual differences respect no racial lines.

In short, there is no scientific evidence to support the belief in the inherent genetic superiority of some groups and the inferiority of others. Such differences as are attested for different groups are best explained as by-products of different social environments. Poverty and lack of education are well known to result in a vicious circle of deprivation. This is why genuine concern has been growing in America to make educational opportunities equal and to assure a decent environment for all citizens, regardless of race. It is becoming more and more obvious that neglect in these areas results in a tremendous waste of invaluable human resources and leaves largely unfulfilled the promise America holds for so many millions of people.

SUMMARY

While approaches to the classification of the races of mankind differ, anthropologists agree on reserving the term "race" for biological groupings only. Traditional classifications of races have been based on phenotypes and have usually distinguished three major racial stocks of mankind—the Caucasoid, the Negroid, and the Mongoloid. Many anthropologists today are moving toward a conception, and therefore a classification, of races as breeding populations sufficiently isolated from one another to produce recognizably different types. The modern classification of races by Stanley M. Garn is of the latter kind; it distinguishes among geographical races, local races, and microraces.

Modern scientific evidence has exploded the myth of "pure" race. Not only are there no "pure" races anywhere in the world, but there is no evidence to suggest the innate superiority of some human groups over others. Nor is there any evidence that racial mixture produces individuals who are biologically inferior or less educable than others. It is not race but culture that shapes the course and destiny of human societies.

Chapter Review

Terms in Anthropology

anthropometry	hybrid vigor	microrace
cephalic index	intelligence quotient (IQ)	nasal index
culture-free test	local race	polytypic
geographical race	mestizo	race

Questions for Review

1. What are some of the criteria upon which traditional classifications of race have been based?
2. How may the natural environment affect the physical characteristics of people over a long period of time?
3. Why are many anthropologists moving toward a new definition of "race"? How do they define "race"?
4. What three categories of races have been distinguished by Stanley M. Garn?
5. What geographical races are represented on the continent of Africa? Asia? North America?
6. What are some of the physical differences between a typical representative of the Northwest European local race and of the Mediterranean local race?
7. What examples can you give of the misleading use of the term "race"?
8. Why is the belief in the existence of "pure" races unwarranted?
9. What is meant by "hybrid vigor"? How have experiments with plants and animals suggested that there may be advantages to racial mixture?
10. What factors may render "intelligence tests" an inaccurate measure of an individual's mental endowment?

Man and Culture
An Introduction to Cultural Anthropology

Man holds a unique position among the
million or more animal species that inhabit
the earth. The only creature to possess
culture, man participates not only in the
natural world that predates his own
existence, but in a world of his own making
with its special advantages and difficulties.
Anyone who has had the opportunity to
travel, or anyone who has roamed the world
vicariously by way of books or motion
pictures, should already have felt the
fascination of culture through observing
the different lifeways created by peoples
living throughout the world.

This unit provides an introduction to
cultural anthropology. It seeks to discover
the origins of culture and to examine
those important aspects of culture, including
social, religious, and artistic activities,
which appear to be universal to all
human societies.

Chapter **9**

Digging Up
the Past

Everyone knows what an archaeologist is. He's one of those people invariably to be found applying a yardstick to crumbling ruins or rummaging about in rubble heaps. He seems to have an insatiable passion for discovering broken pots, pebbles, and old pieces of bone. True? Well, this was the stereotype of an archaeologist not too many years ago.

But there is a world of difference between a "pothunter" or a "bone collector" and a professional archaeologist. The former generally conducts his search for things of the past for private reasons, even if his interest in antiquities is genuine. He is, in other words, a hobbyist. A professional archaeologist, on the other hand, attempts to reconstruct the past systematically in the hope that he may contribute to a better understanding of man's history.

The uncovering of the silent testimony of man's origins and his past ways of life can be as exciting as the fictional adventures of Sherlock Holmes. In this chapter, some of the important aspects of archaeological work—both in the field and in the laboratory—will be discussed. We shall not be concerned with what is generally referred to as "classical archaeology," the study of cultures known through their material remains supplemented by written records. Rather, our concern will be with how an archaeologist reconstructs the prehistoric past—the era of man's history that can be known only through mute material evidence.

A Basic Vocabulary for Archaeology

Like many other specialists, the archaeologist speaks a language not always readily intelligible to people outside his field. Certain of the terms of this specialized language are explained later in this chapter. Some terms that appear in almost all archaeological writing, however, and whose meanings should be clearly understood from the outset are the following:

excavation, or **dig,** referring to the systematic unearthing of ancient ruins by digging out the soil, debris, or other material superimposed on them over the course of centuries;

site, meaning the smallest significant unit of space that is studied by an archaeologist; and.

artifact, referring to any object manufactured or used by man.

The excavation of a site may be a relatively simple matter, or it may require the removal of mountains of debris or modern city buildings. As an example of the latter, the modern city of Hamadan in western Iran is built upon the ruins of Ecbatana, the ancient capital of the Median Empire. The tops of building columns in ancient Ecbatana form the bases for door posts in modern Hamadan. Enticing as this may be to archaeologists, the existence of a living, thriving city atop the ancient ruins may preclude its excavation. Archaeologists are presented with the same difficulty in their study of the ancient Aztec Empire of Mexico. The Aztec capital of Tenochtitlán now lies buried under the mountainous edifices of modern Mexico City.

The nature of a site also helps to determine the difficulty of archaeological excavation. Sites may vary from trash mounds, burial mounds, and masonry pueblos to caves and temples carved out of rock cliffs. The foremost concern of an excavating team is to alter the site as little as possible. But since the excavation of a site almost invariably results in the destruction of the original record, the archaeologist must painstakingly note the original locations of all the artifacts uncovered in relationship to each other. What determines the quality of archaeological endeavor is not so

The building of towns upon ancient ruins has destroyed many an archaeological site. An exception is the prehistoric monument in the English town of Avebury. Because the stone rampart and round inner ditch of this monument form a natural defense to the town, they have remained basically unchanged for centuries.

much *what* one finds but *how* one finds it—how carefully one extracts from beneath the surface of the earth the evidence of man's past.

The Tools of the Trade

A man who told his son, "Go buy yourself a shovel and become an archaeologist," might as well advise him to buy a saw and become a surgeon. Archaeological work requires more than just a shovel and determination. Without patience, skill, and know-how, much evidence can be lost or irretrievably damaged. Yet it is true that the shovel is a trademark of archaeology, inasmuch as a good deal of any excavation involves the moving of dirt.

The variety of tools used by an archaeological party may be limited by the availability of funds, the transportation facilities, and the prevailing field conditions. In general, however, the following items would be found among the supplies of any well-organized archaeological expedition: wooden stakes or long iron spikes to mark the site for excavation; picks of all sizes to loosen ground too hard for shovels to cut through; shovels and spading forks to remove dirt; screens and mesh to sift out small pieces of material that might otherwise remain unnoticed in the loosened earth; various kinds of augurs to sample soil below and around the site; devices to perform both coarse and fine measurements (steel tapes, calipers, and so on); mason's trowels and ice picks for more delicate excavation; paintbrushes of different widths for cleaning excavated portions of the site and artifacts recovered from it;

Three levels of human occupation are clearly visible in this picture of the excavation of Indian ruins in Alaska. The archaeological workers are using hand trowels to remove dirt and debris from the stone layers of the site.

an air pump to remove loose dirt from around fragile specimens; boxes, sacks, and other containers to store and transport artifacts recovered from the site; and magnifying glasses. In special cases, the archaeologist may even make use of heavy earth-moving equipment.

A very important task of the archaeologist is the mapping of a site before and during the excavation. For this, a variety of additional equipment is required. The archaeologist needs drafting equipment, and surveying equipment to establish a point with reference to which other positions are measured or indicated. He needs photographic equipment or the assistance of a good photographer to permit the keeping of a pictorial record while work is in progress.

The Discovery of Sites

An archaeological dig, or excavation, may be prompted either by accident or by design. In some cases, the archaeologist learns of a site that has become exposed by agencies of nature, such as wind or water erosion. He may be informed of a site laid bare by some kind of human activity, such as quarrying, highway or pipeline construction, or simple tilling of the soil. In other instances, the archaeologist becomes suspicious of certain features marking the surface of an area: a small mound covered with trees and underbrush on an otherwise grassy plain, or unexpected surface patterns recorded on aerial photographs. Still other archaeological discoveries have been made on the basis of hints found in old documents or legends.

The archaeologist is sometimes aided in discovering sites by amateurs. You may have heard the story of the discovery of the Lascaux cave in southern France by four young French boys. The boys had lost their dog and, seeking to find him, crawled after him into a hole in the earth. What they discovered has amazed and delighted students of prehistoric man ever since. The Lascaux cave walls are covered with beautifully made paintings of animals—the animals hunted by men living in this part of Europe over 30,000 years ago. Another kind of amateur preceded the archaeologist in uncovering many of the royal tombs of ancient Egypt. Amateurs in archaeology, the discoverers of many of these tombs were professional thieves seeking the legendary treasures buried with the Egyptian kings.

But the majority of archaeological sites have been uncovered simply by patient searching for evidence of ancient human habitation. The techniques of such surveys differ considerably from one type of terrain to another, but they all have in common one thing: prior careful study of the natural history of the area. Once an archaeological party is in the field, its members painstakingly comb the ground for clues to the former presence of man. What they discover is carefully recorded and its location indicated on a detailed map of the area under survey.

The Steps of Archaeology

The very first problem an archaeologist faces after he has mapped the surface of a new site is to decide where to begin excavating. A widely used method designed to save time and manpower is the "exploratory," or "test," excavation. This involves the digging out of strategically located trenches, which will serve as a sampling of the entire cross section of the site. By studying these, the archaeologist determines the proper direction and extent of subsequent digging. When the uncovering of an entire site is contemplated from the very beginning, the archaeologist frequently proceeds by removing layers of deposit within carefully laid-out squares one meter to the side, leaving unexcavated walls of earth between them. Whatever method is chosen by the archaeologist should be flexible enough to allow for modifications after digging has begun. Specific procedures will of course vary not only from region to region but also from site to site.

Once a dig is under way, the archaeologist's chief task is to excavate and record all of the artifacts and organic remains discovered at the site. This crucial step in archaeological excavation will be described in more detail later. The archaeologist may also find it necessary to clean, repair, or even preserve items collected from the site. This he will do with the help of appropriate tools and various solvents, preservatives, adhesives, and hardening agents.

By this time, the excavated materials have generally been moved from the site to a research laboratory, perhaps at a museum or a university, where they will become part of the antiquities collection. But other basic steps in the archaeological process have yet to be taken. For one thing, each of the items collected at the site must be analyzed and dated. It is at this point that the archaeologist must draw upon his knowledge of many different scientific disciplines and their specialized techniques. For example, he must be acquainted with botany in order to identify vegetable remains associated with the site; geology, so that he can relate the characteristics of the site to features of the earth's surface; chemical analysis, so that he can establish the composition of certain artifacts; and zoology, so that he can evaluate the animal remains found in the site.

Not until analysis and dating have been completed, sometimes years after

A good archaeologist throws away all preconceived notions in his search for traces of early man. An amateur might easily bypass the object shown here as merely an old bent stick. The archaeologist recognizes it as a primitive hoe—one of the earliest agricultural implements invented by man.

the first shovelful of dirt is removed from the site, is the archaeologist ready for the final step that justifies all of his previous efforts. This step is the interpretation, or synthesis, of the total evidence yielded by the site. It is at this point that the archaeologist usually writes up his findings, so that others' may benefit from whatever he has learned.

The Collection and Recording of Finds

Since the excavation of a site, even if performed under the close supervision of an archaeologist, may amount to obliterating unique evidence of a bygone culture, the utmost care must be taken to record all the details of the discovery procedure. Notes which seem insignificant at the time they are recorded may easily prove of crucial importance later on, when dating and interpretation are attempted.

All of the significant objects uncovered in a site—whether artifacts, human bones, or other remains—are always left in their original position until their exact location, condition, and relationship to each other have been recorded. If necessary, the finds may also be sketched or photographed in original position. Next, the finds are numbered and, depending on their nature and condition, are carefully packed for shipment to the archaeologist's laboratory. A typical card made out for such an item includes its description, the location of discovery with respect to site boundaries and the depth of occurrence, the specimen number, the date of collection, and the collector's or recorder's name.

Apart from those objects that are removable from a site, the archaeologist is on the lookout for other "features" or evidences of ancient human habitation. Among the surface features he looks for are house-site depressions, quarry sites, and drawings or carvings on rock walls. Such features below ground as house floors, fire pits, storage pits, house postholes, and food remains also attract his attention.

The excavation of burial sites containing skeletal remains requires an extra amount of skill and patience. Such sites are of special importance, since they frequently yield artifacts and other offering remains buried along with the person who died.

Three sets of skeletal remains lie exposed in this burial site in the Chaco Canyon of northern New Mexico. Archaeologists will try to date this site after they have removed the skeletons and artifacts to a museum laboratory. Their first task is to make an exact map of the burial site, showing the relationship of the newly discovered materials to each other.

Sketching and photographing of a burial before the skeleton is removed is essential, as is the noting of all artifacts—typically ornaments, pottery, and weapons—found in association with it. Determination of whether skeletal remains indicate a male or female, adult or child, takes place in the laboratory. The shape of the pelvic region and of certain features of the skull indicate sex with a high degree of accuracy. Such aspects of skeletal development as dentition or the degree of closure between the bones of the skull generally fix age within three years. The identification of animal, plant, and mineral remains found in association with human skeletons permits a more complete reconstruction of the natural environment which surrounded the members of a past culture.

How to Tell Age

The first question most laymen ask about archaeological remains is how old they are. There are two ways that an archaeologist may answer this question. In some cases, an archaeologist is able to assign his discoveries to a specific period of years in the past. In others, he can merely state that certain objects are older or more recent than certain others. The former way of dating archaeological remains is referred to as **absolute,** or **direct, chronology.** The latter is referred to as **relative,** or **indirect, chronology.**

Many of the methods employed in the absolute dating of archaeological discoveries are interesting for their resourcefulness. In tree-ring dating, or **dendrochronology,** the archaeologist attempts to determine the age of wood remains by reference to rings of growth in trees of known age. (See Figure 14, "The Method of Dendrochronology," on page 112.) In **glacial varve chronology,** use is made of distinguishable layers of silt and clay that were deposited annually by the meltwaters of retreating glaciers in certain parts of the world. The carbon-14 method, described earlier, is based on the fact that organic remains decrease their content of radioactive carbon-14 atoms at a regular rate (the half-life of carbon 14 being approximately 5,600 years). Bones are dated for relative age by the fluorine test, which is based on the fact that the flourine content of bones buried in earth tends to increase through time.

Most relative dating of archaeological remains is based on two important assumptions shared by archaeologists and paleontologists. They are that (1) materials found in close association date back to the same period, and (2) the deeper one digs below the earth's surface, the more ancient are the objects one uncovers. It is these assumptions which account for the careful record an archaeologist keeps of the various layers in which artifacts and other remains are found in a site.

One other important method of dating, useful for determining either absolute or relative chronology, is referred to as **cross dating.** According to this method, the distinctive traits of a site of unknown age are compared with those of sites of known or relatively computed age. Thus, the age of one site may be judged approximately equal to that of another, if the type and level of toolmaking in evidence at both sites are about equal.

In recent years, methods of dating the past have been increasing both in

The Method of Dendrochronology

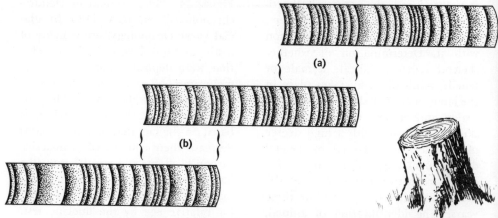

Fig. 14 The Method of Dendrochronology. The crucial factor in tree-ring dating is the discovery of where ring patterns match in different wood specimens. In this diagram, (a) represents where the oldest rings in a tree of known age overlap with the youngest rings in a recent wood remain, (b) represents where the ring patterns in this wood remain overlap with the patterns in an even older wood specimen. American archaeologists have constructed tree-ring scales dating back over two thousand years.

number and in precision. New methods are proving of great help to scientists concerned with probing mankind's obscure past.

The Classification and Interpretation of Archaeological Evidence

It would be erroneous to think of archaeology as a distinct branch of anthropology. Rather, one should recognize the close connection between archaeology and ethnology, even if the methods of these two anthropological studies differ. Just as the ethnologist is concerned with the analysis of cultures in the present or recent past, so the archaeologist is seeking to reconstruct cultures of the more remote past and of prehistory. The extent to which the archaeologist is able

to understand ancient man and his relationship to the physical environment is subject only to the amount of evidence available to him and to his own professional ability. Let us consider now some other aspects of the archaeologist's study of past cultures.

We have already discussed the importance of artifacts. If a site yields a great number of artifacts, description of them is likely to be followed by classification. To begin with, the archaeologist may sort the artifacts according to such features as:

the material of which they are made (for example: stone, wood, fiber, clay, or bone);

the form they possess (in the case of vessels: plaque, plate, bowl, jar, saucer, and so on);

the technique by which they were produced (for example: chipping, grinding, or splitting);

the function they served (hoe for tilling the soil, scraper tools for cleaning skins and other objects, multipurpose axes); and

the type of decoration (in pottery making: black-on-white, red-on-buff, red-on-brown, and other traditional decorative patterns).

The archaeologist is even more interested in using artifacts to classify a site or group of sites in reference to what is already known of the prehistory of an area. To do this, the archaeologist may classify a site as belonging to such larger spatial units as a locality, region, or area. If he is using the **Midwestern system** of classification developed by American archaeologists working in the Midwest, he may describe the site as a "component." The term **component** refers to everything the archaeologist learns about a past way of life by studying a single site or even just one level of the site. In the Midwestern system, a much larger unit that might be comparable to an entire culture is called a **phase.** A set of components or phases occurring successively in time is referred to as a **sequence.**

We have already observed the importance attached by the archaeologist to dating a site and to reconstructing the natural environment that affected it. Beyond this, he seeks evidence about the economy and other aspects of the material culture of an ancient people in order that he may better understand their way of life. Thorough acquaintance with the archaeology of a whole area naturally helps the investigator to understand the importance of culture traits exhibited in a single site.

Emergency Archaeology

Relatively recently, especially since World War II, archaeology has assumed an important new function both in the United States and other countries. That function is the salvage of evidence of past cultures that is threatened by the modern upsurge in building construction. It is referred to as **emergency archaeology.**

A major salvage project is being carried on in the United States by the River Basin Surveys unit of the Bureau of American Ethnology. Since the start of this project in 1945, archaeological surveys and excavations have been undertaken in a total of 269 reservoir areas located in twenty-nine states. Over five thousand sites have been located, of which about one fourth have been recommended for limited testing or partial excavation. Currently, with the rapidly expanding interstate highway system, highway salvage is being organized in more than ten states. As an example of salvage operations elsewhere, recent construction of the Aswan High Dam in Egypt has stimulated a concerted international effort to save Egyptian monuments dating from prehistoric to early Islamic times. At Abu Simbel, the entire face of a rock-carved cliff has been lifted above the rising waters that have resulted from the damming of the Upper Nile River.

Underwater Archaeology

Archaeologists are, for the most part, very versatile people. Since their work often takes them to different parts of the world for extended periods of time, they may be equally at home in the deserts of Egypt, the jungles of Guatemala, or the mountains of Peru. Recently, moreover, some archaeologists have taken to "excavating" under water.

Underwater archaeologists employ many of the same techniques used by their colleagues on dry land. For example, when investigating a sunken ship, they may lay out a grid to help plot its shape and size, map the site with the aid of stereo photographs, and then proceed to excavate in very much the same manner as their earthbound colleagues.

Preservation of the Past

The days of amateur archaeology are fast drawing to an end, owing to the efforts ·of many governments. Apart from instances of willful destruction

Many nations contributed to an emergency fund set up to rescue the famous Egyptian stone temple at Abu Simbel from flood waters gathering above the new Aswan Dam. Four colossal statues of the pharaoh Rameses were cut into over one thousand blocks and moved to a place of safety. This picture shows the reconstructed statues in their new location; the steel arch will support the interior of the relocated temple.

or defacement of historic monuments, there have been many cases of well-meaning but nevertheless damaging efforts by those who have engaged in archaeological work without the necessary training and experience.

An important attempt to preserve the various monuments and objects of antiquity in the United States was made in 1906, when Congress passed the **Antiquities Act.** According to this act, the appropriating, excavating, injuring, or destroying of any historic or prehistoric monuments situated on government lands is punishable by fine or imprisonment. The Antiquities Act further provides for the granting of permits to properly qualified institutions to conduct archaeological investigations for the benefit of the public and the increase of knowledge.

Many states of the United States have laws patterned after the Antiquities Act. The governments of many other nations have taken steps for the protection of objects of historical value found on their lands. But all too often the established rules are inadequate. The increasing hazard that new construction and human curiosity or simple unconcern will do away forever with the evidences of man's past suggests the desirability of even more efforts in this area.

This diver is following the usual procedures of an on-site archaeologist. A grid has been laid over this cluster of jars, the remnants of an ancient Byzantine shipwreck. The diver is noting carefully on a plastic sheet the contents of each square within the grid.

SUMMARY

The task of the archaeologist is to reconstruct the past through the systematic study of its material remains. Archaeological work requires the aid of many specialized tools and techniques, as well as knowledge of many different scientific disciplines. Since much of the evidence the archaeologist is seeking may be destroyed in the uncovering of it, extensive training and considerable skill and patience are required for archaeological fieldwork.

As much of the work of an archaeologist is done in the laboratory as at the site. Once he has made his finds, the archaeologist must classify and interpret them in order to make his discoveries meaningful. In recent years, emergency salvage operations and underwater archaeology have become standard areas of archaeological fieldwork. The archaeologist has also been aided increasingly by measures taken by governments to preserve antiquities.

Chapter Review

Terms in Anthropology

absolute (direct) chronology
Antiquities Act
artifact
component
cross dating
dendrochronology

dig
emergency archaeology
excavation
glacial varve chronology
Midwestern system

phase
relative (indirect)
   chronology
sequence
site

Questions for Review

1. What are some of the kinds of sites that confront an archaeologist? What may complicate the process of archaeological excavation?
2. What does an archaeologist's tool kit typically contain? What are the uses of these various tools?
3. How may an archaeological site be discovered?
4. Why must an archaeologist be acquainted with such fields of knowledge as chemistry, zoology, botany, and geology?
5. What are the basic steps of archaeology? Which of these take place at the site? Which are carried out in the laboratory?
6. What kind of record does an archaeologist make of an excavation? Why must the record be so painstakingly detailed?
7. What are the two ways of dating archaeological remains? What methods may an archaeologist use in determining age?
8. Why and how does an archaeologist classify his finds?
9. Why is emergency archaeology becoming more and more important?
10. What steps are being taken by governments to prevent the destruction of relics of the past?

Chapter **10**

Cultural Prehistory
of the Old World

In the last chapter, we became acquainted with some of the methods used by archaeologists in piecing together the greatest of all puzzles—the story of man's past. Nowhere is this task more challenging than for the period of human history that preceded the keeping of written records, which is formally designated as the prehistoric period. When we consider the facts that the keeping of written records began only some five to six thousand years ago, and that man's origin is dated at perhaps two million years ago with the appearance of *Australopithecus* in the gorges of southern and eastern Africa, we should recognize the immensity of the task that lies before the student of man's cultural prehistory.

Our concern in this chapter is with those hundreds of thousands of years intervening between man's initial struggle for survival and his achievement of greater mastery over his environment. We will mark the stages of man's transition from an apelike creature brandishing the thighbone of an antelope to a home-builder and tiller of the soil. We will examine the tools man invented at various stages better to cope with his environment. We will look also for evidence of man's growing religious awareness, artistic creativity, and capacity for living together with others in society. In short, we will attempt to bridge the gap between man's humble origins and the rise of urban civilizations in the river valleys of the Middle East.

A Timetable of Cultural Prehistory

In our study of fossil man, we made use of the geologic time scale to trace the stages by which our earliest human ancestors evolved into modern *Homo sapiens.* We observed that man first made his appearance late in the Cenozoic era, during the geologic epoch known as the Pleistocene. We also noted that modern man is living in the Holocene, or most recent, epoch of the Cenozoic.

Our task now will be to trace the stages of human evolution with reference to another time scale—that of man's cultural development in pre-historic times. Traditionally, all man's prehistoric cultures have been assigned to three successive phases of the Stone Age: the Paleolithic (Old Stone) Age; the Mesolithic (Middle Stone) Age; and the Neolithic (New Stone) Age. Since man became both a metal-user and a scribe at approximately the same time, the end of the Neolithic coincides roughly with the end of prehistoric times and the dawn of history. How man's early cultural development is traditionally correlated with the geologic time scale is shown in Table 7.

All the evidence of man's cultural activities during the Pleistocene epoch is assigned to the **Paleolithic (Old Stone) Age.** The Paleolithic extended

Table 7 Geologic and Cultural Time*

Recent Geologic Epochs		*The Stone Ages*	
		Neolithic Age ca. 10,000 years ago	
Holocene Epoch ca. 15,000 years ago		Mesolithic Age ca. 12,000 years ago	
Upper ca. 150,000–200,000 years ago			*Upper* ca. 40,000 years ago
			Middle ca. 150,000 years ago
Middle ca. 500,000 years ago			
	Pleistocene Epoch	Paleolithic Age	
			Lower
Lower			
ca. 2,000,000 years ago			ca. 2,000,000 years ago

* The dates given on this chart indicate the approximate date of beginning of the geologic or cultural time periods to which they refer.

up until about 12,000 years ago and, except in its late stages, was characterized by the use of a relatively modest assortment of basic stone tools. Many anthropologists subdivide the Paleolithic age into three periods of unequal length, as follows: the **Lower Paleolithic,** extending from the beginning of the Pleistocene up to about 150,000 years ago (roughly coinciding with the first three of the four glacial advances of the Pleistocene); the **Middle Paleolithic,** terminating approximately 40,000 years ago; and the **Upper Paleolithic,** which lasted until about 10,000 B.C.

Throughout the entire Paleolithic age, man appears to have been a nomadic hunter of game and gatherer of berries, nuts, roots, and other wild plant food. The extent to which he was able to exploit his natural environment depended largely upon what tools and weapons were in his possession. Though the improvement and specialization of man's tool kit came about only slowly, significant changes did take place from one period of the Paleolithic to the next.

The Pebble-Tool Tradition

Probably the oldest of man's stoneworking traditions involved the making of simple pebble tools. Such tools have been discovered in various parts of Africa, including the famous Olduvai Gorge where the Leakeys have been excavating successfully for a great many years. Quite a number of the pebble tools discovered by the Leakeys appeared to have been chipped off from both sides of one end to produce a crude cutting or chopping edge. These Oldowan chop-

This pebble tool was found among australopithecine remains at a site in South Africa. Pebble tools at first puzzled anthropologists: were their crude cutting edges fashioned by man or formed by nature?

pers, as they are frequently called, are very ancient. Although not all scholars agree as to just how old these tools are, the age of one million years or more claimed for them is certainly not extravagant. Moreover, since the making of tools by hand may be assumed to have followed a period during which sticks and rocks shaped by natural causes were already in use, the time of man's first employment of tools must be sought ever further in the past.

At first, anthropologists could not be sure whether pebble tools themselves were man-made or had been shaped by nature. But since the Oldowan choppers were found in association with hammerstones and other crudely worked pieces of stone, anthropologists have concluded that they belong to a definite tool-producing tradition. They have named it the **pebble-tool tradition.** In southern and eastern Asia, the pebble-tool tradition apparently developed into a more advanced chopper and chopping-tool industry that endured throughout the entire Stone Age. In the rest of the

Old World, many new traditions succeeded pebble tools.

Before examining in detail the different types of stone tools that characterized different periods of the Paleolithic, it may be helpful to learn what some of the fundamental techniques of stoneworking are.

The Making of Stone Tools

Not every kind of stone is fit for the making of tools. Among the stones that ancient man chose most commonly for toolmaking were flint, chert, and obsidian. Why? Not only are these stones hard and capable of holding an edge, but they also fracture smoothly when struck or pressed.

The shaping of stone tools was performed by a process of **flaking,** or of removing thin layers of flake from an original stone core. This might be done either by percussion or by pressure. **Percussion flaking** involved the striking of a stone core either against,

The hand ax, the versatile tool of Lower Paleolithic man, was fashioned by chipping flake layers off a hard stone core. Its rounded end was cupped in the hand, its pointed end used for cutting and chopping.

or through the use of, another object until a flake chipped off. The simplest and probably most ancient method of percussion flaking was by the **anvil technique,** which consisted of striking a stone repeatedly against a stationary boulder used as an anvil. Because of the limited control that could be exerted with this method, the tools produced were almost always rather crude. In an improved version of percussion flaking, a stone core was struck with a hammerstone or a baton of hardwood or heavy bone. **Pressure flaking** consisted of pressing against a stone with a blunt tool, such as a pointed stick or the branch of an antler, until a flake was forced off. Pressure flaking was begun only after long use of the percussion techniques.

Archaeologists distinguish among three kinds of tools that were produced by ancient methods of stoneworking. **Core tools** were produced by chipping flakes off a stone until the original core had reached the desired shape and size. The Oldowan chopper is one example of a core tool. Another good example is the **hand ax,** a pear-shaped tool roughly rounded at one end for holding and pointed at the other end for cutting.

Both **flake tools** and **blade tools** were made from the pieces originally removed from a stone core. Of the more sophisticated methods of producing these kinds of tools, two are particularly interesting: the tortoise-core technique and the blade technique. The **tortoise-core technique** made use of a stone core previously shaped to resemble the shield of a tortoise. From this core, flakes suitable for a variety of purposes were separated either by percussion or by pressure. The **blade technique** consisted of removing thin parallel flakes, or blades, from a drum-shaped core that had previously been worked to the proper shape. Blade tools included primitive "knives," scrapers, and **burins,** which were tools with a chisel-shaped cutting edge.

Let us now see where these various traditions of toolmaking show up on our timetable of cultural prehistory.

Lower and Middle Paleolithic Cultural Traditions

While the use of pebble tools ushered in the Lower Paleolithic, the hand ax became its hallmark as the period advanced. This tool was so versatile that in more refined shapes it remained in use throughout most of the Old World until the beginning of the Upper Paleolithic. Another core tool whose use was similarly widespread and of long duration was the cleaver. This massive implement, with one end worked to a somewhat straight cutting edge, was used for tasks involving heavy chopping.

Presumably the users of these simple tools lived primarily as hunters in relatively open country, making temporary camps close to water. The density of human populations must have been very low, and the roving bands of this period were probably no more than twenty to twenty-five members strong. What other items of material culture may have been developed during the Lower Paleolithic is not easy to say. In contrast to stone tools, artifacts made of skin, bone, and wood are too perishable to survive long except under the most unusual circumstances. However, it is quite certain that man's use of wood

for tools is at least as old as his use of stone.

During the Middle Paleolithic, a number of flake tools were added to the kits of primitive hunting bands. Among these new tools were different kinds of projectile points for throwing and various kinds of scrapers. The use, but not the making, of fire must have become relatively common during this period, enabling hunters and their families to discover and enjoy some of the first comforts of life. There is also evidence of the extended occupation of caves, the construction or use of crude rock-shelters, and the intentional burial of the dead by Middle Paleolithic peoples.

Perhaps the best-known cultural tradition of this period is one associated with the Neanderthal people and named after the cave of Le Moustier in southern France. This **Mousterian tradition** was characterized by the use of hand axes, projectile points attached to spears, D-shaped side scrapers employed in cleaning skins, and various bone implements for stoneworking. These people formed their tools with increasing skill, using improved methods of manufacturing. They buried their dead with various tools and offerings, perhaps in the belief that there was an afterlife. And it is reasonable to assume that they possessed both a more highly developed social organization and more effective means of communication than did earlier peoples.

Upper Paleolithic Cultural Traditions

During the Upper Paleolithic period, man came of age culturally. Endowed with full-fledged mental capacity, he

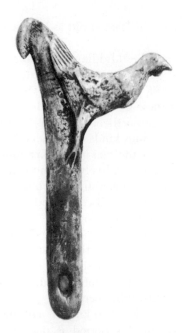

Upper Paleolithic man in Europe added artistry to his toolmaking accomplishments. The skillful carving of this antler-bone dart thrower transforms it from a simple weapon into an object of beauty.

were the **Aurignacian tradition** (*ca.* 28,500–22,000 B.C.) and the **Magdalenian tradition** (*ca.* 15,000–10,000 B.C.). Both of these traditions are associated with Cro-Magnon peoples. Here, we can only sample the advanced level of man's culture during this period.

Most of the stone tools used by Upper Paleolithic man were of the blade type. Included among them were backed blades, which served much as do modern penknives; burins, used for cutting bones and for engraving; borers, used for punching holes in softer materials; and notched tools, used for whittling wood. While these stone artifacts merely extended the established tradition of stoneworking, many new implements made from other materials were being added to man's already versatile tool kit. Out of bone, antler, and ivory, Upper Paleolithic man fashioned eyed needles, awls, barbed harpoon heads, fishhooks, lance heads, and spear throwers. Many of the bone implements were richly decorated with exquisite carvings, equaled in more recent times only by the decorative art of the Eskimos.

But if Upper Paleolithic man excelled in skills of toolmaking, even more significant was his development into an accomplished artist. His artistic sense found expression in at least two forms: drawings and paintings on the walls of caves and rock-shelters, and sculptures modeled from clay or carved out of stone and bone.

What was the subject of his art? Paintings of large animals—woolly mammoths, wild horses, deer, bison, and others—are what appear most commonly on the walls of Upper Paleolithic caves in southern France and

invented additional basic tools, became an excellent hunter, and began to participate in elaborate religious rituals. But Upper Paleolithic man is perhaps best remembered today for his exquisite artistic achievements. Testimony of man's cultural accomplishments during the Upper Paleolithic hails from much of the Old World, but nowhere is it as plentiful and astonishing in its richness as on the painted walls of caves and rock-shelters in northern Spain and southwestern France.

A number of successive cultural traditions, some independent of each other, have been established by archaeologists for the Upper Paleolithic period. The two most distinguished and widespread in Europe

northern Spain. Often these animals are depicted with wounds, as having been pierced by the spears and darts of hunters. Since the Upper Paleolithic artist returned to this subject over and over, it is important that we try to ascertain why. Was the primitive artist a storyteller? Was he recording his deeds as a hunter for the benefit of posterity?

On the contrary, it is believed that these paintings were not intended for the public eye at all. If the artist meant to boast of his achievements, he certainly picked a poor place to exhibit them. For the wall paintings of Upper Paleolithic times do not customarily appear in the places where men made their homes and where they would have been seen daily. Rather, they are to be found in the deep, murky recesses of caves, where the artist must have performed his work by the dim light of stone lamps.

The intent of Upper Paleolithic paintings and sculptured pieces was almost certainly magical. The paintings of animals struck by spears and darts were almost certainly done in the hope of achieving similar success in future hunting forays. Such a practice, based on the assumption that a desired result can be brought about by imitating it, is called **imitative magic.** A similar magical purpose was probably served by the making of numerous female statuettes, the so-called "Venuses," which display exag-

This painting of a bison appears on the wall of an Upper Paleolithic cave at Altamira in northern Spain. Prehistoric cave artists first outlined their subjects on a cave wall, then colored them in with ground earth pigments. Notice how this artist painted over an earlier depiction of a wolf. Does this suggest anything to you about the purpose of his painting?

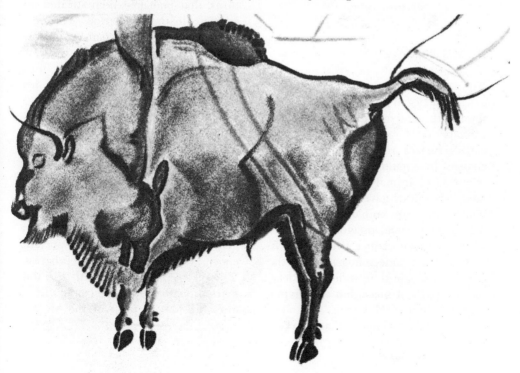

gerated proportions in the areas concerned with reproduction. Such figurines seem to express a hope for fertility.

We see, then, that Upper Paleolithic art was produced with purposes other than admiration or personal satisfaction in mind. Nonetheless, this art is so sophisticated in conception and execution that, more than twenty thousand years later, some of it compares favorably with the best of modern art being created. Both these artistic and other cultural remains give us good reason for speculating that the life of Upper Paleolithic groups was characterized not only by a rich material culture, but also by some degree of professional specialization, by a well-developed social organization, and by the expression of religious beliefs through elaborate rituals. In fact, these early modern humans reached a level of culture characteristic of the vanishing hunting and gathering societies of our own time.

The Mesolithic Age

The ice sheets of the last Pleistocene glaciation began to recede in Europe toward the end of the Upper Paleolithic period. Gradual warming of the earth's surface resulted in profound changes in vegetation and in the distribution of animal populations. Vast areas of tundra gave way to forests. The woolly mammoth and other large mammals that had previously roamed Europe became extinct, while animals such as the reindeer migrated north. On the geologic time scale, the Pleistocene epoch of glaciation was giving way to the milder Holocene.

The climatic changes that marked the end of the Pleistocene also led to a gradual shift in the cultural traditions of western Europe. Adjustment was taking place from an older economy, based primarily on hunting and supplemented by gathering, to an economy in which intensive foraging for food was of central importance. Wild plant food now provided the mainstay of man's diet, which was supplemented by catches of small game, fish, and fowl. This period of cultural transition in Europe and elsewhere is referred to as the **Mesolithic (Middle Stone) Age.**

The technological hallmark of the Mesolithic was the **microlith.** This tiny blade tool, usually triangular in shape, was set into a bone or wooden haft to form a composite tool. There is evidence, too, that use of the bow and arrow was becoming more and more common.

What else have archaeologists discovered about the Mesolithic? They think that man first domesticated an animal during this period. The dog, which in its wild state had kept a safe distance away from Upper Paleolithic camps except when scavenging, now became tame and joined man at his campfire.

The Mesolithic lasted several thousand years, the length of time varying for different areas of the Old World. Yet man's rapid adjustment to his new environment during this period, and his trend toward inhabiting a given locality far longer than ever before, soon caused the Mesolithic to give way to an even more important epoch in man's cultural progress. This new epoch began with the formation of small farming communities atop hillsides in parts of the Middle East.

The Birth of Civilization in the Middle East

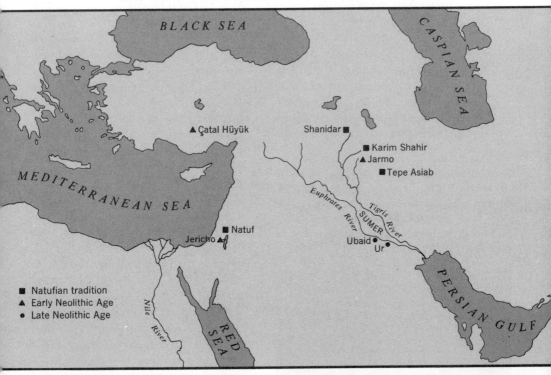

The Neolithic Revolution

The **Neolithic (New Stone) Age** has sometimes been referred to as the first revolution in human history. What happened some ten thousand years ago in the hills of the Middle East was indeed a revolution, and perhaps the most peaceful revolution the world may ever hope to see. There man first domesticated plants and animals and founded the first truly permanent towns.

For the beginning of this story, we shall need to travel to such excavated sites as Shanidar and Karim Shahir in northern Iraq, Tepe Asiab in western Iran, and Natuf in historic Palestine. Here, about ten to eleven thousand years ago, men were becoming more familiar with their habitat as they searched intensively for food in the areas surrounding their semipermanent communities. Archaeological finds of grinding stones and flint sickle blades on the sites mentioned above indicate that these peoples came to be dependent on wild cereals and other plant foods for their diet. Archaeologists refer to the tradition of these preagricultural peoples as the **Natufian tradition.** In brief, the Natufians were foragers who, aside from hunting and fishing, collected large quantities of seeds, probably including wild wheat and barley seed. In a good year, they managed to gather enough seed to provide a surplus. This was stored in plastered, bell-shaped pits beneath the floors of their stone-walled houses.

The step to be taken next now seems inevitable. Some peoples began to plant the seeds they gathered deliberately, and perhaps in a location with a more reliable water supply. We may assume that this development took place between ten and nine thousand years ago, for we have definite evidence of farming centers dating earlier than 6000 B.C. Among the best

As archaeologists worked their way down to the lowest levels of ruins at Jericho, they discovered this ancient stone watchtower. It dates from early in the Neolithic Age, when Jericho grew from a hunting camp into a permanent walled town.

known are three that have been excavated systematically since World War II: Çatal Hüyük, on the Anatolian plateau in southern Turkey; Jericho, near the Dead Sea; and Jarmo, located near the Iranian border in northeastern Iraq.

The recently excavated mound (*hüyük* in Turkish) of Çatal, rising fifty feet above the surrounding plain, has yielded a wealth of valuable information about the way of life in early Neolithic farming communities. Remains of at least twelve building levels have been identified, with a variety of artifacts found at the different levels. Clay figurines of both humans and animals, elaborate wall paintings, and shrines decorated with plaster heads of bulls or rams, leave no doubt that this was a remarkably well-developed civilization. There is testimony also that Neolithic man had become a pottery maker, some form of container now being necessary for storing seeds, grain, and other food surpluses. As a result of several calamities that befell the inhabitants of Çatal Hüyük—ancient fires that it must have been impossible to control —a great variety of normally perishable materials have been preserved in carbonized form. Among these are remains of domesticated wheat, barley, peas, and lentils dated by carbon 14 at about 6400 B.C. Further evidence indicates that these people may have raised sheep for wool and meat. The domestication of cattle appears to have followed less than a thousand years later.

Prior to the discovery of the ancient city buried under Çatal Hüyük, Jericho and Jarmo were the best-known monuments of the Neolithic Age. The ancient Jericho, uncovered under seventy feet of debris during the 1950's, was once a fortified town at the site of a well-watered oasis. It replaced an ancient Natufian hunting settlement of about 8000 B.C. The town itself dates from about a thousand years later. Among the different kinds of evidence found on its site, grinding stones and sickle blades suggest that the domestication of plants was probably achieved by its ancient inhabitants.

The results of excavations at Jarmo suggest very strongly that its inhabitants practiced farming and had domesticated goats. At Jarmo, as at Çatal Hüyük, there are indications that the inhabitants carried on trade with peoples living some distance away. What are some of the evidences of trading activity? For one thing, tools made of obsidian were recovered from the Jarmo site. The closest source of this material is some two hundred miles to the north.

What appears to be the oldest Neolithic farming community in Europe has only recently been excavated. This newer site, located on the Macedonian plain in northern Greece, takes its name from the nearby village of Nea Nikomedeia. Tentatively dated at about 6000 B.C., Nea Nikomedeia appears to have been characterized by many of the same features discovered in the Middle East. There is evidence that its inhabitants grew wheat, barley, and lentils and kept goats and sheep.

It may be that there are similar sites throughout southeastern Europe only awaiting discovery by archaeologists. If so, the region that is believed to have provided the starting point for the Neolithic revolution may become substantially extended.

The Rise of Cities

The practice of farming went hand in hand with the establishment of permanent settlements during the Neolithic. Both before and during the growing season, fields require frequent care and cultivation. This precludes a nomadic existence. Once a harvest has been brought in, a settlement can draw on the stored grain until the next harvest. This makes the nomadic life unnecessary. The keeping of animals, which seems to have followed closely after the domestication of plants, not only served to supplement Neolithic man's vegetable diet, but it also enabled a Neolithic village to survive whenever the supplies of grain proved insufficient between harvest times. Then, too, large domesticated animals serve as an excellent source of power for the various activities that a farming economy requires.

Those Neolithic communities that solved the problem of subsistence and even achieved food surpluses inevitably began to grow. The result was that as the Neolithic advanced, cities of substantial size began to develop. The surpluses of food did not come about, however, without the introduction of new techniques in farming. Without question, the most important of these was the use of irrigation. It is therefore no coincidence that the first large cities in the Middle East developed mainly along the banks of the Tigris and Euphrates rivers and their tributaries. The hilly terrain that provided a birthplace for the Neolithic revolution could not support the needs of advanced farming communities.

The first period of true urbanization dates back to around 4000 B.C.

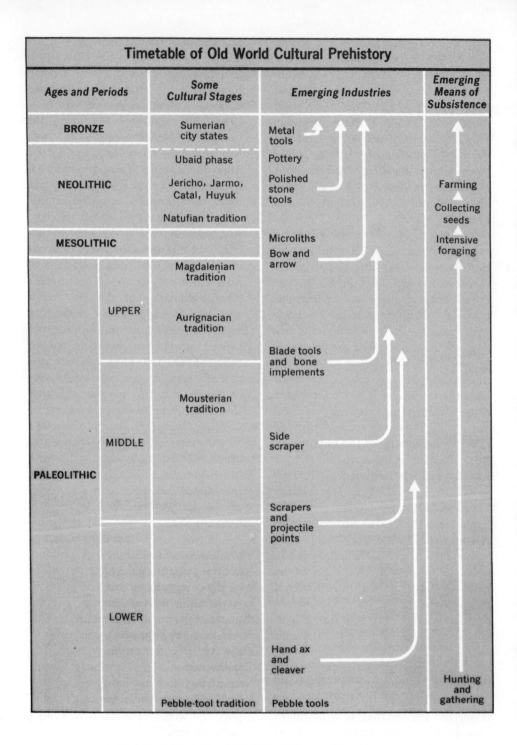

Fig. 15   Timetable of Old World Cultural Prehistory.

and is referred to as the **Ubaid phase** of urbanization. Ubaid, located near the Euphrates River in southern Mesopotamia, was the first site discovered to document this period. Ubaid economy was based upon agriculture. The dwellings were built of mud and straw or sometimes of sundried brick, and Ubaid town dwellers erected impressive temples to their gods.

The Ubaid phase belongs still to the era of prehistory. But not long after came the introduction of record-keeping, a preliminary step in the development of writing. Curiously enough, the earliest records were of a mixed religious and economic nature. They consisted of lists of business transactions useful to temple priests, who supervised economic as well as religious activities.

Sumerian Civilization

The urban revolution in Mesopotamia reached fulfillment with the emergence of the **Sumerian city-states** between about 3200 and 2500 B.C. Most important among these was the city of Ur, located on the banks of the Euphrates in present-day southern Iraq. The size of the Sumerian city-states was considerable; it is estimated that they averaged well over ten thousand inhabitants. Within their city walls, the Sumerians constructed monumental temples, palaces, and other public projects, such as reservoirs and irrigation canals.

Sumerian civilization was characterized by a relatively high degree of specialization in occupation. A typical city would have its potters, bakers, weavers, oarsmen, brewers, scribes,

Atop the royal temple of Ur stood a sacred shrine reserved for religious ceremonies involving the priest-kings of Sumer. The sanctuary has been destroyed, but most of this ancient monumental structure is still standing. The great terraced temple was built of mud-brick and later encased in fired brick. Three great stairways led to the first terrace, the middle stairway continuing upward through two more levels just visible in this picture.

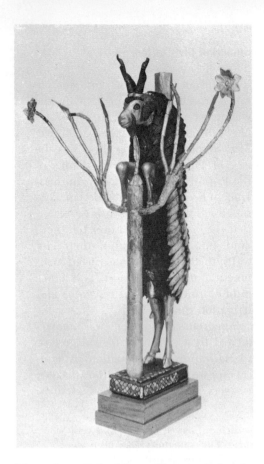

Many beautiful objects discovered in the great royal burial pit at Ur attest to the ancient Sumerians' skill in metallurgy. This delicately carved statue of a goat was decorated with gold, silver, and other precious materials.

cessful military leader, as warfare was frequent among the city-states. The social life of the city-states seems to have been quite elaborate. As an example, mosaic panels found in the city of Ur portray vividly the circumstances surrounding a royal banquet: the servants busily refilling cups, a musician with his harplike instrument, an entertainer of some sort, the king dressed in an elaborately tasseled skirt, the guests in less conspicuous garments.

The warfare already mentioned as characteristic of the city-states gave rise to many new inventions. Chief among these were the wheeled vehicle and certain practices of metallurgy, or metalmaking. Signs of developing skill in metallurgy were everywhere in evidence. Metal ornaments and metal implements replaced countless objects made of polished stone or fired from clay. At first, only metals that occur uncombined in nature, such as gold or copper, were used by the Sumerians. Many objects discovered during the excavation of Ur—for example, a golden helmet hammered from a single sheet of metal and painstakingly engraved—show how rapid was the development of the skills needed for working these new materials.

The separation of metals from their ores, known as smelting, was the next important step in the development of metallurgy. This process enabled man to produce both more and better metals for different purposes. The use of bronze, an alloy of tin and copper, eventually became so important that it gave its name to a new epoch in man's cultural development. The **Bronze Age**, which coincided with the first keeping of written records,

musicians, goldsmiths, bricklayers, and scores of others—not to mention the important warrior and priestly classes. But the great majority of inhabitants of a city-state were the peasants who tilled the fields.

Each Sumerian city-state was thought to be owned by one of the many Sumerian gods and was administered on his behalf by a high priest. Civic affairs were handled initially by a council of elders, in later times by a king. The king was most likely a suc-

marks the passage from the era of prehistory into historic times. Man, who had come of age culturally during the Upper Paleolithic, was now ready to do even more than exploit his environment at an unprecedented rate; by means of writing, he was prepared to pass on his accumulating knowledge to subsequent generations of men.

SUMMARY

This chapter has traced mankind's cultural development in the Old World from its crude origin with the use of pebble tools to the rise of urban civilizations in the Middle East. Humble as the story may seem at its beginning, it was early man's dawning recognition of how he might use tools to extend his own powers that laid the foundation for subsequent cultural advances.

The era of cultural prehistory is traditionally divided into three successive phases of the Stone Age. During the Paleolithic Age, man lived by hunting and gathering. He developed certain techniques of toolmaking, which he perfected throughout the period. In addition, toward the end of the Paleolithic, he demonstrated great artistic ability in works of art thought to have been created for magical purposes.

During the Mesolithic, man showed his ability to adjust to changing circumstances in the environment. He became more and more a forager, content to remain in one locality for a long period of time. The Mesolithic gave way to the Neolithic whenever and wherever groups of people settled in semipermanent communities and began the collection of seeds to provide a surplus diet. To our knowledge, this occurred first in various highland areas of the Middle East. The Neolithic Revolution was in full swing when man learned to plant crops and to domesticate animals. It had reached fulfillment when, in the city-states of ancient Sumer, man invented writing and crossed the threshold into historic times.

Chapter Review

Terms in Anthropology

anvil technique
Aurignacian tradition
blade technique
blade tool
Bronze Age
burin
core tool
flake tool
flaking
hand ax

imitative magic
Lower Paleolithic
Magdalenian tradition
Mesolithic (Middle
  Stone) Age
microlith
Middle Paleolithic
Mousterian tradition
Natufian tradition

Neolithic (New Stone) Age
Paleolithic (Old Stone) Age
pebble-tool tradition
percussion flaking
pressure flaking
Sumerian city-states
tortoise-core technique
Ubaid phase
Upper Paleolithic

Questions for Review

1. Into what three ages is the entire period of man's cultural prehistory divided? What do the names of the three ages suggest about prehistoric culture?
2. What do anthropologists consider to be the earliest of man's stoneworking traditions? What methods of stone toolmaking succeeded this tradition?
3. Describe the cultural traditions of the Lower and Middle Paleolithic Ages in terms of (a) the type of economy, (b) the tools in use, (c) the type of shelters, and (d) evidence of religious belief.
4. Describe a typical tool kit of an Upper Paleolithic band.
5. What was the main subject of Upper Paleolithic art? What is meant by "imitative magic"?
6. What explains the shift in the economy of western European peoples during the Mesolithic Age?
7. What is meant by the term "Neolithic Revolution"?
8. What form of economy characterized the Natufian tradition? the cultural traditions of Jericho, Jarmo, and Çatal Hüyük?
9. How can one explain the origin of the first great cities in the Middle East?
10. Describe the culture of a typical Sumerian city-state. What invention of this period brought to an end the Stone Age? What invention of this period brought to an end the era of cultural prehistory?

Chapter **11**

Cultural Prehistory of the New World

Some hundred and twenty-five years ago, three books published almost simultaneously in the United States caused a considerable stir among scholars of New World history. These books were *Incidents of Travel in Central America, Chiapas, and Yucatán* (1841) and *Incidents of Travel in Yucatán* (1843) by John Lloyd Stephens and *History of the Conquest of Mexico* (1843) by William H. Prescott. Both of the authors were Americans, but of very different personal backgrounds. Stephens was a former lawyer turned occasional diplomat and constant world traveler. Stimulated by reports of ancient ruins in Central America and armed with letters of recommendation and a diplomatic appointment as a United States representative to the area, he traveled extensively in Honduras, Guatemala, and the southern portions of Mexico and the Yucatán during the late 1830's. Wherever he went, Stephens discovered with growing excitement the all-but-forgotten mon-

uments of the ancient Maya civilization. At the same time, Prescott was gathering together a great deal of information on the civilization of the Aztecs, but through the pages of dusty volumes rather than by actual travel in Mexico. Prescott brought to light again the empire of the Aztecs as it had been seen by men who traveled with Cortés, the conquistador.

The Pyramids of the New World

One of the things "rediscovered" through the writings of Stephens and Prescott was the existence of magnificent pyramids in various parts of the New World. These pyramids soon became the object of much speculation among scholars. Could there be any connection between them and the pyramids of ancient Egypt? They do indeed appear similar at first view. But upon closer study, differences between them both in form and function turn out to be quite significant.

Is there any historical connection between the pyramids of the Old and New Worlds? New World pyramids (example above) were elevated platforms on which temples were built for use in religious ceremonies involving high priests and rulers. Egyptian pyramids (example below) were built as tombs and permanently sealed off after the death of a pharaoh.

Today no anthropologist would suggest that they are of common origin or that their appearance in both places is the result of cultural diffusion. The classical Egyptian pyramid was fundamentally a tomb; its side walls were without steps and came to a point. In the New World, pyramids evolved from raised platforms serving as foundations for a temple or an altar. They were terraced and had one or more stairways leading to the ample ceremonial platform on the top.

If there is no connection between these two types of monumental structure, then one must acknowledge that the ancient Indian inhabitants of the New World made spectacular advances on their own. Far from being savages as was once thought, these people developed advanced civilizations quite independently of the revolutionary events that occurred in the Old World from the Neolithic Age onward. In the rest of this chapter, we shall briefly discuss some of the remarkable achievements made by the first Americans before they were conquered by Europeans during the Age of Discovery.

Ancient Man in America

As we learned in our discussion of the varieties of *Homo sapiens,* the best available estimates place man's coming to the New World from northeastern Asia at about 30,000 years ago. Whether or not there were subsequent contacts between the early inhabitants of America and peoples across the Pacific during the **pre-Columbian** (before Columbus) period has not yet been satisfactorily resolved. However, there are some striking similarities between the cultures of pre-Columbian America and of Asia at that time. These include certain decorative motifs and musical instruments (nose flutes and panpipes), the manufacture of bark cloth, and the use of a particular kind of loom for weaving. Many anthropologists are willing to admit that crossings of the Pacific between South America and either Asia or Oceania may indeed have occurred, but they doubt that these would have had significant effects on the cultures of the New World.

The earliest sure evidence of man's presence in the Western hemisphere, based on accepted carbon-14 dates, reaches back to about 14,000 B.C. It seems likely that future archaeological discoveries will at least double this time span. The latest such claim (1967), made for primitive stone tools found buried in volcanic ash at a site near the Mexican city of Puebla, is based on two conflicting sets of carbon-14 dates. One set dates them at 20,000 years old and the other at more than 40,000 years old. The earliest uncontested human remains, the Midland man found in western Texas in 1954, appear to be about 12,000 years old.

Two Ancient North American Cultural Traditions

One of the two earliest known cultural traditions of the North American continent is referred to as the **Big-Game Hunting tradition.** Dating back to at least 10,000 B.C., this New World tradition coincides in time with the end of the Upper Paleolithic period in the Old World. The Big-Game Hunting tradition most probably developed first in the grassy plains of North America and then spread out rapidly both eastward and southward. Piecing together the way of life of these peoples from the evidence now available, archaeologists picture them as camping on high ground overlooking well-used watering places and as hunting the large animals of the time, including the now extinct mammoth and a species of bison. Small game and wild plants no doubt served to supplement the basic diet. Various types of scrapers, knives, and other tools, including some made of bone, were in use.

The Big-Game Hunting tradition was characterized, moreover, by the use of various kinds of weapon points named after the place of discovery. **Clovis points,** named after a site near the town of Clovis in eastern New Mexico, are lance-shaped spearheads of stone, usually between three and five inches in length. These points have a fluted base, that is, a base from which a long flake has been carefully extracted to form a center groove. **Folsom points,** more delicately flaked and fluted on both faces for almost the entire length of the point, are named for a site in northeastern New Mexico. Still another type of projectile point, thought to be somewhat older, was discovered in Sandia Cave near Albuquerque, New Mexico. **Sandia points** are characterized by having one side of the base slightly extended and by only a semblance of fluting.

Contemporaneous with the Big-Game Hunting tradition was a less specialized way of life that extended over much of North America west of the Rockies. The Indians of this second ancient tradition were apparently dependent for nourishment on smaller game, fish, and wild plants. The characteristic stone implement of these peoples was a percussion-flaked blade shaped like a willow leaf, which was probably used as a knife as well as a projectile point.

The Period of Cultural Transition

Beginning about 8000 B.C., and coincident with the postglacial warming of the Holocene epoch, there occurred a period of cultural transition in the New World. From a predominantly hunting way of life, New World peoples were moving toward economies better suited to the changing environments of the continent. One of the new traditions—the **Desert tradition**—represents an adaptation to the increasingly arid climate of certain regions of western North America. This tradition eventually resulted in the rich cultures of the North American Southwest and of Middle America (the region including Mexico and Central America). Another major cultural tradition—the **Archaic tradition**—was developing in the East and Midwest. In the Great Plains of North America, however, the Big-Game Hunting tradition continued basically unchanged for about another four thousand years.

From the point of view of material culture, there were significant innovations during this long era of cultural transition. Archaeological evidence points to the use of grinding stones of various kinds, indicating a greater dependence on collected seeds. From

Folsom points were delicately flaked and fluted almost the entire length of each side. The fluting provided a firm base for attaching the point to a spear shaft.

Timetable of New World Cultural Prehistory

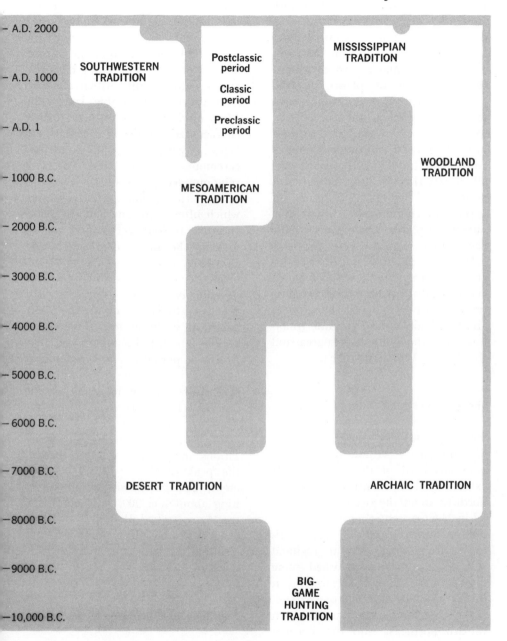

Fig. 16 Timetable of New World Cultural Prehistory.

about 5000 B.C. on, stone artifacts began to be polished and their varieties increased. Intensified foraging next brought about a semisedentary life in some regions and the first signs of New World man's turning toward the cultivation of plants. A full-fledged agricultural tradition began in Central America about 2000 B.C., to be followed by similar traditions in the Southwest and other regions of North America. These traditions were all characterized by the production of pottery and by the settlement of permanent communities, which in a number of places reached very sizable proportions.

We shall now single out three major archaeological culture areas of North and Central America and discuss their traditions in more detail. These areas are the Mesoamerican (Middle American) area, the Southwestern area, and the Eastern Woodlands area.

The Mesoamerican Cultural Tradition

The **Mesoamerican tradition** of Middle America was without question the most advanced of the continent. It extended from central Honduras north to about the twenty-fifth parallel in Mexico, centering on the Mexican upland. Within the Mesoamerican culture area, several regional cultures may be distinguished—some located in the Valley of Mexico, one in the Valley of Oaxaca, and one extending from Chiapas state in southern Mexico northeast into the Yucatán peninsula and southeast to the western border of Honduras.

In general, the Mesoamerican tradition was characterized by the cultivation of maize and a large assortment of other plants—squash, beans, cacao, chili, and others. Among the principal farming techniques in use were irrigation, field terracing, and the **slash-and-burn method** of agriculture. The latter consists of felling trees and cutting down brush, which are then burned to create arable land. The Mesoamerican tradition was further characterized by life in sedentary villages organized around numerous **ceremonial centers.** These centers of religious activity served as the seats of the ruling and priestly classes, which often were one and the same. In some regions, ceremonial centers took on the aspects of urban centers elsewhere, that is, they became commercial centers with ordinary citizens in residence.

It is customary to divide the Mesoamerican tradition into three major periods of cultural manifestation. The **Preclassic period** (*ca.* 2000 B.C. to A.D. 300) was marked by the adoption of agriculture as the mainstay of the economy. It was primarily during the **Classic period,** lasting from about A.D. 300 to A.D. 900, that most of the civilizations of Middle America reached the peak of their cultural development. The **Postclassic period,** beginning about A.D. 900, saw the rise of the Aztec state followed by a rapid general decline throughout the area terminating with the Spanish conquest of Mexico.

Teotihuacán: "The Place of the Gods"

Some thirty miles to the northeast of Mexico City, in the Valley of Mexico, lie some of the most spectacular ruins of ancient civilization to be found anywhere in the world. These are the

The Cultures of Mesoamerica

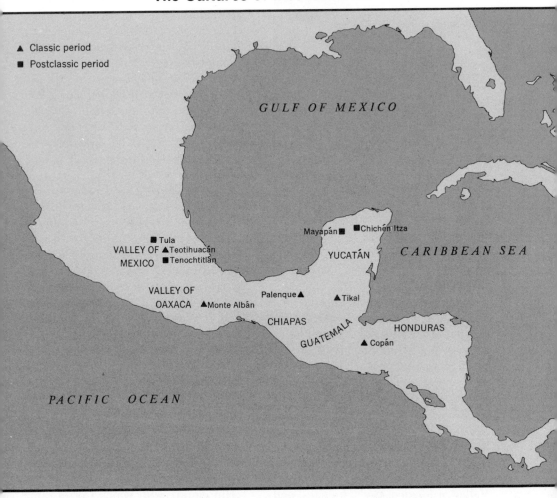

▲ Classic period
■ Postclassic period

GULF OF MEXICO

■ Tula
VALLEY OF ▲ Teotihuacán
MEXICO ■ Tenochtitlán

Mayapán ■   ■ Chichén Itza

YUCATÁN

CARIBBEAN SEA

VALLEY OF
OAXACA ▲ Monte Albán

Palenque ▲   ▲ Tikal

CHIAPAS

GUATEMALA

HONDURAS

▲ Copán

PACIFIC OCEAN

monumental remains of the great pre-Aztec ceremonial center of Teotihuacán. During a good part of the first thousand years of the Christian era, the influence of this metropolis spread throughout most of Mesoamerica. About A.D. 700, Teotihuacán was conquered and burned to the ground. The little we now know about its life and people is based exclusively on the material evidence that survived the holocaust and the subsequent encroachment of more than a thousand years.

At its peak, the population of Teotihuacán must have reached nearly a hundred thousand inhabitants. The city was dominated by the flat-topped Pyramid of the Sun, which towered over two hundred feet above the surrounding site and measured seven hundred feet along each side of its base. It is estimated that some ten thousand people must have labored

This sculptured head of Quetzalcoatl, the feathered serpent god, decorates a temple wall amidst the ruins of Teotihuacán. Worship of Quetzalcoatl was a continuing tradition in the Valley of Mexico.

twenty years to build this pyramid. The immensity of their effort is one index of the importance played by religion in the lives of the inhabitants.

There is also monumental sculpture at Teotihuacán. Among the best examples are the ten-foot-high representation of the "Water Goddess" and the carved heads of feathered serpents which adorn the walls of one temple. These latter carvings symbolize the Mexican god Quetzalcoatl, who was worshiped by many peoples in the Valley of Mexico. Gods, humans, and animals are depicted in a realistic style in wall paintings that decorate the palaces and courtyards of Teotihuacán.

Toltec Civilization in the Valley of Mexico

Soon after the destruction of Teotihuacán, another large ceremonial center developed at Tula, north of today's Mexico City. According to Aztec stories recorded after the Spanish conquest, warlike Toltecs and other tribes coming out of the northwest founded Tula in the latter part of the tenth century. When seen today, the complex of structures surrounding Tula's main plaza—including two temple platforms, two ball courts, and a colonnade—is not so much impressive for its size as for its rich work in stone. Four giant statues of warriors, together with additional carved pillars, supported the original wooden roof beams of the main temple. Friezes representing jaguars, coyotes, eagles feeding on human hearts, feathered serpents, and skulls and crossbones bear testimony not only to Tula's preoccupation with the arts but to a militaristic way of life as well. However, in spite of the military force it wielded and its advantageous defensive position atop a hill overlooking a river, Tula, like Teotihuacán before it, fell about A.D. 1160 to another wave of barbarians pressing down from the north. Out of the ensuing power struggle among the several groups that occupied the Valley of Mexico, the Aztecs emerged victorious. These people evolved another highly advanced civilization and established the powerful empire with which Cortés came face to face when he entered its capital on November 8, 1519.

The Aztec Empire

What Cortés saw spread out before him in the Valley of Mexico filled him with both astonishment and admiration. Tenochtitlán, the city of the Aztecs, had been built up on a marshy island in shallow Lake Texcoco; Cortés called it "the Venice of the New World." Four great causeways connected it to the mainland, and over the widest one, on which eight horsemen could ride abreast, Cortés entered the city. The inhabitants then numbered several hundred thousand, making Tenochtitlán one of the largest cities in the world at that time. There were wide streets with one- and two-story dwellings, which often fronted on one of the many canals that ran throughout the city. At the center, on the same spot as the *Zócalo* (public square) of present-day Mexico City, was the main ceremonial plaza with its two-hundred-foot-high pyramid crowned by two temples. Several smaller pyramids, as well as the residence of the priests and other important buildings, lined the great plaza. Nearby, great aqueducts brought clear water to the city from hillside springs on the mainland.

Part of the central plaza was given over to the market, where the people came together from time to time to hear their leaders address them. Aztec society included twenty great clans, each represented by one member in a supreme council. At one end of the plaza stood the palace of the priest-king. Ruling at the time of Cortés's arrival in Tenochtitlán was Moctezuma, whose palace covered as large an area as did the plaza itself. Besides the sumptuous living quarters of Moctezuma, there were quarters for hundreds of guests from other allied city-states. The palace also housed the numerous officials of the government and the vast tribute exacted from the conquered areas of the Aztec empire.

At the time of the Spanish conquest, Aztec society was divided into several classes. Besides the royalty, there were nobles, soldiers—who were held in high esteem, since war was a profession bearing much honor—priests of many ranks, merchants, common freemen, propertyless laborers, and slaves. The slaves came from among criminals, prisoners of war, and those Aztecs unable to meet their obligations. Slaves could not be sold to another master without their own consent, and their children were always freeborn.

Aztec art was in the service of Aztec religion, whose harsh gods demanded the sacrifice of human hearts and

Monumental stone art in celebration of a militaristic way of life is much in evidence at Tula. These imposing warrior statues helped support the roof of the main temple in the Toltec capital.

human blood. The Aztecs offered up many sacrifices to their sun-god to aid him in his daily struggle against enemies as he journeyed across the sky. Immense carved stone figures of the sun-god and other Aztec gods, most of them monstrous in appearance, were set among the many temples and plazas of Tenochtitlán. Temples were also decorated with sculptured friezes and intricately carved columns. But not all Aztec art work was created for religious purposes. A great many pieces were for secular use, among them beautifully molded pottery and handsome jewelry of gold, silver, copper, and exquisitely carved jade.

Perhaps the best-known example of Aztec art is the massive "Stone of the Sun," also called the "Aztec Calendar Stone." This circular stone, weighing about twenty-four tons and measuring over twelve feet in diameter, depicts in relief the history of the world. The sun, in the center, is surrounded by the signs for the twenty days of the Aztec ceremonial calendar. In addition, the stone is filled with symbols

A gaping sun-god fixes his gaze outward from the innermost circle of the Aztec Calendar Stone. Around him in the third stone ring are the signs for the twenty days of the Aztec ceremonial year, surrounded by still other celestial signs associated with worship of the sun-god. The Aztec Calendar Stone was discovered under the site of Mexico City's cathedral.

of stars, the heavens, previous world ages, time, and other aspects of the universe.

The counting of time was common to many Mesoamerican peoples and probably had very ancient roots in the area. The Aztecs shared with the Mayas and other peoples both a solar calendar of 365 days and a ceremonial calendar of 260 days. The 260-day ceremonial cycle, reckoned of the utmost importance by the priests, resulted from the meshing of thirteen numbers with twenty "day names," such as "house," "serpent," "monkey," "eagle," "flint knife," and others. The resulting "year" was divided into twenty "weeks" of thirteen days each. The solar year consisted of eighteen months of twenty days each, plus five additional "unlucky" days—a total of 365 days. Fifty-two solar years formed a cycle, at the end of which the Aztecs experienced a great fear that the world might come to an end. This period was marked consequently by the performance of particularly elaborate rituals and many sacrifices.

We are fortunate in knowing a great deal more about the way of life of the Aztecs than about that of any other Mesoamerican people. Our information comes direct from chronicles such as the one by Bernal Díaz del Castillo, a member of Cortés' expedition and one of the original conquerors of Mexico. Castillo's *The True History of the Conquest of New Spain,* written in the 1560's and first printed in 1632, provides invaluable information about the civilization discovered by the Spaniards in Mexico. So do the illustrated volumes of Aztec history prepared by Bernardino de Sahagún. The story of the Aztecs thus combines prehistory with history, and luckily so, since today the Aztec capital of Tenochtitlán lies beneath the pavements of Mexico City.

Civilization in the Valley of Oaxaca

At about the same time that the city of Teotihuacán was a thriving religious and economic center, the farming Zapotec people of the fertile Valley of Oaxaca were developing a most impressive ceremonial center of their own. In order to create a large plaza—one several times the size of a football field—they leveled an entire hilltop and then built along its sides a vast complex of pyramids, platforms, temples, and a ball court. One interesting feature uncovered by archaeologists is an underground tunnel which made it possible for priests to walk unobserved from one of the pyramids to the ceremonial buildings in the middle of the great plaza.

The priests of this ceremonial center, known as Monte Albán, employed an elaborate calendar. The artists of Monte Albán were not behind others in creating monumental stone carvings in the service of a highly ritualistic religion.

The Maya Civilization

Our sampling of the major centers of ancient Mesoamerican culture must already have been sufficient proof of the impressive achievements attained in this area. Yet we have not mentioned the most spectacular of all Mesoamerican civilizations, that created over several centuries by the Maya Indians. Maya civilization consisted not of one but of countless cere-

The construction of elaborate ball courts for playing what may have been a ceremonial game was common to many peoples of ancient Mesoamerica. The Aztecs played a game the goal of which was to pass a rubber ball through a ring using only elbows, hips, and legs. The game was also popular among the Mayas, who built this ball court at Copán in Honduras.

monial centers, extending from Chiapas in southern Mexico northeast through the peninsula of Yucatán and southeast to the western border of Honduras. This was the civilization whose achievements came as such an overwhelming surprise to Stephens, traveling in this area in the 1830's.

The Maya civilization must have been many centuries abuilding. By about A.D. 300, it came to flower in numerous places in Central America. Among the greatest centers of the Classic period (*ca.* A.D. 300–A.D. 900) were Tikal in Guatemala, Copán in Honduras, and Palenque in Mexico. During the Postclassic period (*ca.* A.D. 900–A.D. 1520) new heights were again reached, this time primarily in northern Yucatán. The best-known centers from this period are Chichén Itzá, which came under heavy Toltec influence, and Mayapán, which became the leading center when the

power of Chichén Itzá came to an end at the beginning of the thirteenth century.

Maya ceremonial centers, like those of the Aztecs, were dominated by large truncated pyramids topped with temples. Unlike the Aztec capital, these places apparently did not serve as permanent living centers for the Mayas. Instead, the people were scattered about the countryside, convening in the centers for religious ceremonies, judicial proceedings, and the usual marketing of goods.

Serving individual ceremonial centers were many specialists who made astonishing achievements in a number of fields. Among these achievements were the invention and use of the corbeled arch (see Figure 17 on page 146), painstaking calendrical computations that included very accurate tables for predicting solar eclipses, and the invention and use of a symbol for the zero concept. The Mayas also developed hieroglyphic writing, which was both carved in stone or wood and painted in folding books of bark paper. Much of this writing still awaits deciphering by scholars. Moreover, the Mayas were superb architects and artists who worked in stone, clay, and wood. During the Postclassic period they also made use of metal imported from regions farther to the south, such as Panama. The art created by the relatively unwarlike Mayas served many purposes but rarely celebrated the military virtues.

Anthropologists have always been intrigued by the unexplained sudden collapse of the Maya civilization of the Classic period. One theory has it that farming exhausted the land surrounding the Maya ceremonial centers at the same time that local populations were rapidly increasing, with widespread famine as the result. According to another theory, the collapse was the result of civil strife between the priesthood and the populace. This theory considers it possible that the people may even have driven the priests out of the temples. Since the priests regulated the planting of the crops according to an elaborate calendar which only they were able to compute, crops might then have failed and the large Maya populations been

This great step pyramid at Chichén Itzá dates from the period of heavy Toltec influence on Maya civilization in the Yucatán. The step pyramid may have been dedicated to Kukulkan, the name under which Quetzalcoatl came to be worshiped in the Yucatán. The court of columns, foreground, is architectural evidence of Toltec influence on Chichén Itzá.

A Mayan Corbeled Arch

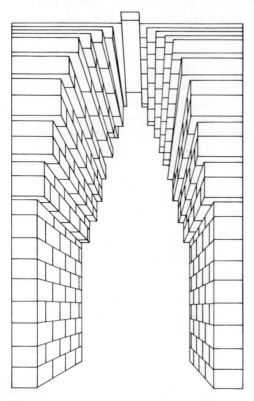

Fig. 17 **A Mayan Corbeled Arch. This type of arch construction uses projecting layers of masonry to narrow the distance between two walls until an arch is formed. The Mayas used the corbeled arch in many buildings.**

left incapable of supporting themselves. Some evidence for this latter theory was recently obtained in British Honduras. There archaeologists discovered a tomb that had been desecrated in a manner that suggests popular fury.

Today, with a number of Maya centers excavated and reconstructed at least in part, one cannot help wondering how many other riches lie buried in the scores of Maya sites yet to be explored.

The Tradition of the North American Southwest

The principal factor that influenced the cultural development of the Southwest—an area including present-day Arizona and New Mexico as well as portions of Utah, Colorado, and northern Mexico—was its proximity to Mesoamerica. The northward diffusion of maize, bean, and squash cultivation, coupled with the eventual settlement of permanent farming villages, produced in this area the **Southwestern tradition**—the most distinctive prehistoric Indian tradition in what is now the United States.

By about A.D. 500, several regional traditions had begun to take shape in the Southwest. Centering in the Gila valley of southern Arizona, a way of life developed which archaeologists refer to as the **Hohokam culture.** Traces of this culture uncovered to date show that the Hohokam people made use of irrigation in agriculture, played some kind of game on ball courts, produced pottery, fashioned ornaments from stone and shell, and practiced cremation. To the east of the Hohokam, in what is today southeastern Arizona and southwestern New Mexico, the **Mogollon culture** developed. The Mogollon were sedentary people who lived in pit houses and attached about equal importance to hunting, gathering, and agriculture. They too were pottery makers. Unlike the Hohokam, the Mogollon did not practice cremation but buried their dead.

The most fully developed regional Southwestern tradition, however, was the **Anasazi culture,** remains of which are found in the higher elevations of the northern Southwest. Today, many visitors to Mesa Verde National Park in southwestern Colorado or to the Navajo National Monument in northeastern Arizona are able to inspect the colorful masonry cliff dwellings dating back to the end of the thirteenth century.

The famous Cliff Palace at Mesa Verde is an impressive sight even today. In its heyday it must have been a busy, prosperous settlement. Built under the protective overhang of a large cave, it contained more than two hundred rooms, numerous small storerooms, and twenty-three **kivas**—circular subterranean structures probably used as ceremonial chambers and men's clubrooms. A four-story-high tower with a commanding view of the canyon spreading out below may have served as an observation post or a fortress or possibly both.

The Anasazi people were excellent craftsmen. Their pottery was well-shaped and richly decorated, their baskets and cotton cloth solidly woven, and their ornaments of polished turquoise and other materials very handsome. The high degree of specialization attested to by these skillfully made artifacts suggests correspondingly complex forms of government and religion.

Toward the end of the thirteenth century, certain areas of the Southwest experienced an extended period of severe drought. Apparently not even the advanced techniques of water storage and irrigation used by the Anasazi (one of the canals at Mesa Verde was four miles long) were of any avail. At the same time, nomadic raiders ancestral to today's Navaho (Navajo)

The famous Cliff Palace at Mesa Verde in southwestern Colorado is among the most impressive remains of the Anasazi culture. Sheltered under the protective arm of a massive rock ledge, the stone-and-mud walls of its dwelling rooms and kivas have survived well the passing of time. The Cliff Palace was constructed during the twelfth and thirteenth centuries A.D.

and Apache Indians were moving into the region from the north. A combination of these factors, and quite possibly developing dissension among the Anasazi villages themselves, are probable causes of the rapid desertion of the northern Anasazi outposts.

Today, the descendants of the Anasazi are the Hopi Indians of Arizona and various Pueblo peoples of New Mexico. Farmers and weavers like their forefathers, they are among the very few Indian tribes who have managed to preserve their cultural traditions unbroken down to the present day.

The Cultural Traditions of the Eastern Woodlands Area

The Eastern Woodlands area includes the territory ranging south of a line connecting Lake Winnipeg (Manitoba) with the Gulf of St. Lawrence and east of a line running from Lake Winnipeg to the Sabine Pass (where the Sabine River empties into the Gulf of Mexico). The earliest cultural tradition of this area was the Big-Game Hunting tradition, later to be succeeded by the Archaic tradition. In the course of the last three thousand years, two regional traditions evolved in this area.

The **Woodland tradition,** which was first to develop, had an economy based on a combination of maize farming, hunting, and gathering. A characteristic feature of this tradition was the burial mound, which frequently contained richly furnished tombs. The pottery of Woodland peoples was typically marked by impressions of cord or fabric that had been wrapped around the paddles used to smooth out the surface of a vessel before firing. The most common type of vessel produced was a simple pot with a conical bottom. A number of artifacts made from polished stone, such as ornamental smoking pipes, were also in use among these peoples.

Much later, around A.D. 700, the Woodland tradition evolved into a new and distinct variety along the lower and central Mississippi River. Under the more immediate influence of Mesoamerican cultures, the peoples of the **Mississippian tradition** gained more than half of their subsistence from the cultivation of maize; the rest was provided by hunting and gathering. Mississippian settlements were larger and more permanent than elsewhere in the East. Mississippian artifacts were improved in quality by the addition of a variety of new decorative styles; some were engraved or painted, others incised, and still others dotted with minute depressions.

SUMMARY

This chapter has traced the development of New World cultures, beginning with the earliest times for which we have sufficiently firm evidence. The chapter has concentrated on the prehistoric cultural traditions of Mesoamerica, the North American Southwest, and the Eastern Woodlands.

Outside the community of anthropologists, it has been customary to single out the Middle Eastern regions of the Old World as the principal sources of those innovations that enabled higher civilization to come into being. One of the purposes of this chapter has been to point out how much cultural originality and creativity also characterized the New World.

Although most of the inventions in native America came about later than they did in the Old World, they were achieved independently and in some instances actually surpassed those of the Old World. For example, while Mesoamerican peoples failed to domesticate large animals for agricultural purposes, some Mesoamerican peoples made use of a much greater variety of domesticated plants than did the Europeans who conquered them. Furthermore, the Maya invention of the zero concept seems to have preceded a similar achievement in the Old World by several centuries.

In short, though man was late to arrive in the New World, he rapidly adjusted to his new environment and rose to a remarkably high cultural level in the early centuries of the Christian era.

Chapter Review

Terms in Anthropology

Anasazi culture	Folsom point	pre-Columbian
Archaic tradition	Hohokam culture	Postclassic period
Big-Game Hunting tradition	kiva	Sandia point
ceremonial center	Mesoamerican tradition	slash-and-burn method
Classic period	Mississippian tradition	Southwestern tradition
Clovis point	Mogollon culture	Woodland tradition
Desert tradition	Preclassic period	

Questions for Review

1. Compare the pyramids of prehistoric Mesoamerica with the classical pyramids of ancient Egypt.
2. What evidence exists for contact between peoples of Asia and America after man's original migration to the New World and before the arrival of Columbus?
3. What traits were characteristic of the Big-Game Hunting tradition? How long did this tradition last in various parts of the North American continent?
4. Which cultural traditions of North and Central America are akin to the early Neolithic traditions of the Old World?

5. What regional cultures within the Mesoamerican culture area are described in this chapter?
6. What culture traits were held in common by the peoples of Mesoamerica? In what significant ways did the regional cultures of Mesoamerica differ?
7. What were the most important regional cultures of the North American Southwest in prehistoric times?
8. What is known about the people who left behind the magnificent cliff dwellings at Mesa Verde?
9. How did the prehistoric cultural traditions of eastern North America compare with those of the Southwest?
10. How does the prehistoric cultural inventiveness of New World peoples compare with that of the peoples of the Old World?

Chapter **12**

Family, Kinship, and Marriage

Man is a social creature; that is, his development is shaped by society. He must depend upon society—upon other persons—for a considerably longer period of his life-span than does any other animal. There are both biological and social reasons for this. Evolution seems to have made man both less fully developed at birth and slower to mature than other animals. Strange as it may seem, however, this slower initial development possesses a crucial survival value in the long run. For while man's slower maturation makes him dependent far longer than his fellow primates, man's larger brain enables him to acquire during this period many uniquely human skills— including the mastery of language— that more than compensate for his initial helplessness and dependency. Man's prolonged immaturity may thus be considered as prerequisite for the long, complex process of socialization, or adjustment to society, that occurs after his birth. Moreover, this aspect of human development undoubtedly was instrumental in causing the for-mation of a universal social institution that has lasted until the present —the human family.

The Nuclear Family

Because of his helplessness in infancy and his dependency during most of his early youth, the human child requires the constant care of the mother. From earliest times, this responsibility must have significantly restricted woman's role in gathering food and in the other pursuits of subsistence. This restriction, in turn, would have increased her reliance on the male. If our speculations are sound, we may assume that the special family bonds of cooperation in raising children are as old as man himself. They have remained essentially the same to the present day.

The simplest form of the human family is the **nuclear family,** which is a family group consisting of father, mother, and children. From the point of view of the child, the nuclear fam-

The nuclear family is one of the oldest human social institutions. Its strength lies in the protection it provides to children and the emotional satisfaction it furnishes to adults.

ily in which he is raised is his family of orientation. Upon reaching adulthood, an individual marries and creates another nuclear family, his family of procreation, which becomes fully established with the birth of the first child.

The very basic needs which the nuclear family serves explain its long existence. Among these needs are the caring for and training of the young, the gratification of sexual drives, and the provision of emotionally satisfying relationships based upon companionship and cooperation between husband and wife, between parent and child, and among the children.

Monogamous and Polygamous Families

In most modern societies, the nuclear family practices monogamy—that is, one man and one woman live together in a union recognized and approved by other members of the society. In a number of societies, however, families may practice polygamy; that is, the husband or wife may have more than one mate at the same time. As suggested, there are two forms of polygamy: polygyny, in which the man has two or more wives, and polyandry, in which the woman has more than one husband, more frequently than not the brother or brothers of her primary husband. This second type, polyandry, occurs in very few societies. Rarer still are instances of group marriage, in which several husbands are married jointly to several wives.

Even when a society encourages polygamous families, the fact remains that many monogamous unions exist side by side with them. One reason for this is the fact that the number of males and females born is almost equal; any disparity between the number of males and females in a society is usually due to some selective cultural factor, such as prolonged warfare, and is not likely to be sufficiently great to permit every adult male (or female) to have more than one mate.

Then, too, a polygynous family is economically very demanding of the husband. To cite one example, among the Ganda, a Bantu-speaking people of Uganda in eastern Africa, a male may practice polygyny, but each wife he takes must be given a house and garden of her own. Many of the poorer peasants of the tribe simply cannot afford such an arrangement.

Polygynous families are to be found, therefore, largely among the wealthier men. The main causes of the surplus of women among the Ganda are the custom of male infanticide in the chiefs' families, the heavy losses of men in wars frequently waged with neighbors, and the large number of women captured in these wars.

Monogamy has had such a long history among most Western societies that we have become accustomed to view polygamy as a strange, even an immoral, institution. Therefore, it is important to remember that those societies which sanction polygamous marriages usually have well-founded reasons for doing so. By the same token, many of our ways of behaving are sometimes judged strange by other societies.

The Extended Family

The nuclear family group may become an **extended family** by the inclusion of near relatives, or even of another nuclear family. Only a few generations ago, it was customary in the United States to find a set of grandparents, an aunt, or an uncle living in a common household with a nuclear family. Today, for many reasons, independent nuclear families have become the regular pattern in

The extended family system is the preferred kinship arrangement in many societies of Asia and Africa. This extended family belongs to an Ivory Coast tribe whose subsistence is based upon food gathering. The members of this family can count upon each other for help in times of scarcity.

the United States. In many other societies, however, extended families constitute the expected and preferred social arrangement and as such are culturally regulated.

There are two important types of the extended family, the patrilocal family and the matrilocal family. In the **patrilocal family,** the bride customarily leaves the household of her parents to live in or near the household of her husband's parents. In the **matrilocal family,** the groom moves away from his parent's home to live with his wife's parents. In some societies, a newly married couple may live with or near the parents of either spouse or even in the household of the groom's maternal uncle. In American society, the residence of newlyweds is almost always apart from the household of either set of parents.

Kinship

The term **kinship** refers to the state of being related. Kinship ties may be classified in two basic categories: **consanguinity,** or relationship by blood, and **affinity,** or relationship by marriage. In theory, every person is likely to have both consanguineal and affinal kin; the extent to which it is important to distinguish them by special terms and a particular social relationship differs from one society to another.

Most Americans tend to minimize kinship ties. Such a term as "cousin" may be used by an American to include a large number of relatives regardless of sex, generation, or biological distance. There are many reasons for this development. Not the least important historically was the pioneer settlement of the American frontier, which could not have been accomplished without the readiness of many Americans to give up the security of traditional kinship ties and set out on an independent course. More recently, the industrialization and urbanization of the United States, and the ever-increasing mobility and independence of its young people, have continued the trend begun earlier. By contrast, the members of most of the small, close-knit societies of the world regard kinship ties and the associated behavior toward different kinds of relatives with the utmost seriousness.

Among the criteria used commonly to distinguish different types of kinsmen are the generation level (as in the terms "grandfather," "father," "son," and "grandson"), the sex of the kinsmen (as in "aunt" and "uncle"), and relative age within the same generation, especially the distinction between older and younger brothers or sisters. We noted earlier another distinction in the nature of relatedness, that between consanguineal and affinal ties (as in "father" and "father-in-law"). Distinction is also drawn between **lineal** (direct) and **collateral** (nondirect) ties. One's relationship to one's father is lineal, that is, in a direct line of descent; one is related to one's uncle collaterally. Finally, the sex of the person speaking may be indicated by a kinship term. For example, the Haida Indians of the American Northwest coast have two separate terms for "father," one used by sons and the other by daughters.

The kinship terminologies of most peoples faithfully reflect the kinship ties important in their society. Since the expected behavior among kinsmen is commonly regulated by the degree and kind of relationship, anthropologists consider the study of kinship systems as one of their important tasks. To represent and analyze the often very complicated maze of relationships, they find it helpful to resort to diagrams.

In diagraming kinship systems, anthropologists use a triangle to symbolize male relatives and a circle to symbolize female relatives. A single line running from left to right connects **siblings**—brothers and sisters—while two parallel lines (an equal sign) indicate a marital tie. Different generations are indicated by the relative position of the symbols, with children represented below their parents. A nuclear family consisting of a father, mother, son, and daughter would be diagramed as shown in Figure 18.

A kinship diagram may be labeled from the point of view of a particular individual, usually an adult male, who is designated as **ego** and set off graphically. Figure 19, "The American Kinship System," on page 156 is a simplified diagram of the most common type of kinship system found in the United States. It is labeled from the point of view of an adult male ego. Even this diagram, however, does not quite indicate the full complexity of American kinship terminology. For instance, it gives for ego's parents the **terms of reference,** meaning the terms ego is likely to use when talking about his parents; but when speaking to his parents, ego may use another set of terms—the **terms of address**—perhaps in this case "Dad" and "Mom" or "Pa" and "Ma." Some of us would term our father's or mother's uncle our "great-uncle" or "grand-uncle," but others would not actively

The Nuclear Family

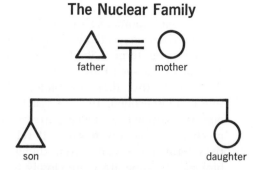

Fig. 18 The Nuclear Family. This kinship diagram illustrates the relationships between members of a nuclear family.

use these terms. The distinctions among the terms "first cousin," "first cousin once removed," "second cousin," and "cousin-in-law" are still made by some Americans, though these usages are becoming rarer and rarer.

Some Differences Among Kinship Systems

It is customary for most Americans as well as for the members of other Western cultures to limit the terms "father" and "mother" to the two immediate biological ancestors. By the same token, the terms "brother" and "sister" are usually reserved for children of the same parents. Members of other human groups classify their kin differently. In the Hawaiian type of kinship terminology, ego's brothers and sisters and the children of his parents' brothers and sisters are all lumped together under two terms, the only distinction being that between the sexes. The result is to extend the terms "brother" and "sister" to all those relatives whom most Americans designate as "first cousins."

Similarly, in some societies, ego's mother, ego's mother's sister, and ego's father's sister may all be referred to by the same term. Clearly, what is emphasized in such kinship systems is the social rather than the biological role of motherhood. In such systems, one is expected to behave in very much the same way toward all relatives termed the same, even though biologically some are more closely related than others.

Another interesting feature of many kinship systems is the distinction made between parallel cousins and cross-cousins. A **parallel cousin,** from ego's point of view, is the child of a father's brother or of a mother's sister—that is, of a parent's sibling of the same sex. By contrast, a **cross-cousin** is the child of a father's sister or of a mother's brother—that is, of a parent's sibling of the opposite sex. When cousins of these two types are sharply differentiated, the distinction is invariably reflected in some important aspects of life in the society. For example, it may affect marriage practices.

The American Kinship System

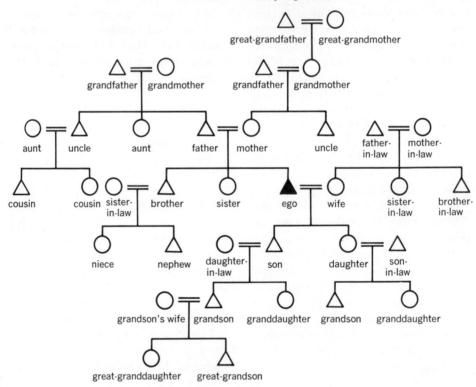

Fig. 19 **The American Kinship System. This diagram represents a typical American kinship system, using the point of view of an adult male ego. What terms of address could be substituted for the terms of reference used in this diagram?**

Lineages and Clans

It was mentioned earlier that the nuclear family may become an extended family by the inclusion of near relatives within the same household. Whether the nuclear family or the extended family is the more favored pattern of family life in a society is to some extent dependent upon the means of livelihood. Those peoples who base their subsistence on hunting, fishing, and gathering are by necessity limited in the size of their groups. At the same time, a social organization based on extended families suits their circumstances particularly well, since it encourages teamwork and permits easy mobility. Complex industrial societies with great concentrations of population and specialization in occupation tend to favor small, independent family units.

Between these two extremes are the many societies, intermediate in size, which draw their livelihood from hoe or plow farming or from herding animals. As a rule, their communities are organized by extending the kinship network to include a large number of members, frequently all those tracing their descent from a common ancestor. If a member of such a group identifies himself with one line of relatives only, the organizing principle of the group is termed **unilateral**. Where descent is traced through the father's line, the organizing principle is further termed **patrilineal**; descent through the maternal line is referred to as **matrilineal**. All the unilateral descendants of a common ancestor who can be named consider themselves the members of a **lineage**.

Several related lineages, the members of which claim to have common ancestry even though it may be so remote as to be mythological, form a **clan**. The members of a clan may not all reside in one locality. For instance, the several clans among the Iroquois Indians were spread throughout the tribes that composed the Iroquois political league. But members of a clan are obligated to assist and remain loyal to each other. Such loyalty is reinforced by special ritual observances and the common possession of certain myths and other symbolic bonds. Because clans practice **exogamy,** that is, they require one of the marriage partners to come from without the group, clans are prevented from becoming a divisive factor within the fabric of a society.

In contrast to the reckoning of one's descent through one line only, some societies practice double descent, combining patrilineal and matrilineal principles. In still other societies, the United States included, families tend to be linked with close relatives of both parents.

Marriage: Preferential Mating and Taboo

All societies direct their members to some extent with respect to whom they may or may not marry. Marriage according to the guidelines generally set by a society is referred to as **preferential mating.** Not only are there preferred marriages; all societies possess **incest taboos,** or regulations that prohibit marriage among certain close relatives. The incest taboo on mating between siblings or between parent and child is universal except for a very few special cases. In aborigi-

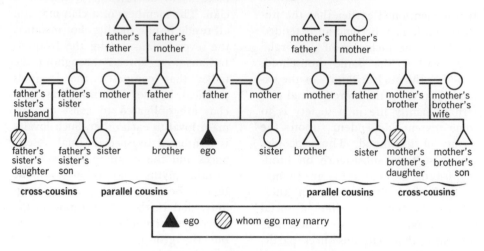

Cross-Cousin Marriage Among the Kariera

father's father — father's mother | mother's father — mother's mother

father's sister's husband — father's sister | mother — father | father — mother | mother — father | mother's brother — mother's brother's wife

father's sister's daughter | father's sister's son | sister | brother | ego | sister | brother | sister | mother's brother's daughter | mother's brother's son

cross-cousins | parallel cousins | parallel cousins | cross-cousins

▲ ego   ⬭ whom ego may marry

Fig. 20 Cross-Cousin Marriage Among the Kariera. The Kariera people of western Australia consider the difference between parallel cousins and cross-cousins very important. "Ego" in this chart addresses his parallel cousins as "brother" and "sister." He is prohibited from marrying a cousin who is his "sister," but he may marry either of his female cross-cousins.

nal Hawaii, in ancient Egypt, and among the Incas of Peru, mating between brothers and sisters was at one time permitted so that the noble or divine blood of the few would not become contaminated through marriage to ordinary mortals. These instances are sometimes referred to as "dynastic incest."

Beyond the basic restriction on mating within the nuclear family, each society defines incest differently; that is, each society differs concerning which categories of kin its members may marry. For instance, some peoples strongly encourage, and even expect, marriage among cross-cousins but prohibit marriage among parallel cousins as incestuous. An example are the Kariera people of Australia (see Figure 20, "Cross-Cousin Marriage Among the Kariera"). Among some of the nomadic groups of the Middle East, on the other hand, marriage to a parallel cousin is considered almost requisite. The cultural definition of incest is so arbitrary that within the United States, the degrees of kinship within which marriage is prohibited by law vary among the fifty states.

Since the regulations on who may marry whom vary so greatly among the societies of the world, it is difficult to explain, on a strictly biological or psychological basis, the almost universal taboo on marriage within the nuclear family. One important reason for this restriction may have been early man's need to maintain a stable nuclear family free of sexual rivalries. Perhaps another reason was his desire to broaden the scope of his social relationships by means of marital alliances across family boundaries.

Marriage: Bride Acquisition and Divorce

Judging by the marriage customs of most Americans, one might easily assume that the decision to enter into a marital union is made by the couple concerned only. As a matter of fact, there are very few societies which leave the decision entirely to the two individuals themselves. In many cultures, sanction of a marriage is effected by the transfer of property, which of necessity involves a number of the couple's close relatives.

Among the most common transactions accompanying marriage is the giving of a **bride-price** (or **bride-**wealth). In this arrangement, very common to African societies, a certain amount of money or property is given by the prospective husband to the family of the bride. The husband is customarily assisted in this by his family. The bride-price serves to compensate the bride's relatives for the loss of a productive worker and of the children she may bear. It also tends to ensure that the bride will be treated well in her new household.

A contrasting tradition, still observed by people in many European societies, is that of the **dowry.** There are variations of this custom, in which the bride's parents assist the young

This picture of a Burmese wedding shows the bride's mother assisting in a ceremony between bride and groom that symbolizes the permanence of their marriage union. In Burmese society, marriage is as much a concern of families as of two individuals.

Here, a newly married couple of northern Cameroon carry a bride-price to the home of the wife's family. The husband is presenting this gift in recognition that his wife's family is losing a valuable member. The bride-price is one goat, one lamb, and a pot of grain.

couple in establishing a household with a gift of money, goods, or both. In still other societies, the groom is required to provide services for the bride's family in exchange for the girl, or he may substitute them for the payment of a bride-price. In another arrangement, the groom's sister may actually be exchanged for the bride. In general, the more effectively a young woman contributes to the subsistence of her family, the greater the price that must be paid for her. It follows, then, that in some of those societies which expect the parents of the bride to provide a handsome dowry along with their daughter, young women are thought of as dependents rather than as productive and indispensable members of the family.

As all societies set up some guidelines for marriage, similarly all provide for the dissolving of marriage ties in at least some circumstances. No society encourages divorce or even approves of it in principle. Yet in spite of the fact that various economic transactions contribute to the stability of marriage, marriages in the smaller, less complex societies are no less fragile than in modern, technologically oriented societies. The grounds for divorce vary from one group to another. Dissolving a marital union may be as simple as the wife's putting her husband's belongings outside the house, as the matter is customarily handled among the woman-centered Hopi Indians of Arizona.

SUMMARY

Man is a social animal; he chooses to live in groups. The most basic and universal of all human groups is the nuclear family, consisting of a set of parents and their children. A nuclear family may be enlarged by the inclusion of additional marriage partners, as happens in those societies which sanction polygamous marriages. A nuclear family may also become an extended family, if it joins with closely related nuclear units in maintaining a common household.

Kinship refers to the state of being related. Kinship ties tend to be minimized in highly industrialized societies. In most societies of the world, however, a number of kinship ties are well defined and the relationships resulting from them are reflected in social organization, marriage regulations, and other aspects of culture.

All societies regulate marriage to the extent of imposing some incest taboos. An almost universal prohibition is placed upon marriage within the nuclear family. Marriage in many societies involves an economic transaction between two families. It is rare, in fact, for marriage to be considered the concern of the marriage partners only.

Chapter Review

Terms in Anthropology

affinity	group marriage	patrilineal
bride-price (bridewealth)	incest taboo	patrilocal family
clan	kinship	polyandry
collateral	lineage	polygamy
consanguinity	lineal	polygyny
cross-cousin	matrilineal	preferential mating
dowry	matrilocal family	sibling
ego	monogamy	term of address
exogamy	nuclear family	term of reference
extended family	parallel cousin	unilateral

Questions for Review

1. How has man's prolonged childhood dependency upon adults helped to make him a "social animal"?
2. Why do anthropologists assume the nuclear family to be a very ancient form of social grouping?
3. What factors may tend to discourage polygamy even in a society that approves its practice?
4. What is an "extended family"? What are the two important types of the extended family?
5. What may the study of kinship terminology reveal about a culture? What

kind of society tends to minimize kinship ties? What kind of society tends to maximize their importance?

6. What are some of the criteria commonly used to distinguish different types of kinsmen? How are each of these criteria indicated on a kinship diagram?

7. Distinguish between a clan and a lineage. What helps to prevent clans from becoming a divisive factor within a society?

8. What is meant by "preferential mating"? What is an "incest taboo"?

9. What are some of the preferred types of marriage described in this chapter? What are some of the types of marriage prohibited in different societies, including American society?

10. What is the difference between the giving of a bride-price and the giving of a dowry? What does each custom suggest about the position of women within a society?

Chapter **13**

Societies:
Cooperation and Conflict

The American people are known as the world's greatest joiners. American society abounds with organizations of every conceivable sort, and most Americans discover quite early in youth that they enjoy participating in a number of different associations. Students often join fraternities or sororities and may participate in various other interest groups. Adults have their men's and women's clubs as well as a host of professional, service, recreational, and other associations. It seems to be the rule rather than the exception that an average American holds membership cards for more organizations than he can possibly participate in effectively. This tendency to organize in groups whose members engage in similar activities, share like experiences, or pursue common interests is not limited to populous and complex societies. It is just as true of small tribes. Along with the universal trait of kinship grouping, it is an important expression of man's intensely social nature.

Associations Based on Sex

An **association** may be defined as a social group whose members are joined in the pursuit of a common interest. A study of the various associations found throughout the world indicates that such groupings are most commonly based on sex, age, or both. Of those groupings based on sex, fraternities and men's associations decidedly predominate over the clubs whose membership is limited to women. The greater frequency with which men's associations occur is not the result of a higher degree of sociability among men as compared with women. Rather, the explanation lies in the nature of women's activities, which tend to restrict them to the household.

A good example of one type of male association formerly existed among the Ona, a tribe who inhabited the island of Tierra del Fuego off the southern tip of South America. The most important social and religious event among the Ona was an elaborate ceremony frequently lasting several months of the year in which it was held. Participation in this ceremony was limited to adult males of the tribe and to adolescent boys who were candidates for tribal initiation. On the ceremonial occasion, a spacious hut was erected some distance from the village. This hut served as the center of ritual activities, and women and uninitiated children were strictly forbidden to come near.

During the ritual period, Ona men impersonated traditional spirits and appeared in disguise before the women of the tribe to exact their obedience under the threat of severe punishment. During the ritual period also, adolescent candidates for initiation were subjected to a variety of physical hardships and were given long and concentrated instruction in the responsibilities of adulthood. Only through participation in this initiation rite could a young Ona male attain full-fledged membership in the tribe. In effect, the Ona had a **tribal fraternity,** or an association admitting all male members of the tribe after a required formal initiation.

More common than the tribal fraternity is a type of male association in which membership is limited or carefully chosen—the **nontribal fraternity.** Nontribal fraternities are no less widespread in some parts of sub-Saharan Africa than they are on large American campuses. In the latter situation, fraternity members choose from among incoming classes certain young men to join their ranks. The functions of nontribal fraternities vary widely, ranging from secret terrorist activities to benevolent actions known to and approved by other members of a society.

Associations Based on Age

Of special interest to anthropologists are those societies that are characterized by age-grades. **Age-grades** are associations of persons not only of the same sex but also of approximately the same age. Age-grading occurred among several of the North American Plains Indian tribes. It was, and to an extent still is, even more common in parts of Africa. What purpose is served by age-grading in a society? The following examples may serve to answer.

Among the Arapaho Indians of the Great Plains there once existed eight age groupings into which the male members of the tribe were organized. The youngest group, the Kit Fox men, consisted of adolescent boys and very young men. This group had no special insignia by which it was known, nor could its members claim any ceremonial sponsorship from among the respected elders of the tribe. One step above this group were the Stars, who were still relatively undistinguished members of the tribe. The next five age-grades consisted of adult males who were full-fledged members of the tribe. Except for the fifth group, each of these age-grades was characterized by distinctive insignia and by a carefully regulated dance performed under the direction of ceremonial sponsors.

The highest and the most distinguished Arapaho age-grade was a group called Water-Sprinkling Old Men, believed to have consisted of only seven members, who were usually men in their seventies. These old men embodied all that was held holy in Arapaho life. They were the guardians of the sacred tribal bundles and the directors of all the activities of the five age-grades below them. For their own ceremony, they sang songs to the accompaniment of sacred rattles in a large sweathouse during the four days of the annual ritual period.

The ceremonial progression of Arapaho men through eight age-grades served two general functions. It reinforced the greater respect and confidence accorded to older members of the tribe. And it set forth clearly the obligations of each age-grade in times of urgent need or in encounters with enemies of the tribe.

Among the Nyakyusa, a Bantu-speaking people who live north of Lake Nyasa in southeastern Africa, all social grouping is based upon age-grading. At the age of ten or eleven, Nyakyusa boys leave the huts of their fathers and join with other boys of their age in what is termed an **age-village.** This village is built on the edge of their parent village. By the time the oldest boys in the group have reached fifteen or sixteen, the village

Here, members of a New Guinea tribal fraternity meet in their private clubhouse. All adult male members of the tribe may enter the clubhouse once they have been initiated. Women are barred from approaching the meeting place except when bringing food to the men.

is usually closed to further young boys, who must begin building another. A typical young men's village is made up of between twenty and fifty males with an age range of only five years or so. In their late twenties, the young men of an age-village marry, and their wives join them.

Among the Nyakyusa, then, the local unit of social organization consists of a group of age-mates who have shared a common life from late childhood, together with their wives and children. The Nyakyusa also share in common the landholdings of the village, which are administered for the good of all. Under such an arrangement, getting along with one's con-

This picture was taken during an age-grade ceremony in an Aboure tribal village in Ivory Coast. A headdressed warrior "captain" is showing a member of a lower age-grade how he would defeat his enemy.

temporaries is of prime importance. Cooperation is stressed as a necessity if one is to live what the Nyakyusa consider "the good life"—harmonious companionship with one's equals.

Three age-grades exist among the Nyakyusa at any one time: the young men of an age-village, who help with the common defense but have no supervisory or administrative duties; males between approximately thirty-five and sixty-five years of age, the generation of authority who are responsible for defense and administration; and those over sixty-five, whose leaders perform certain ritual functions but no longer possess administrative responsibilities. A great ritual is held among the Nyakyusa once every generation, at which time a general moving-up occurs. The middle age-grade, itself replacing the elders, gives up its duties in favor of the junior age-grade, whose youngest members wait several years before assuming their administrative duties. This ceremony, referred to as "the coming out," also involves the complete redistribution of the landholdings of all the villages. While the villages of the young men become formally established on their own lands, the inhabitants of the older villages make room for the new generation by moving to a new location as a unit. In doing so, they remain together in the company begun many years earlier.

Institutionalized Kinship

In the Spanish-speaking societies of the world, located chiefly in Latin America, a special type of relationship exists among individuals who are neither kin to each other nor members of the same formal association. This practice, known as the **compadre relationship,** bears some resemblance to the custom of godparenthood, but is characterized by stronger ties among the individuals involved. The compadre relationship may be described as ceremonial, or institutionalized, kinship formally established between a child and an adult willing to sponsor him. The relationship extends to the parents of the godchild as well. Moreover, it is not rare for a child to have several compadres, perhaps even a dozen or more, and to maintain a warm and devoted relationship with each through such special occasions as name days and weddings.

Compadres are frequently sought from among those individuals who are able to give material assistance to a godchild when the need arises. In small villages, where winning a dispute may be determined in part by the number of loyal supporters one can command, compadres can always be counted upon.

Social Classes

The different types of human associations and relationships described so far have an important element in common. All are formal organizations in which membership is gained through a ceremony and is thus well defined. Social classes, on the other hand, most frequently lack formal organization. What is a "social class"? For the time being, let us define a "social class" as a group of individuals within a society who are ranked together at a certain level according to some attributes they share. This is a very broad definition. Let us now consider a few representative examples of how the members of a society may be ranked.

Societies whose members are not ranked into two or more levels are termed "classless." Classless societies have been relatively rare; they are characteristic of peoples whose economies do not permit or encourage the accumulation of goods. The Eskimos, the Bushmen of southern Africa, and the various groups of Australian aborigines serve as good examples of classless societies. All these, you may notice, are hunting and gathering peoples. There is a direct relationship between the mode of subsistence, the degree of cultural complexity, and the population density of a society, on the one hand, and the number of social classes on the other. An exception to this is, of course, the type of classless society that now characterizes many communist nations of the world.

Differentiation of a society into social classes may be based upon property, descent, conquest, or a combination of these and other factors. Three social classes seem to have had worldwide occurrence: the class of nobles, the class of common freemen, and the class of slaves. For example, these three classes characterized a number of Indian societies of the northwest coast of North America.

Among the Indians of the Northwest Pacific coast, each individual at birth joined a tightly organized tribal group bound by ties of kinship but differentiated into distinct social classes. Joint ownership of property characterized the group. Fishing, hunting, and gathering rights, as well as lands and waters, houses and canoes, belonged to the group as a whole. Serving as administrator of the group's material wealth and "privileges"—including such intangible things as names, ancestral crests, songs, dances, and rituals—was the chief. Customarily, the chief was the male who traced his descent most directly to the ancestor from whom the group derived.

Below the chief, members of the group were generally identified with one of two social classes: nobles or commoners. Within these classes, each individual held a rank determined by how closely he was related to the chief. The higher his rank, the more marks of prestige were in evidence. These included more elaborate clothing and special ornaments, a preferred portion of the rectangular plank house shared with several other families, and leadership in such group activities as hunting or fishing. Although an undistinguished commoner could scarcely hope to better his position, he was safe from oppression or exploitation by reason of his kinship with everyone in the tribe, including the chief himself.

A third class of individuals could not hope for so much. These were the slaves, generally captives taken in warfare, who were regarded as property and held no formal position in the society. Whenever possible, they were ransomed by their relatives with generous settlements. In some cases, slaves were treated well, but they were completely at the mercy of their owners and at times were even put to death in an ostentatious show of the owner's utter disregard for the valuable property they represented. Clearly, only a chief or rich noble could afford such a display of wealth.

American society is frequently said to consist of six social levels, ranging from the upper-upper class at the top and continuing through the lower-upper, upper-middle, lower-middle, and upper-lower to the lower-lower class at the bottom. American social classes are based primarily on economic standing and such related factors as type of occupation, kind and location of residence, level of education and manner of spending leisure time. However, any analysis of American society that ignores the importance of race in determining social position is obviously incomplete.

This Chinese woman, photographed on a street in Peking, is one of the few remaining members of the old Chinese nobility. Born an aristocrat, she has no recognized place in the classless society of modern Communist China.

American society is also frequently said to be characterized by a good deal of mobility. It is not difficult for a member of one social class to move into another class, such movement usually reflecting a change in economic standing. Yet race as a criterion of social standing has frequently rendered such movement very difficult, and in some places practically impossible, for Negroes and other nonwhite American citizens.

Status and Role

The position or rank of an individual in relation to others within a society is frequently referred to as his **status.** An individual may come to enjoy a specific status in one of two ways. He may do so by the application of his own efforts; the respect accorded to a skillful hunter among the Eskimos, to a successful and brave war leader among the Aztecs, and to a self-made man in American society all mark a high degree of **achieved status.** Or he may possess a status that is fixed by reason of his age, sex, or race, and is thus beyond his personal control. Status that an individual comes to hold automatically is termed **ascribed status.**

Any one person invariably holds a number of different statuses in his society at the same time. An adult male in American society usually holds the status of father and head of the family when at home. In his work, he may be a member of a professional group, such as a school faculty. If he belongs to a bowling club or a fraternal order, he is one of a number of members who are equal in privileges. The parts he plays in these various settings vary considerably. While he is expected to exercise his authority at home as a father, he may restrain himself in voicing his opinions among his older colleagues at work. But at the bowling club or on the golf course his behavior is largely unaffected by whether he is playing against his son or his boss. On occasion, an individual has to distinguish among several statuses at the same time. In the company of his wife, son, and mother, he is expected to act alternately as husband, father, and son. One can readily see that associated with any particular status is an appropriate, distinctive way of behaving, termed a **role.**

We are now ready to define a **social class** as one of two or more groups within a society whose members derive a sense of unity from the number of distinctive statuses that they share in common.

Caste

When membership in social classes becomes completely frozen within a society, anthropologists speak of a **caste system.** Caste systems are characterized by ascribed, or hereditary, status. They are characterized further by **endogamy,** the requirement that both parties to a marriage come from within the same social grouping, or caste. In a society divided into castes, it is impossible for an individual to change the social position he has inherited even through the most outstanding personal achievement.

A rigid caste system has been a part of Hindu civilization in India during most of that nation's history. Today the government of India is trying to put an end to this system, but such aspects of culture are not easily changed. According to ancient tradition, four principal castes make up the Hindu caste system. The highest caste is that of the Brahmans, the priests and scholars of Hinduism. Next below the Brahmans are the Kshatriyas, the rulers and warriors of India. Next below them are the Vaisyas, merchants and small farmers, and finally the Sudras, landless peasants and laborers. In the course of centuries, these four castes have become less specialized and may include members of many different occupations. Moreover, several thousand different castes and subcastes have been added to the four principal castes.

Outside the caste system entirely are those people whom Hindus refer to as "casteless" and whom Westerners term **untouchables.** The mere nearness of untouchables is believed by some Hindus even today to defile and degrade anyone of a higher caste. Not too long ago, members of the subcaste who washed the clothes of these people were permitted outside their quarters only at night. It was thought that even to look upon untouchables would pollute persons of higher castes. When India gained independence after World War II, the practice of untouchability was abolished, and subsequently a law was passed making discrimination against former untouchables a criminal offense. Nevertheless, the deep-rooted traditions of caste still rule many aspects of Indian life.

Underlying the fixed social pattern of Hindu society and making it practicable has been the basic assumption that people of differing backgrounds are inherently unequal in social worth. The "ideal" attitude under such circumstances is to accept one's role and to perform one's duties faithfully. The son learns from his father the occupation practiced by his caste and brings honor to his group and to himself by behaving and performing according to its highest standards. If one can look past the inherent inequalities of the Hindu caste system—which from the American point of view seem intolerable—it is easy to see that it can produce a steady stream of accomplished specialists. Moreover, by eliminating competition and rivalry, the society may attain to a high degree of stability.

Those Indians who insist that their nation must rapidly modernize to ensure the survival of its fast-growing population are aware of the inevitable conflict between the caste system and the spirit of social equality that usually follows on the heels of technological advancement.

Law and the Social Order

We have seen man entering the world as a member of one social unit, the family. We have seen young men, upon reaching adolescence, joining with others in a network of social groupings based on sex, age, and other characteristics. Man's tendency to associate with others is doubtless a very ancient trait of humanity. Not only did early man derive from membership in a group a measure of security in an environment that must otherwise have appeared very hostile, but most of the stupendous accomplishments of the past were the result of the cooperative effort of well-organized human groups. In short, to be human is to be involved in a variety

Indian untouchables, who are outside the caste system, have for centuries been shunned by other members of their society. Their choice has been to accept the lowest forms of work or to live by begging. The modern Indian government has outlawed the practice of untouchability, but social traditions as firmly rooted as this one are slow in dying.

of social relationships, some of which are necessary to survival itself.

When people are in close association with one another, it is inevitable that some conflicts should arise. Conflicts may occur not only among individuals but also among various groups within a society as well. In order to ensure the necessary amount of cooperation among their members, societies have come to employ a variety of methods for dealing with conflicts. The laws governing actions among members of a society may be embodied in formal legal codes, as is characteristic of large, highly developed civilizations. Or they may be part of an enduring but unwritten body of legal tradition, as characterizes many

of the nonliterate societies of the world. Let us now look at a few representative examples of how social order is maintained in the latter type of society.

A very simple procedure for settling disputes is found among the Eskimos. The members of an Eskimo society are well aware of what is right and wrong in terms of their culture. However, they have no formally organized system of redressing wrongs when they occur. While it may be generally recognized that right in a particular case is on the side of the **plaintiff**—the person who claims to have been injured—it is up to him to assert it. If a man's wife has been stolen, which is not at all uncommon among the Eskimos, he may decide to kill the offender. But since murders are expected to be avenged, this action could result in a feud that would disrupt the life of the entire community.

One alternative to killing an aggressor is to challenge him to a **song contest.** Songs scathing in their abuse of an opponent are composed for such an occasion, the idea being to humiliate and discredit him. According to custom, the winner of a song contest is he who receives the most applause from the audience. Although there may seem to be little connection between the right or wrong of a case and its outcome as determined by this method, the Eskimo song contest does settle the dispute—thus freeing the community from the threat of violence.

Another alternative open to an Eskimo claimant, particularly in cases of serious and repeated abuse, is to secure the permission of the entire community to cast out a wrongdoer or to execute him. Such permission may be sought from the members of the society by their informal leader or by the injured party himself. Quite commonly, a close relative of a condemned man is asked to carry out the execution on behalf of the community. This custom tends to preclude the possibility of a feud arising.

Ifugao Law

Let us now look at the Ifugaos of the northern Philippines for some more examples of how disputes may be settled among nonliterate peoples. The Ifugao people live in small settlements scattered throughout the valleys of the mountainous island of Luzon. Ifugao economy is based on the cultivation of rice in narrow fields

These members of an Eskimo society are witnessing a song contest between an injured party and the man accused of wronging him. The disputants, facing each other in the left foreground, will continue beating their drums and hurling abuses at each other until the audience applauds a winner.

created by terracing the steep mountain slopes.

The Ifugaos are highly competitive and acquisitive people. Although they lack formal political organization and central authority, they possess an elaborate code of customary law. In this unwritten code of law, penalties and obligations are fixed in surprising detail once the exact nature, circumstances, and degree of an offense have been established. Damages for assault, adultery, theft, and other offenses are paid in kind, and debts must be satisfied by repayments together with proper interest. In general, an adequate amount of reparation wipes out any offense or injury.

The Ifugaos take offense easily and engage readily in legal contests to avoid losing face. Just as among the Eskimos, offenses are prosecuted by individuals who consider themselves wronged. But the Ifugaos carry this procedure one step further. If a plaintiff fails in his attempts to settle a dispute with an opponent, he engages a **go-between,** customarily a member of a high social class who is respected for his generosity, courage, and negotiating skill. The go-between represents the public interest, but he cannot render a decision in a case, nor can he enforce a settlement once it is reached. His only function is to try—for a fee—to bring disputing parties to a settlement by using his skills of persuasion.

The go-between hears the complaint of the injured party and then presents these charges to the offender, who in turn explains his side of the case. Claims are customarily met by counterclaims, and the go-between visits back and forth, trying to balance the case of the two parties in

order to bring them together. In the meantime, both the claimant and the defendant may gather their relatives and play host to them, in preparation for a feud should the case between the two parties not be resolved. While the go-between is active, the two parties are pledged to peace, and nonobservance of this truce may lead to loss of the plaintiff's case. If no settlement is reached and the go-between withdraws, a period of compulsory truce must still be observed. But following this, the plaintiff with the help of his kinsmen may undertake to redress by force the wrongs done him.

There is one additional legal means that may be resorted to in order to avoid a feud. This is the use of an **ordeal,** a dangerous or painful test of innocence or guilt, supposed to be under supernatural control. A party to a dispute may be challenged to recover a pebble from boiling water or to touch a red-hot knife with his bare hands without suffering injury. Refusal to submit to such a test means loss of the case; to pass it successfully gives one the right to collect damages. Barring the case of an innocent person put to such a test, ordeals are frequently quite effective. Rather than face the prescribed ordeal and supernatural punishment, the guilty party tends to confess.

Native Court Procedures of Africa

Very highly developed legal institutions exist among some of the nonliterate peoples of Africa, particularly among the Bantu-speaking peoples of its southern half. In contrast to the Eskimos and Ifugaos, among whom the injured party plays the main role

A tribal chief renders judgment in a native court in western Nigeria. According to custom, he has heard the testimony of witnesses and received legal advice from elder counselors of the tribe. Most native courts in present-day Nigeria are restricted to the handling of minor disputes between individuals.

in redressing wrong done him, these peoples make use of court procedures similar to those that characterize Western societies. Cases are quite commonly tried before a panel of judges, who base their verdict on two things: the statements made by parties to a dispute and evidence presented by competent witnesses. Court procedures follow established custom, similar cases dealt with in the past are cited as precedents, and the merits of a case are carefully weighed before a decision is rendered.

African methods of enforcing law have in many places given way to Western methods of legal procedure. The Tswana tribes of Botswana (formerly Bechuanaland) at one time were served by a system of lower and higher courts. Lower courts existed at the local level and chiefs' courts at the tribal level. The chiefs' courts handled particularly difficult or serious cases. Among the Ashanti people of present-day Ghana, trials formerly were open to the public, and, at least in theory, anyone present could question either of the two parties to a dispute. Cross-examination was commonly the business of the elders who participated in the legal judgment. The person who lost a case had the right to appeal the decision to the royal court.

We have now examined a variety of methods by which different societies ensure their own survival by keeping the friction among their members to a minimum. In the small groups in which Eskimos live, there seems little need for an elaborate code of law or for a specialized organ to administer justice. An Eskimo who has been wronged is expected to make use of **self-help,** that is, the right of redressing an injury by his own action without judicial intervention. The institution of the go-between among the Ifugaos represents a transition toward formal legal procedure. While the go-between's function is to mediate a conflict between two quarreling parties, he does not render a judgment nor can he enforce a settlement. Once a society has reached a certain size and complexity, impersonal and formal legal machinery becomes a necessity. We have seen it represented in fully developed form among some of the nonliterate peoples of Africa. Since in all human societies the survival of the group must take precedence over the caprice of any of its members, all societies have developed certain methods of social control that are effective for their cultures.

SUMMARY

If societies were organized solely on the basis of kinship, a frequent result might well be intense rivalry between the kinship groups. Societies avoid the weakening of their structure by cross-organizing on a nonkinship basis as well. Associations based on sex, age, or common interests are found in societies throughout the world. In addition to possessing such associations, the majority of societies are also subdivided into social classes. Some few even have a rigid caste system that is maintained by the practice of endogamy.

To ensure that peaceful and cooperative conditions prevail, societies have developed various means to resolve the inevitable conflicts among their members. These methods range from the self-help practices that characterize many of the smaller societies of the world to the highly complicated legal machinery that is generally characteristic of more populous and complex societies.

Chapter Review

Terms in Anthropology

achieved status	endogamy	self-help
age-grade	go-between	social class
age-village	nontribal fraternity	song contest
ascribed status	ordeal	status
association	plaintiff	tribal fraternity
caste system	role	untouchable
compadre relationship		

Questions for Review

1. What is the distinction between a tribal fraternity and a nontribal fraternity? What examples does this chapter provide of each?
2. Define "age-grade." What purposes did age-grading serve among the Arapaho Indians?
3. Describe a Nyakyusa age-village. What happens during the Nyakyusa "coming out" ceremony?
4. What are some of the factors upon which the division of a society into social classes may be based?
5. What is meant by "achieved status"? by "ascribed status"? What are some of the statuses held by someone you know well?
6. What does the anthropologist mean when he says that "associated with any particular status is an appropriate role"?
7. What distinguishes a caste system from a society divided into social classes? Why do you think that the Hindu caste system has been able to maintain itself for such a long period?
8. What is the function of an Ifugao go-between?
9. What is the most important difference between the Eskimo way of settling disputes and the procedure used by Bantu-speaking peoples as described in this chapter?
10. What types of evidence indicate to you that man is an intensely social being, bent on preserving the society of which he is a member?

Chapter **14**

Religion and Magic

Man is a reasoning animal. Early man first employed reason to make stone tools, which helped him adapt to his environment. Since this humble beginning, the possession of reason has enabled man to achieve mastery over his environment to an astonishing degree. Yet there remain many aspects of existence for which reason does not prepare man adequately—for which reason has no adequate explanations. It has been common for man, confronted with things beyond his understanding, to conceive of such things in terms of the "supernatural." The term **supernatural** denotes that which cannot be explained as resulting from natural causes. Or, put another way, the supernatural refers to what is beyond or above human reason.

The attitudes of different peoples toward the supernatural vary, since what is mysterious and awe-inspiring to some peoples may not necessarily appear so to others. But belief in the supernatural is common to all human societies. Such belief generally takes one of two forms—the form of religion

or the form of magic. Both religion and magic may be described as attempts to deal with the supernatural. Both religion and magic are alike, too, in that they involve the performance of learned rituals by skilled practitioners. But there is an important difference between religion and magic. What this difference is, and how it is reflected in the religious and magical practices of different peoples, is the subject of this chapter.

The Origin of Religion

We will use the term **religion** to refer to man's concern with the supernatural and his expression of this concern in his beliefs, attitudes, and actions. The fact that religion is a part of every culture has important implications. It implies, for one thing, that the origin of religion should be sought in man's remote past. Many theories of how religion arose have been put forth, but whether they seem more or less plausible, they will always remain mere speculations. For this reason, modern anthropologists are generally wary of adding new theories to the many already in existence.

What are some of the well-known theories of the origin of religion? Perhaps the best-known theory is that presented by Edward B. Tylor in his classic work, *Primitive Culture,* in 1871. Tylor offered a psychological explanation of religion. He asserted that "belief in spiritual beings" was at least partially common to all religions and hence very ancient. The belief in spirits, which Tylor termed **animism,** was the result of man's quest to understand such puzzling conditions of the body and mind as the states of being awake, asleep, or in a trance, and of being alive or dead. According to Tylor, man's explanation of these conditions rested on the concept of the human soul, which was thought to leave the body temporarily during sleep or unconsciousness and permanently at death. The next step, so Tylor argued, was for man to extend the concept of the soul to other living creatures and even to inanimate objects of various kinds. When several of these souls, or spirits, or supernatural beings, acquired special and more or less equal importance, the result was a religious system of polytheism. **Polytheism** is defined as the belief in, or worship of, more than one god. Since it was to be expected that one god would eventually outrank all the others, polytheism must have paved the way toward belief in a single supreme being, or **monotheism.**

Tylor's explanation of the origin of religion remains highly esteemed today. But a number of other theories have also attracted the serious consideration of scholars. Friedrich Max Müller, a German-born philologist of the nineteenth century, held that religion had its origin when early man, having experienced an awe of such natural phenomena as fire, wind, sun, and moon, personified them and began to worship them. The early religion of the Greeks and Romans provides one example of Müller's theory. The Greek god Zeus (Roman Jupiter), chief of all the gods, was a sky god recognizable by his thunderbolt. Phoebus (Roman Apollo) personified the sun, Hephaestus (Roman Vulcan) fire, and Poseidon (Roman Neptune) the sea. These gods gradually acquired more and more human attributes, but they still retained their original characters of representing natural phenomena.

At the beginning of the twentieth century, an Englishman named James G. Frazer presented still another theory of the origin of religion in a book entitled *The Golden Bough.* Frazer attempted to show that before what could be termed "religion" developed, there existed magic. Magic, according to Frazer, was a primitive form of science, an attempt by man to control his environment. The emergence of religion was early man's acknowledgment that magic does not always work and that man's control of the universe is limited.

For the French sociologist Émile Durkheim, the origin of religion was to be found in the collective behavior of society. More specifically, Durkheim believed that religion arose out of those tribal rituals that were designed to celebrate the symbolic identity and sacredness of a group.

Anthropologists today are in agreement that belief in the supernatural is an important aspect of any culture.

Moreover, judging from the archaeological evidence, this must have been true for many thousands of years. As to the ultimate source of religious beliefs and the behavior associated with them, anthropologists do not accept that it must have been uniform for all men, and they are convinced that no amount of research will result in a final answer to the question.

The Earliest Evidences of Religion

The earliest definite evidence of man's developing religious consciousness is found in Mousterian (Neanderthal) burial sites of the Middle Paleolithic period, which are estimated to be at least 50,000 years old. Among the Neanderthal graves at La Ferrassie, an ancient rock shelter in southern France, the skull of an infant was discovered under a stone slab. The underside of this primitive tombstone was marked by man-made indentations believed to have had some symbolic significance. Archaeological discoveries show that elsewhere in Europe at about the same time, Neanderthal peoples were burying their dead surrounded with finely made flint tools. Both forms of anthropological evidence, the primitive tombstone and the grave goods associated with human remains, serve to indicate that the Neanderthal dead received special attention and were furnished with objects thought to be helpful to them during their after-life.

Much more dramatic evidence of belief in the supernatural is available for the Cro-Magnon people of the Upper Paleolithic period. The bodies of their dead were customarily decorated with shells and red ochre and were supplied with a variety of tools before being covered with heavy stones for protection. Besides caring for the dead, Cro-Magnon man extended his dealings with the supernatural into some of his daily activities. Cave paintings and carved figurines, found in large numbers over much of Europe, were doubtless magical in their function, suggesting not only a sizable body of beliefs concerning the supernatural, but also different methods of dealing with it.

A painting discovered in the cave of Les Trois Frères in southern France has especially excited the imagination of anthropologists. This painting, which depicts a creature part man and part animal, has been entitled the "Sorcerer." The figure, which appears to be dancing, is indeed a mixture of elements. It has the beard, legs, and feet of a human and the antlers of a stag, while its ears, front limbs, and tail are characteristic of other animals. Whether the "Sorcerer" portrays a masked magician during a ritual, a god of the hunt, or some other kind of being, no one can say. But we must accept, beyond any doubt, that for Upper Paleolithic man, religion and magic were very much a part of life.

The Concept of Mana

The concept of the supernatural varies greatly. It may be conceived of in personal terms, that is, as a being with some humanlike characteristics. Or it may be conceived of in impersonal terms. Among the impersonal conceptions of the supernatural, the concept of mana, to be found in Melanesia and Polynesia to the present day, is probably the best known.

Mana refers to an impersonal super-

Part man, part animal, and a mystery to scholars is the figure of the "Sorcerer," discovered on a cave wall in southern France. Is he a god of the hunt, a hunter disguised for pursuing game, or perhaps a masked magician performing a ritual?

natural force which may be concentrated in persons or inanimate objects and which may be acquired by a variety of means. Mana is highly communicable, and all persons are anxious to possess it and to control as much of it as possible. Success in personal undertakings is due to mana, as are an abundant harvest and healthy and fertile domestic animals. In Polynesia, where the amount of mana an individual possesses depends on his social standing, high chiefs are believed to be so highly charged with it as to be dangerous to people of lower ranks. Such people, particularly the commoners, are consequently protected by a variety of taboos designed to shield them from undue exposure. Mana, in this view, is not unlike high-

voltage electricity which, helpful as it may be, spells deadly danger in the hands of the layman.

Magical Practices

The fact that there are some important similarities between religion and magic has already been mentioned in this chapter. Moreover, we have already had occasion to mention magic several times in context. In simpler cultures especially, the distinction between magic and religion is not always obvious. But, in general, the term **magic** refers to those dealings with the supernatural which attempt to manipulate it for the benefit of some individual. When magic is performed with the intent to do good, it is commonly termed **white magic.** When magic is employed to harm or kill, anthropologists speak of **black magic,** or **sorcery.**

Two main types of magic have been practiced by peoples the world over for many thousands of years. These are the practices of imitative and contagious magic. The principle underlying imitative magic—the belief that like affects like—is already familiar to you. It is probable that the Cro-Magnon cave paintings of game animals pierced with spears or arrows were made in the belief that they would ensure a successful hunt. Similarly, the stabbing, burning, or other mutilation of an enemy's image is believed by some peoples to cause the sickness or death of the individual involved. Another form of imitative magic is commonly practiced by peoples whose subsistence depends upon a certain amount of moisture for growing crops. Magical practitioners among such peoples may imitate the action of flowing water or falling rain in order to induce the necessary moisture.

The principle upon which **contagious magic** rests is that things which have been in contact at one time continue to exert influence upon each other even when separated. A common application of contagious magic involves securing nail clippings, a lock of hair, or a piece of clothing from a person and burning the object in order to cause that person suffering. Another example of contagious magic was formerly practiced in some parts of Melanesia. If a man was wounded

by an arrow, both his friends and his enemies were anxious to secure possession of the arrow. The friends of the injured man would put the arrow in a cool, moist place to effect a smooth healing; the opponents, by contrary means, hoped to aggravate the wound.

The custom of eating the flesh of certain animals in order to gain some of their characteristics is an interesting extension of contagious magic. Tiger flesh is highly prized by some peoples, since it is believed to impart courage and strength to those who eat it. In other societies, young men avoid eating deer meat for fear they may become timid.

Japanese farmers of Hiroshima begin each new rice-sowing season with the ceremonial planting of a rice shoot in the paddy field of a sacred shrine. The farmers form a protective circle around the shrine and pray that their agricultural deity will protect their rice crops during the growing season. What kind of magical practice is this?

Magical Practitioners: Shamans

Magical activities are usually limited to specialized practitioners who have acquired the power to manipulate supernatural forces through a highly personal experience, such as a trance or vision. Best-known among the practitioners of magic are **shamans,** also known as **medicine men** among the American Indians, whose main function is to cure others.

Since the word "shaman" derives from one of the native languages of Siberia, it seems appropriate to look among the nomadic Chukchee of

Purification of their bodies through a rite of contagious magic—inhaling the fumes arising from the charred remains of a sacrificial goat —gives these women supernatural powers. They will be able to detect the causes of illness and other evils that afflict members of their South African society.

northeastern Asia for an example of a shamanistic performance. The account that follows summarizes the typical practices of a Chukchee shaman at about the end of the nineteenth century.

The Chukchee shaman customarily performed at night in the inner compartment of a tent shelter. Stimulated by the smoke of strong pipe tobacco, he began singing to the beat of his carefully tuned drum. By placing the drum at various angles in front of his mouth, he surrounded his crowd of listeners with sounds that seemed to originate in all corners of the tent. After about half an hour the drumbeat quickened, and rapid, indistinct sounds marked the arrival of the shaman's supernatural assistants. Many Chukchee shamans were not only excellent imitators of natural sounds but also very skillful ventriloquists. Among the assisting spirits whose voices were now heard might be the raven, the horsefly, the grasshopper, the fawn, and the wolf. On occasion, these spirits broke into a strange language and the shaman introduced yet another supernatural character—a voice interpreting what the spirits were saying.

Next, through the voices of particular spirits, the shaman shared his magical knowledge with others. Sometimes he issued a warning to those who had broken a taboo or forgotten some important observance. Quite frequently, at the peak of his performance, the shaman fell into a trance, during which his soul visited the spirit world seeking advice for his patients.

Shamans are present in many small, nonliterate societies of the world. Even the very small bands of hunting and gathering Bushmen recognize among their members individuals who have acquired special powers as a result of having fallen into a state of trance. Such individuals are believed to be able to cure others simply by laying their hands upon them. While it is true that the position of shaman has generally been filled by men, there are some outstanding exceptions. Among the Yurok Indians of California, for example, shamans were exclusively women.

The most common method of curing that shamans employ is to pretend to remove from the body of a patient an object claimed to have caused his sickness. The object frequently has some relationship to the patient's habits. It may be a piece of tobacco, a fish bone, a worm, an insect, or simply a chip of stone or wood. The removal of the object may be accomplished manually or by suction through the surface of the skin. Though the shaman produces the object by a skillful sleight of hand, his purpose is less trickery than to convince the patient of the magical effectiveness of his method. The patient, believing in the curing power of the shaman, quite commonly derives from the shaman's ministrations noticeable psychological benefit.

Divination and Witchcraft

Two other categories of supernatural activity are usually mentioned in connection with magic. They are the practices of divination and witchcraft. **Divination** is a practice aimed at foretelling the course of future events by supernatural means. Not only is divination common among many nonliterate peoples, but it also

Shamans among the Northwest Coast Indians wear elaborate costumes and facial masks when performing magical activities. These medicine men belong to the Haida tribe of British Columbia.

persists in various forms in highly advanced societies despite the ever-increasing reliance upon science. Even today, in any large American city, one can have his fortune foretold by a crystal-gazer or a palm-reader. Where water is known to lie deep under the earth's surface, the services of a water witch (dowser) may be requested along with those of a geologist.

The oracle of Apollo at Delphi in ancient Greece serves as a well-known example of the practice of divination. Within this sanctuary the priestess Pythia, seated upon a ceremonial tripod, inhaled vapors said to rise through a fissure in the ground and was inspired by the god Apollo to utter prophecies. These prophecies were interpreted by priests and handed

Within the oracle of Apollo at Delphi, the priestess Pythia writhed in trance-like states and delivered prophecies about the future happiness of mortals. Temple priests interpreted her frenzied utterances to the ancient Greeks who journeyed to Delphi to request knowledge of the oracle.

on to the ordinary mortals who had asked questions of the oracle.

In ancient Rome, where gods were asked to approve or disapprove of a proposed undertaking, specialists called **augurs** provided answers based on such omens as the flights of birds or the direction of lightning. Unusual problems were handled by even more specialized diviners, who based their predictions on an examination of the entrails of sacrificial animals.

Witchcraft, like sorcery, involves the manipulation of supernatural powers that are malevolent. But unlike sorcery, which is a learned activity, the power of witchcraft is believed to be inherited. Moreover, witchcraft supposedly can take possession of an individual involuntarily.

As far removed in time as we are from the Salem witch trials, when a number of individuals accused of witchcraft by several young girls were arrested and some even hanged, we usually find it difficult to understand how witchcraft can be taken seriously. The explanation is actually quite simple. A person who thinks himself under the spell of a witch and who believes in the potency of such supernatural forces may suffer or even die as the result of physiological changes produced by his nervous system under the relentless stimulus of deadly fear. We all have experienced bodily discomfort resulting from mental or emotional stress. The cause may have been a first airplane flight, an important examination inadequately prepared for, or some similar circumstance.

Interestingly enough, anthropologists find that the anxiety which invariably accompanies reports of witchcraft may be offset by a positive value which the belief in witchcraft frequently generates. During periods of intense crisis or at times of unexplainable catastrophe, the belief that witchcraft is responsible may serve as an effective scapegoat, relieving the accumulated frustrations and venting the suppressed aggressions of a society. However, this hardly justifies the effects of the belief in witchcraft on the unfortunate individuals who are accused of it.

Religious Practices and Practitioners

Among the main religious practices designed to deal with the supernatural are sacrificial offerings and rituals of worship accompanied by prayers of appeal or thanksgiving. Sacrifices of one form or another are particularly common and widespread. In the New World, ritual sacrifices reached their highest significance among some of the peoples of ancient Mesoamerica.

For the Aztecs, we are fortunate to have a detailed account of the annual ritual sacrifice as described by Bernardino de Sahagún, who arrived in the Aztec capital ten years after Cortés. In the fifth month of their year, the Aztecs held a festival in honor of their principal god, the sun-god. To this god, the Aztecs sacrificed a youth whose preparation for this moment had begun immediately following the ceremony of the previous year. The youth was chosen from among the most handsome and able of the Aztecs' captives, and for an entire year he

was carefully instructed in the good manners and the social graces which befitted a member of the nobility. He went about the city freely, elaborately clothed and attended by eight pages dressed as well as those belonging to the palace. All who met him accorded him the greatest respect and kissed the ground in his honor.

Twenty days before the ceremony, the youth was married to four young maidens, with whom he spent the last days of his life. On the day of the feast, accompanied by his wives, who attempted to console him, he was taken by royal canoe on the first part of his journey to the sacrificial temple. When he disembarked, his pages accompanied him to the foot of the temple steps. Slowly he climbed alone to the top, where the priests threw him onto the sacrificial stone and held him while one of them thrust a knife deep into his breast. Immediately the heart was drawn out and offered to the sun. According to Aztec belief, the soul of the youth thus sacrificed was carried to a most desirable afterworld reserved for the souls of fallen warriors.

In both the Old and New World, acts of worship were frequently accompanied or preceded by ceremonial cleansing. Among many American Indian tribes, such cleansing was accompanied by sweating in a sweathouse, a custom continued by some Indians even today. Chanting or group singing as well as dancing very commonly were combined with acts of worship, intensifying the experience of the participants.

Most religious practices are directed either toward supernatural beings or toward objects that symbolize them. Souls of the dead, or ghosts, are thought by many peoples to linger near their original homes and, more often than not, to be potentially dangerous. When such departed spirits are believed to be concerned with what happens to their earthly relatives and become the object of much veneration and even appeasement, anthropologists speak of **ancestor worship.** Until recently, when the structure of Chinese society began to change profoundly under Communism, ancestor worship was particularly strong in China. The members of Chinese families periodically worshiped in their homes in front of ancestral tablets, small carved pillars representing or symbolizing a departed forebear. The oldest living male in each family acted as the head of the family worship and was accorded the highest respect and unquestioned loyalty. As a result, the traditional Chinese family was an exceedingly strong, though inflexible, social unit.

The worship of deities is likewise widespread and ranges from worship of but one supreme being, as in Christianity or Islam, to the worship of plural gods, as in Hinduism. Some of the supernatural creatures worshiped by different peoples may seem to have surprisingly few godlike qualities.

These Balinese men with arms upraised are playing the role of monkey warriors who helped the hero Rama to defeat a demon king. The monkey dance traditionally performed on Bali (Indonesia) is based on a sacred Hindu epic. It honors the monkey god, Hanuman, whose wisdom and courage aided Rama to rescue his bride from the demon.

Among the American Indians, and elsewhere in the world, there are many tales that tell of the adventures of a trickster, customarily some kind of animal, whose behavior is inherently treacherous and deceitful and who in turn is gulled and deceived by others. One should remember that the ancient Greek gods were also not above trickery and petty anger. By the Greek poet Homer's account, the Trojan War was believed to have been instigated by a goddess enraged because she had not been judged the most beautiful.

Objects may be worshiped for their meaning or because they are considered sacred in themselves. The enclosure of the Great Mosque at Mecca in Saudi Arabia contains a stone shrine, known as the **Kaaba,** which holds a sacred black stone. This stone is considered holy by the Moslems, who believe that it was sent down from heaven by God himself. The high point of a Moslem's pilgrimage to this holy city is the kissing of the sacred black stone.

A great many of the world's societies have specialized religious practitioners, or priests. The term **priest** customarily refers to a person who through special ability or training acts as an intermediary between the supernatural and the members of a religious group. A priest does not usually attempt to manipulate the supernatural. Moreover, a priest gains power not through his own person but through his office in an organized religion. The term priest, then, is customarily reserved for the official religious practitioners in more complex societies with correspondingly more elaborate bodies of religious beliefs.

A Buddhist priest prepares for his religious role by retiring to a monastery for long instruction in the teachings of Buddhism. Only then is he qualified to lead a congregation along the path to a good and moral life.

The Role of Religion in Society

The fact that belief in the supernatural is very ancient and, in some form or other, is present in all human societies, is an indication that it must serve some important universal need.

What are some of the roles religion plays in human societies? To begin with, religion helps to define the relationship between man and the world that he inhabits. It thus serves to reduce the many uncertainties he must face during his lifetime. Religious rituals very commonly mark critical moments in the lives of individuals—for example, birth, the onset of sexual maturity, marriage, illness, or death.

A particularly interesting religious

custom associated with the birth of a child is **couvade,** found among many different peoples of the world but with special frequency among South American Indian tribes. According to this custom, when a child is born, the father is expected to act as though he himself were experiencing the pains of childbirth. He is therefore subjected to various restrictions for a given period of time. The basis for couvade is a belief in the magical relationship between parent and child and the consequent need to protect a child by protecting his parents.

Rites of passage mark changes in an individual's position in society at certain important stages of his life. Puberty rites and marriage ceremonies are common examples of rites of passage. Through their mysteries, these ceremonies produce an appeal to supernatural forces. They also serve as occasions to stress the responsibilities that an individual assumes with change in his status. Rites of passage thus enhance the solidarity and working relationships among the members of a society.

Rites that are associated with periodic or seasonal events of importance to a society are referred to as **rites of intensification.** During the late summer of alternate years, the Hopi Indians of northeastern Arizona hold snake dances in the plazas of their villages, or pueblos. This ancient and sacred performance of the snake dance terminates a ritual period designed chiefly to offer prayers for rain and abundant crops. During the dance, the many snakes previously collected, poisonous and harmless alike, are handled by the painted and costumed dancers, who hold the snakes between their teeth until they are released to carry messages to the gods. This very impressive ceremony has a profound effect upon all the members of the pueblo, who either witness it or actively participate in it. The ceremony brings into focus the common stake all have in securing a livelihood in an environment far from hospitable to farming. It serves also to weld the Hopi group into a unified, cohesive whole by making matters which may have divided them seem unimportant.

We have not yet mentioned the role played by religion in guiding the ethical conduct of individuals. It is probable that early religion was concerned exclusively with the role of the supernatural in human affairs. The religions of more sophisticated peoples have generally coupled awe of the supernatural with a code of moral behavior for everyday living. In modern American society, for example, there are persons for whom religion represents the moral code governing their relationships with others and persons for whom religion is primarily a body of beliefs and periodic ritual observances. Nor is this situation unique; it has been and is characteristic of many other societies.

Religious Movements

The behavior associated with an established religion almost invariably represents the more conservative features of a culture. Nevertheless, one must not overlook the dynamic nature that religious beliefs and observances may sometimes acquire. Human history is full of examples of prophets and religious reformers who have had profound influence not only upon their own cultures but upon other cultures as well. The spread of religious ideas through conquest, missionary activity, or simply intercultural contact has likewise occurred throughout the ages.

A religious movement known as the **ghost dance** swept many of the Plains Indian tribes of North America late in the nineteenth century. There were two waves of this stirring cult. The more important was the second, originated in the late 1880's by a Paiute Indian of Nevada named Wovoka.

Wovoka claimed to have had a vision in which he saw God and all of the long-departed Indians living a happy life in a land of plenty where they practiced the old customs of their cultures. God instructed Wovoka to return to his people with a message of goodwill and a dance ritual, which was to be performed for five consecutive days at frequent intervals. God promised Wovoka that if these instructions were carried out, he and his brethren would see the return of the good life and be reunited with their dead relatives and friends.

From the Paiutes, the ghost-dance religion spread to the Arapaho, the Cheyenne, the Dakota, and other Plains Indian tribes, where it suffered various changes and additions. Among the additions was the idea of the impending destruction of the white man, who had taken away Indian lands and

These Apache dancers, costumed as benevolent Mountain Spirits, are taking part in an annual rite that celebrates the passage of Apache girls into womanhood. The mysteries of this ceremony are designed to appeal to the supernatural forces that determine success in all human undertakings.

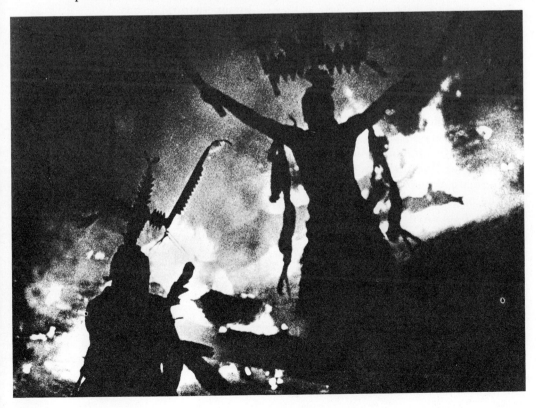

destroyed the herds of buffalo. The Plains Indians were quick to embrace a religion that predicted the destruction of the white intruders and the return of the good life. Ghost dances were carried on with increasing fervor. Dancers would fall from exhaustion into trancelike states in which they would see their dead relatives and friends or relive the joys of a successful hunt. Some groups began decorating their shirts with various symbols of the ghost dance in the belief that these symbols would make them safe from enemy bullets.

When none of the predictions concerning the revival of Indian power came true, the passion with which the ghost dances were carried out gradually died down. But the religion did not die out until after the massacre at Wounded Knee Creek, South Dakota, of several hundred Sioux men, women, and children who were gathered together for a ghost dance ceremonial.

SUMMARY

Belief in the supernatural is common to all human societies. That such belief is very ancient is indicated by the discovery of burial sites in Europe dating back to the time of the Neanderthals. Various theories concerning the origin of religion in human culture have been set forth. However, modern anthropologists do not believe that it will ever be possible to determine precisely the original sources of religious belief and behavior.

Anthropologists also find it very difficult to draw a precise boundary between religious and magical practices. However, while magic customarily involves the attempt to manipulate the supernatural, religion generally attempts only to guide the expression of man's concern with the supernatural. Two main types of magic have been practiced by people in societies throughout the world. Imitative magic attempts to determine the outcome of events by imitating the desired result. Contagious magic attempts to bring about results by manipulating objects that have been in contact with the person who is to be affected. Magic may be turned to either good or evil purposes. The best-known practitioners of magic, called "shamans," are believed to have the ability to cure by supernatural means.

Priests, unlike shamans, usually do not try to control the supernatural. They derive their power to act as intermediaries between man and the supernatural through their offices within organized religions. There is no question but that religion plays an important role in human culture. It helps man to cope with and adjust to the many mysterious forces of the universe for which he has no satisfactory explanation. In the sharing of religious beliefs, societies maintain a powerful source of social values to which they may turn in times of crisis.

Chapter Review

Terms in Anthropology

ancestor worship	Kaaba	religion
animism	magic	rites of intensification
augur	mana	rites of passage
black magic (sorcery)	medicine man	shaman
contagious magic	monotheism	supernatural
couvade	polytheism	white magic
divination	priest	witchcraft
ghost dance		

Questions for Review

1. How are religion and magic alike? On what basis do anthropologists generally distinguish between them?
2. Describe some of the well-known theories of the origin of religion.
3. What evidence suggests that the Neanderthal people thought about the afterlife of their dead? that the Cro-Magnon people did?
4. Why is the possession of mana deemed valuable by the peoples of Melanesia and Polynesia? How do these peoples guard themselves against too great an amount of mana?
5. Explain the principles underlying the two main types of magical practice. What are some examples of each type of magic?
6. How does the practice of magic by a shaman differ from its practice by a sorcerer? How does witchcraft differ from both shamanistic magic and sorcery?
7. What are some of the main religious practices designed to deal with the supernatural? How are these practices exemplified among different peoples?
8. Do Americans observe any customs that could be termed rites of passage or rites of intensification?
9. What are some of the functions of religion that appear to be fairly universal for all cultures?
10. What social and psychological functions were served by the ghost-dance movement that stirred many Plains Indian tribes toward the end of the nineteenth century?

Chapter **15**

The Arts

According to a common definition, "art" results whenever something is produced with more care than is necessary for its practical use. According to another definition, "art" depends upon a distinctive element of creative power possessed by some individuals but not by others. In this latter view, "art" is characterized by an appeal to the human sense of beauty that gives satisfaction both to its creator and to its audience.

For an anthropologist, there are obvious difficulties in accepting either one of these definitions of "art." With regard to the former, it is frequently impossible to establish the precise boundary between finishing an object for maximum efficiency and elaborating it for artistic purposes. If "art" is primarily intended to give satisfaction to an audience, how would one classify the exquisite Upper Paleolithic paintings by Cro-Magnon peoples, which were executed in such dark and remote underground caverns that it was virtually impossible to contemplate their beauty?

An additional factor enters the discussion of where ordinary utilitarian activity ends and "art" begins. In modern technological societies, so much emphasis is placed on specialization that generally one has little difficulty in sorting out mere utilitarian objects from deliberate artistic creations. They may be distinguished by their function and by their maker's purpose. But this was not the case in prehistoric societies, nor is it the case in many of the small nonliterate societies of today. There is no question whatever that the Upper Paleolithic cave paintings, carvings, and other artifacts represent artistic creations of extraordinary skill and beauty. Yet at the same time there is convincing indirect evidence that they were created primarily for magical or religious purposes—for example, to ensure success in hunting. One must also realize that in prehistoric societies, as well as in many societies of the present day, most cultural activities were so thoroughly integrated into everyday life that to discuss forms of "art" without constant reference to religion and even the mode of subsistence would be quite misleading.

The forms of "art" are manifold. They range from art forms that are primarily appreciated visually—such as painting, sculpture, and the decoration of common objects—to forms that are appreciated through the several other senses. Sculpture may also appeal to the sense of touch. Musical artistry is appreciated through our sense of hearing and in the form of opera is also a visual art. "Art" can apparently be smelled and tasted if one acknowledges the compliments often paid to master chefs. And in the

Hopi Indian craftsmen strive for the utmost realism in carving kachina dolls. This is a wolf kachina. It represents a supernatural being who acts as an intermediary between men and the gods.

enjoyment of literature, all the senses are involved in the working of the imagination. In this chapter, we will be concerned with those human activities that are most customarily designated "the arts." We will observe how different peoples derive enjoyment from the visual arts, folklore, and music.

Some Forms of Visual Art

When an object of practical use is provided with ornamental designs for the sole purpose of enhancing its beauty, we speak of **decorative art**. In any particular culture, the nature of decoration customarily follows established patterns considered appropriate for certain objects. Nevertheless, an artisan may exercise a degree of creative imagination great enough for him to be considered an artist. The potters and pottery painters among the Pueblo Indians of the North American Southwest carefully study an undecorated vessel before planning its design. The women speak of sleepless nights spent in trying to visualize how best to decorate the bowl or jar that will claim their creative concentration on the following morning. Copying the designs of others is strongly disapproved of, and the decorative work is invariably approached with the desire to paint "one's own thoughts."

All of the forms of visual art fall into one of two general categories. When an artist emphasizes the form of an object rather than its meaning or its likeness to something else, **formal art** results. When an artist is primarily concerned with the portrayal of nature or life, we speak of **repre-**

sentative art. In many cases, a given piece of art will combine features of both categories.

The term **style,** when used in the visual arts, refers to a characteristic mode of artistic expression. Styles of art vary no less among the nonliterate peoples of the world than they have varied from period to period in historical Oriental and Western art. Art that deliberately strives for faithful representation of an object is referred to as **realistic,** or **naturalistic, art.** When an accepted way of expressing the subject matter predominates over the desire to produce an exact likeness, the result is **conventionalized,** or **stylized,** art. When an art object is intended to have a meaning for those who behold it, and that meaning is conveyed by the use of symbols, we speak of **symbolic art.** More often than not, symbols in art have become so highly stylized that they bear little or no resemblance to what they represent. For example, a circle may be used to represent the entire annual cycle of the four seasons. However, symbols used in art may also be realistically depicted. In European art, a bishop's crown was commonly used to represent not only its wearer but the entire hierarchy of the universal Christian Church.

Now let us examine how art styles were used by some of the Indian peoples of North America.

Art Styles of the Plains Indians

Two principal styles of decorative art were used by the Plains Indians, one customarily applied by men, the other by women. Men used a naturalistic style in painting figures of buffaloes,

This carved wooden idol from northern Luzon in the Philippines is a good example of highly conventionalized art. The figure represents a minor agricultural deity.

horses, and people on ceremonial or everyday objects made from animal hides. These figures were usually painted in flat colors obtained from clays, and in a majority of cases they represented exploits of war.

By contrast, the decorations made by women were geometrical in design. Some of these decorations were painted. Others were embroidered with softened and dyed porcupine quills or, in later times, with glass beads obtained in trade. Among most of the Plains Indians, the geometrical designs and the colors used had symbolic values. Their meanings varied greatly from one tribe to another and even to some extent among individuals of a tribe. The symbolic art of the Arapaho Indians at the beginning of this century has been particularly well recorded. Let us examine one Arapaho design in detail.

An unfolded rawhide bag once used by Arapaho women for gathering cherries is shown in the illustration on this page. The meaning of the designs on the front side of this bag (at right in the illustration) was explained as follows: The earth as it appeared after its emergence from primeval waters is represented by the rhombus in the center. The central portion of this rhombus, green in color, symbolizes the earth; the bisecting line, in red, symbolizes the course of the sun. The earth at the present time is represented by the entire rectangle. The triangles within it stand for mountains, and the two short lines on top of the two small triangles are the first people, duplicated in the overall design to achieve symmetry.

The design on the back side of the gathering bag (at left) symbolizes the sacred tribal hoop used by the Arap-aho in playing games. It might also be considered to represent a shield, similar to a hoop in size and shape. The border on the triangular flap of the bag (far left) symbolizes a bow.

Arapaho painted designs frequently employed symbols which differed from those used on embroidered objects. For example, horse tracks were represented on embroidered objects by the symbol ⊓ , while in paintings two spaced dots . . were used. Such design elements as triangles and diamonds also had a variety of symbolic meanings.

Art Styles of the Northwest Coast Indians

Probably the most striking and distinctive native art of this continent north of Mexico is that created by the Northwest Coast Indians. The tribes of this area engaged extensively in wood carving and produced impressive totem poles, which honored the ancestors of their clans. The primary

This Arapaho rawhide bag is decorated in the geometric style traditionally employed by Arapaho women. An explanation of the symbolic meaning of the design appears within the text on this page.

use of these elaborate carvings was in the many ceremonials associated with the supernatural beliefs of these Indian tribes. However, the element of prestige in possessing objects of value was doubtless also significant.

The characteristic feature of Northwest Coast Indian art is the symbolic representation of animal forms. For instance, the beaver is identified by two large upper incisors, a large round nose, a scaly tail, and often by a log held in its forepaws. The hawk and the eagle are distinguished by the shapes of their beaks; the hawk's beak is curved back so that it touches the face, while the beak of the eagle is merely turned downward. The sea monster is symbolized by the head of a beaver, a bear's paws with flippers attached, and various elements representative of the killer whale.

These powerful carvings were further enhanced by the bold use of color. A passion for symmetry and a tendency to fill all of the space available on a surface was also characteristic of the Indian artists. An animal might be represented by two profiles arranged along a vertical axis, or its face might be shown from the front with various portions of its anatomy symmetrically arranged in the remaining space. The ingenious interlocking of carved figures on totem poles and on objects made of horn or ivory was common practice and resulted in great richness of form.

The masks carved by the Northwest Coast Indians for use by dancing societies or in the curing ceremonies of shamans were unusually elaborate and are among the most striking found anywhere in the world. Some had hinged movable parts that were manipulated by strings. Others were dou-

Symbolic representations of human and animal forms decorate this Northwest Coast Indian totem pole. The carved figures lack realism, but they are perfectly symmetrical.

This carved wooden mask of an old woman of the Niska tribe, British Columbia, is a fine example of realistic character portraiture. The woman is wearing a labret, a lip ornament here inlaid with abalone shells.

ble or triple masks consisting of several layers of carving that were revealed successively during a ritual performance. But the inventiveness of these Indian artists went beyond the creation of strong and exaggerated forms. Some masks display character portraiture so finely carved and startlingly realistic as to leave no doubt of their creators' mastery of technique and deep understanding of the material with which they worked.

The Uses of Folklore

The term **literature** is customarily used to refer to prose or verse that is written and especially to writings that are distinguished by excellence of form and universal appeal. Does this mean that peoples who have not adopted a writing system have noth-

ing comparable to literature? Nothing could be farther from the truth. Both the art of storytelling and the practice of reciting poetry as part of ritual observances are common among nonliterate peoples and reach very far back in time.

The oral traditions, the beliefs, the dances, and the songs preserved by a people through custom over centuries make up their **folklore.** The study of folklore has gained increasing attention among anthropologists since the end of the nineteenth century. The subject matter of a people's oral traditions, including their myths, tales, riddles, and proverbs, can reveal a great deal about the moral values of a society. Moreover, similarities in the folklore of different peoples may yield important clues to ancient migrations and contacts between cultures.

The African peoples south of the Sahara have developed a particularly rich body of folklore. It has been estimated that they possess as a group at least five thousand distinctly individual tales. These peoples also make wide use of proverbs to warn, to praise, and to guide. For instance, an outsider in a group who shows a disposition to meddle may be set straight by the impersonal reminder, "Chicken says, 'The feet of the stranger are small.' " Proverbs are also considered an effective means of supporting arguments in native courts of law.

While tales have worldwide distribution, true proverbs and riddles are characteristic of the Old World only. Probably they are of more recent origin than are tales. At any rate, it is likely that they did not spread throughout the Old World until the migration of man into the Western hemisphere was nearly completed.

The Tales of the North American Indians

The first collection of North American Indian tales was made as early as 1633 by Jesuit priests who were living among tribes of the northeastern coastal area. From that time on, Indian tales have been recorded from the Arctic lands of the Eskimos to the desert lands of the Pueblo Indians. As a result, the oral traditions of the North American continent are very well known.

All of the North American Indian tribes have been found to possess a rich body of traditional stories, greatly cherished by the people and carefully handed down from generation to generation. The many thousands of distinct tales recorded for different tribes may be grouped into several classes according to their subject matter.

One group of Indian tales is concerned with origins: the origin of the universe, the earth, and various kinds of animals, and the appearance of the first human beings and of particular tribes of people. A common tale describes a legendary hero who finds himself floating on an expanse of primeval water. The hero persuades various animals to dive to the bottom in an attempt to bring up a bit of soil. When at last one of the animals—frequently a toad or a muskrat —is successful, the hero creates the earth from the clod of soil brought to him. Usually he goes on to provide the earth with living creatures, including men and women.

Another group of tales found almost universally among the North American Indians describes the adventures of a trickster figure, who may be man, or animal, or a combination of both. The trickster has supernatural powers, and he may use them either to help or to deceive others. Sometimes the trickster is thought of as a hero, despite the unheroic traits he possesses in great measure. In a tale common among the Plains Indians, the trickster is given the power of sharpening his leg so that he can hunt by thrusting it into a buffalo. Although the trickster has been told that he can use this power only four times (a magic number with American Indians), he becomes so pleased with his new skill that he continues to kill wantonly. But soon he finds his leg thrust through a buffalo from which he cannot free himself and is so badly kicked that he almost dies.

Still another group of tales concerns the adventures of a hero conceived of as human although his feats are surrounded by many supernatural circumstances. The birth of this hero is quite commonly miraculous, as in the much-liked Plains tale that has him formed from a clot of buffalo blood. His adventures usually involve a succession of seemingly insurmountable tests, in which he receives aid from both humans and animals.

A fourth group of tales relate journeys into other worlds. A particularly good example of this kind of tale is "The Star Husband," a favorite with the storytellers of many tribes. In a typical version of this tale, a young girl sleeping out under the stars wishes that she could marry the brightest of them. The next day she sees a porcupine in a tall tree and climbs up after him. As she climbs, the tree grows taller and taller. When she can no longer see the earth below, the porcupine speaks to her and reveals that he is the brightest star of all; he has heard her wish and has come to take her away to the sky with him. The two go to a sky village, where they live very much as they would on earth. In time, they have a son who is named Star Boy.

One day, as the girl is digging for roots, she finds a variety of root that her husband has told her never to disturb. But her son wants this root, and she does not like to refuse him. She finds that the root is very long, and when at last she pulls it up, she notices that her digging has broken through the sky floor. She makes the hole bigger so that she can look through it, and when her eyes have grown accustomed to the light, far below she sees the tepees of her village and her people moving among them. Thinking about all she has left, she becomes very sad. Another day, when the girl is digging, she hears a voice nearby. An old woman has called to her, and she answers, saying how much she wishes to return to her people. The old woman offers to help her if she will bring one hundred sinews —no more, no less—from which to make a rope. When the rope is ready, the girl waits until her husband is away on a hunt and then takes Star Boy with her to the hole in the sky.

Now the old woman ties the rope around the girl's waist, helps her through the hole, and tells her to keep her eyes closed until she feels the earth under her feet. But the rope stops moving and the girl finds herself looking down on tall grass, too far above the ground to jump. The old woman calls to her that the sinews were not counted correctly and that she can do no more for her. When the Star Husband returns home and does not find his wife and son, he begins to search for them and dis-

covers the hole with the rope descending. Looking down the rope, he sees his wife and son suspended at the end of it far below. He takes a heavy rock and, directing that his wife be killed but his son saved, sends it down along the rope. When the rock hits, the woman drops to the ground dead, but Star Boy is unhurt. He is found and cared for by the people of his mother's village and grows up to perform many great feats. His deeds become the subject of a sequel, a tale belonging to the group of hero stories already mentioned.

Nearly a hundred versions of the Star Husband tale have been collected from tribes widely scattered over North America, from the northeastern Canadian coast to the southwestern desert and from Alaska to the southeastern mountains. A careful study of the differences among all these versions has not only established the existence of several regional subtypes of the tale, but has also produced a tentative account of where it most likely originated and how it traveled.

Today, the telling of tales is becoming a lost art. Most of the tribal storytellers are rapidly passing from the scene. With the spread of television and drive-in movies to even the most remote areas of America's Indian reservations, a majority of the young people have lost interest in the oral traditions of their past. It is small wonder that much anthropological fieldwork today is of such urgency.

Musical Traditions

Some form of musical expression is characteristic of all human societies, although the style and purpose of musical performances may vary greatly from one culture to another. The specialized problems associated with the study of music in cultures outside of the Western tradition have given rise to the field of **ethnomusicology,** or the anthropology of music. The scope of this study may be defined narrowly or broadly. At its narrowest, it is limited to the musical behavior of nonliterate peoples. At its broadest, it also includes Oriental music and the folk music of the Western world.

Even though no one as yet has convincingly accounted for the origins of music, its universal presence in the cultures of the world and its close relationship to language and ritual behavior suggest great antiquity. The importance of music appears to be greater among nonliterate peoples than in highly advanced societies. This may be due in part to the small size of many tribal societies and the tendency of more members to participate in the various ceremonial functions of the group. In such societies, too, there tends to be more frequent use of instrumental performances for religious, social, and other purposes.

A great variety of musical instruments and singing styles are to be found in different areas of the world. We will return to an example as we discuss now the variety of artistic expression that characterizes Navaho Indian culture.

The Arts of the Navaho Indians

We have already suggested that in small, nonliterate societies the various aspects of culture—religion and the arts especially—are so closely integrated that it is difficult to discuss any one without reference to the others. This is true of the culture of the Navaho Indians of the American Southwest. The Navaho celebrate a number of ceremonies that combine painting, poetry, dance, and music to provide a very intense emotional experience for all who observe or participate in them. One of these, a nine-day ceremony termed **Yeibichai,** or the **Navaho Night Way,** serves the primary function of an initiation or curative rite.

During the Yeibichai, the ceremonial leader with his assistants create **sand paintings,** or dry paintings, as they are sometimes called. Sand painting is an art at which the Navaho excel. The colors for a painting are obtained from powdered minerals, colored sands, charcoal, and other vegetable materials. The painting, done upon a flat surface of sand or buckskin, requires a great deal of skill and training. The artist picks up the powdered color in his fingers and allows it to trickle from them as he slowly moves his hand. He usually begins in the morning and performs with concentration, since Navaho custom requires that a sand painting be destroyed on the same day that it is begun.

A sand painting made on the sixth day of a Night Way ceremony is shown in the illustration on page 202. This painting represents the vision which a mythological chanter named "the Visionary" saw near a lake. The outer figures on the north and south of this painting are harvest deities appearing in the form of sheep. They are known as the Bighorn Gods. Each god carries a black bag of plenty on his back and leans on a staff decorated with feathers. The masks of the Bighorn Gods are decorated with red woodpecker feathers, which represent sunbeams; broken white lines symbolizing lightning; and two blue horns suggesting a mountain sheep.

To the east in this painting stands the Talking God, god of dawn and the eastern sky, of animals and the chase. He wears a white mask with eagle plumes, a tuft of yellow owl feathers, fox-skin ornaments under his right ear, and various mouth and eye symbols. The pouch he carries is made of a squirrel, whose color and markings are carefully depicted. In the west appears the black figure of the chief House God, wearing a blue mask crowned with eagle plumes and owl feathers and carrying a black wand. Ringing the picture on three sides is the Rainbow Goddess. She wears a rectangular mask that identifies her as a female and carries at her waist an embroidered pouch tied with four strings.

A bowl of water in the center of the painting symbolizes the lake seen in the chanter's vision. Floating on the lake are two crossed spruce logs,

This Navaho sand painting, created during a Night Way ceremony, represents what the mythological chanter named "the Visionary" saw near a lake. Its symbolic meaning is explained within the text on pages 201–03.

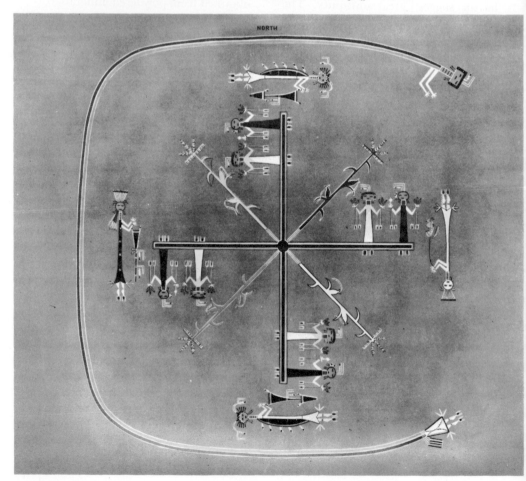

NORTH

represented by black bars. The Bighorn Gods and the chief House God are supposed to be causing the spruce logs to whirl around, while the Talking God scatters pollen from his pouch. Extending outward from the shores of the lake are four corn stalks, each painted a color symbolizing one of the four cardinal directions—white for the east, blue for the south, yellow for the west, and black for the north.

Four pairs of deities are represented as sitting on the floating logs, their feet hanging below. The figures dressed in black are males, as is indicated by their round masks, their two eagle plumes and owl-feather tufts, the gourd rattles in their right hands, and their white arms. Men are said to have been created of white corn. The figures in white are females. Their arms and chests are yellow, since women were created of yellow corn, and they wear rectangular masks and hold a wand of spruce in each hand.

What is the purpose of creating so elaborate a painting, if it is to be destroyed at day's end? The Navaho believe that sand paintings offer a way for the gods to enter the bodies of the sick. When a painting is completed, a patient may take his place in the middle of it for a curing ceremony. Following the ceremony, the members of his family may also apply some of the sand to their bodies in order to restore themselves to full health.

Poetry and Music in the Navaho Night Way

The most impressive moment of the Night Way comes on the ninth and last day of the ritual. After the arrival of the masked ceremonial dancers, the medicine man begins the final proceedings with a long prayer addressed to the thunderbird. The thunderbird is a male deity believed to dwell with some of the other divinities at Tsegihi, a particular place on the Navaho reservation. Parts of the prayer delivered on the last day of one Yeibichai are given here in free translation:

In Tsegihi,
In the dwelling made of the dawn,
In the dwelling made of the evening twilight,
In the dwelling made of the dark cloud,
In the dwelling made of the male rain,
In the dwelling made of the dark mist,
In the dwelling made of the female rain,
In the dwelling made of pollen,
In the dwelling made of grasshoppers,
Where the dark mist stands in the doorway,
The trail to which is the rainbow,
Where the jagged lightning stands high above,
Where the male rain stands high above,

With your moccasins of dark cloud,
Come to us.
With your leggings of dark cloud,
Come to us.
With your shirt of dark cloud,
Come to us.
With your headdress of dark cloud,
Come to us.

With the dark thunder overhead,
Come to us soaring.
With the heavy cloud at your feet,
Come to us soaring.
With the far darkness of the rain cloud overhead,
Come to us soaring.
With the far darkness of the dark mist overhead,
Come to us soaring.

The Navaho artist creates a sand painting by skillfully sifting grains of colored sand through his fingers onto a flat surface, either the ground or buckskin. Why don't the Navaho preserve their sand paintings?

With the jagged lightning flung high
    above you,
Come to us soaring.
With the rainbow arching high above you,
Come to us soaring.
With the near darkness of the dark cloud,
    of the male rain, of the dark mist, and
    of the female rain,
Come to us.
With all of these may the foam float on
    the water
As it flows over the roots of the great corn
    plant.

I have made a sacrifice for you.
I have prepared a smoke for you.
Restore my feet for me.
Restore my legs for me.
Restore my body for me.
Restore my voice for me.
Restore my mind for me.

Happily the old men will regard you.
Happily the old women will regard you.
Happily the young men will regard you.
Happily the young women will regard you.
Happily the children will regard you.
Happily, as they scatter in various direc-
    tions,
They will regard you.
Happily, as they approach their homes,
They will regard you.
Happily may their trails home
Be on the pollen path.

In beauty I walk.
With beauty before me, I walk.
With beauty behind me, I walk.
With beauty below me, I walk.
With beauty above me, I walk.
With beauty all around me, I walk.
So be it in beauty.
So be it in beauty.
So be it in beauty.
So be it in beauty.

The orderly and repetitious nature of Navaho poetry serves an important function. In the Navaho view, it helps to restore harmony and order in both the natural and supernatural realms. And in the case of illness, it helps to provide a sick patient and his family with a renewed sense of security.

Navaho music also may serve to provide individuals with a sense of well-being. Every Navaho family possesses a number of protective songs, in many cases handed down over several generations. These "good luck songs" are considered to be of aid in raising crops, weaving blankets, silversmithing, and many other undertakings.

Navaho chanting may at first appear both monotonous and impossible to distinguish from the music of other Indian peoples. But to the anthropologist, Navaho music has some distinctly characteristic features. Its melodic range is wide; melodies may rise to a climax, then suddenly descend as much as an octave. As a rule, there are no more than two different rhythmic patterns in a song. And the Navaho use vocal tension and pulsation and a clear falsetto voice which, except for the music of the Plains Indians, is relatively rare. For the Navaho, chanting is not an optional activity. It is an integral part of his whole culture.

SUMMARY

For the anthropologist, the artistic activities of a society cannot be studied in isolation from other aspects of the culture. The art of many peoples —and of nonliterate peoples especially —tends to be closely associated with religious beliefs and practices. The anthropologist is concerned not only with a people's visual arts but also with their folklore and music. Each in its own way may reveal to him a great deal about the character of a society.

The visual arts—painting, sculpture, and decoration—have been important in most human societies. This chapter has used as examples the art of two North American Indian groups. Among the Plains Indians, men employed a naturalistic style of art to depict their exploits in war and hunt-

ing. The Plains Indian women customarily used geometrical designs to convey symbolically their feelings about life and nature. The Northwest Coast Indians employed still other styles of art in the creation of elaborate wood carvings that served ceremonial purposes.

The folklore of a people is also of great interest to the anthropologist. He has found that myths and tales, proverbs and riddles, are often very indicative of the traditional values of a society. A people's conception of how the world was created, which is often embodied in myth, may help to explain their view of how they relate to the supernatural. The folk heroes of a people may suggest the human qualities they find most admirable or appealing. Then, too, the subject matter of traditional literature often provides a great deal of information about the past history and previous cultural contacts of a society.

Finally, the study of the music of nonliterate peoples has convinced anthropologists of the fallacy of thinking that "it all sounds the same and therefore is the same." The anthropologist finds a considerable variety of distinct musical styles among peoples the world over. He knows that the songs of the African bush or of native southwestern America exhibit no less intricate patterning than the traditional music of Europe and Asia.

Chapter Review

Terms in Anthropology

conventionalized (stylized) art	formal art	sand painting
decorative art	literature	style
ethnomusicology	realistic (naturalistic) art	symbolic art
folklore	representative art	Yeibichai (Navaho Night Way)

Questions for Review

1. Why is it difficult for an anthropologist to give a precise definition of "art"?
2. What are the two main categories of visual art described in this chapter? Compare and contrast the three styles of art defined in this chapter.
3. What are the differences between the two decorative styles found in the art of the North American Plains Indians?
4. What were the most prominent characteristics of the art produced by the Northwest Coast Indians?
5. What does the study of the folklore of a people customarily entail?
6. What may the study of a people's oral traditions reveal to an anthropologist about their society?
7. What evidence suggests that proverbs represent a much later form of oral tradition than either myths or tales? Describe the use of proverbs among the peoples of sub-Saharan Africa.
8. Why may ethnomusicology be considered a subdivision of cultural anthropology?
9. What characteristics of Navaho sand paintings make it meaningless to discuss this form of artistic expression without reference to Navaho religion?
10. What function is served by the orderly repetition that characterizes Navaho ritual poetry?

Chapter **16**

Theories and Methods of Cultural Anthropology

In our study of human culture, we have examined some aspects of culture that seem nearly universal for human groups. We have noted, for example, the importance of the family as a basic unit of organization in all societies. We have observed how members of a society are grouped according to ties of kinship and according to other bonds that may help to strengthen the fabric of the society. We have noted some of the ways in which men settle conflicts among themselves. We have observed the differences between magic and religion, and we have also seen how both help man to deal with circumstances that seem to defy rational explanation. We have examined some of mankind's artistic creations. We have even looked back in time to discover as best we could the origins of various aspects of human culture.

Yet we have barely scratched the surface of anthropology, for the study of man is infinite in scope. Although we have observed some of the characteristic ways of keeping peace in socie-

ties, we have seen these methods in practice in only a few selected societies. We can relate some of the magical activities of a Chukchee shaman, but we have not examined how these vary in detail from the practices of medicine men among the North American Indians. While we have become more familiar with the visual arts of certain American Indian tribes, we have had to exclude from our discussion the artistic activities of hundreds of other human groups. The anthropologist who attempts to describe human culture in general can only begin to draw upon the vast body of knowledge about human cultures that is now available to him. He must remember also that this body of knowledge is constantly expanding because of the current work of anthropologists in the field.

How does an anthropologist arrive at any general theories about culture? Should he even try to do so? About a century ago, when anthropology was just becoming established as an independent branch of study, many leading anthropologists theorized broadly about human culture without seeming to be troubled by the gaps in their knowledge of human societies. This is not to say that their work has not been valuable to succeeding generations of anthropologists. However, anthropologists today tend to apply more rigorous tests to theories of culture. How the methods of anthropology have changed over the last century and what the goals of modern anthropology are form the subject of this chapter.

The Concept of Cultural Evolution

In our discussion of physical anthropology, we noted how profoundly the theory of evolution has affected our understanding of man's place in nature. Natural scientists have not been alone in applying the concept of evolutionary change to the human past. Many early anthropologists used it to explain mankind's cultural development as well. This kind of thinking was stimulated by new discoveries about human culture made during the nineteenth century.

Throughout the nineteenth century, travelers, soldiers, and missionaries were bringing to light new information about cultures little known to Europeans. At the same time, archaeologists were greatly extending our knowledge of man's cultural prehistory. How was all this new information to be interpreted? At least some anthropologists of the period interpreted it as evidence that man's cultures—no less than man himself—are subject to evolutionary change. Their idea that human culture has progressed, and is constantly progress-

ing, from simpler to more advanced states is referred to as the theory of **cultural evolution.**

One of the scholars who helped to develop the theory of cultural evolution was an American, Lewis Henry Morgan, who first gained recognition for his study of Iroquois Indian culture (1851). Morgan's aim was to establish the general principles underlying human cultural progress. According to Morgan, such progress came about through several successive stages. Since apparently all men everywhere were characterized by basically similar mental processes, Morgan further reasoned that all societies could be expected to pass through these successive levels.

What were these stages of human cultural development? Morgan named three: savagery, barbarism, and civilization. Savagery, the lowest stage, was subdivided by Morgan into three levels: a lower period in which man was only slightly advanced over animals; a middle period characterized among other things by the use of fire; and a higher period marked by the invention and use of the bow and arrow. Barbarism, the middle stage, was similarly subdivided into a lower period marked by the art of pottery making; a middle period characterized by the domestication of animals and plants; and an upper period during which man came to depend upon the use of metals. The highest stage of Morgan's scheme was civilization, made possible by the invention and use of alphabetic writing and divided into ancient and modern periods.

Morgan's analysis of human cultural development into stages was based chiefly upon advancements made in technology at each level. But far from limiting his theory of cultural evolution to advancements in technology, Morgan extended it to many other aspects of culture, particularly social and political institutions.

It is not easy to evaluate Morgan's contribution to the general theory of culture. He was on firm ground in describing the general progress of man's material culture from the tools and techniques used in food gathering to those used in food production. On the other hand, Morgan was far from successful in extending his theory to cover other aspects of man's cultural development. He argued, for example, that the monogamous nuclear family was the latest form of man's kinship grouping and was inevitably associated with other advanced cultural achievements. Subsequent work by many anthropologists studying different cultures of the world has shown that this argument cannot be proven.

Today, with an abundance of ethnographic data on which to draw, it has become obvious that broad generalizations about human cultural progress are often contradicted by the available evidence. Owing to historical, geographic, and other factors, individual societies have moved through different stages of cultural development at varying rates. Also, a particular society may have remained at a relatively simple stage of technology while other aspects of its culture may have developed to a more complex level. The Australian aborigines are said to have an Old Stone Age culture, or a material way of life just as simple as that of early man tens of thousands of years ago. However, we cannot assume that Australian aboriginal culture mirrors early man's religious and social institutions as well. The few Eskimo groups that have managed to stay unaffected by new settlements or by encroaching military bases have a material culture which resembles that of the Mesolithic Age. Eskimo toolmaking and exploitation of the environment by fishing, hunting, and fowling are similar to the Mesolithic way, but any other parallels between the Eskimos and Mesolithic peoples are likely to be accidental rather than inevitable.

The Modern Study of Culture

In their attempt to develop a science of culture, modern anthropologists work toward relatively modest goals. Those who believe to any extent in cultural evolution tend to limit themselves to comparing specific societies or to comparing only certain aspects of human culture. The mass of data recorded since Morgan's time is used to support statements about culture that are less sweeping but far more solidly grounded.

Opposition to the theory of cultural evolution first appeared around the turn of the century. In America, this reaction centered around the work of Franz Boas, a German-born scholar who is now widely acknowledged as the father of modern American anthropology. Boas was a vigorous advocate of anthropological fieldwork. He believed that good descriptive studies of specific cultures were necessary before any attempt should be made to speculate about culture in general. Having been trained originally in the natural sciences, Boas stressed the use of scientific methods in anthropology. He criticized Morgan and others for

These pictures illustrate two fundamental types of economy: food gathering and food producing. Bushman hunters (lower l.) and Dahomey fishermen (lower r.) represent food gathering economies; Lapp herders (above) and a Moroccan farmer (middle) represent food producing economies. Subsistence economy based on food gathering cannot support large populations. Farming, on the other hand, has made possible urban civilization and thus helped to bring about specialization and technological advancement.

approaching anthropology more as philosophers than as scientists. Even though Boas was probably more familiar with cultures throughout the world than any other anthropologist of his time, only a very small part of his extensive writings concerns itself with general conclusions about the cultural history of man. However, this does not mean that he was against attempting such conclusions once enough data became available.

An attitude even more strongly opposed to viewing cultures historically was exhibited by a group of anthropologists who followed the lead of a Polish-born ethnographer, Bronislaw Malinowski. During the early decades of this century, Malinowski introduced an approach to cultural anthropology that departed from all previous efforts in this field. According to Malinowski, no less than a complete account of all that the members of a society do must be the goal of ethnographic fieldwork. Moreover, the anthropologist should interpret the various elements of a culture within the context of the total culture to which they contribute. Malinowski himself spent several years of his life as a "participant observer" of the natives of the Trobriand Islands in the southwestern Pacific. He described their way of life in several volumes, each centered around a major theme of the Trobriand culture.

Contemporary American anthropologists employ the methods of Boas and Malinowski along with additional specialized approaches to the study of culture. For example, one group of anthropologists has traced the movements of various Indian tribes in order to determine what land they controlled or held when they first came into contact with white men. Other anthropologists have been making use of comprehensive data collections prepared for many different cultures in their attempts to make wide-ranging cross-cultural comparisons. These data collections yield statistical information concerning relationships between different aspects of culture. For example, among the seventy or so animal-herding societies so far represented in this survey, nearly four fifths trace descent patrilineally. This seems to suggest a definite correlation between a basic economic activity and a particular type of kinship organization.

Of special interest is the study of the relationship between culture and personality, which dates back to the 1930's. This approach attempts to answer some of the questions concerning human cultural activity by using knowledge gained in the psychological study of human behavior. Let us examine this approach in more detail.

The Study of Culture and Personality

Studies of the relationship between culture and personality proceed from the recognition that the total behavior of an individual, or his **personality,** is to a large extent determined by those members of his society who are responsible for his upbringing. Newborn children everywhere, although they possess a definite biological inheritance, are free of any learned—that is, cultural—behavior. From the moment of birth on, they begin their long adjustment to the pattern of rearing practices characteristic of their particular society or social group. A child's physiological needs, for exam-

The Eskimo child carried on his mother's back has little freedom of movement, yet is introduced to a wide variety of experiences each day. Some anthropologists consider very important the effects of child-rearing practices on adult personality.

ple the need for food, may be met kindly and immediately, or sympathetically but according to a definite schedule, or in a manner that brings about more frustration than comfort. To use another example, a child may be tightly swaddled or bound on a cradleboard during most of the day, or he may be given freedom of movement by being placed in a crib or playpen. Different societies follow different practices as they go about introducing members to their cultural traditions. The variety among these child-rearing practices is thought to contribute to the formation of different personality characteristics.

The study of culture and personality requires thorough grounding in both anthropology and psychology, as

well as an extended period of field-work. The following examples provide some idea of what can be learned in this field of anthropological inquiry.

Among the Comanche Indians, children were given a great deal of freedom as they were growing up. Parents rarely if ever used punishment in dealing with their children but instead were generous with praise and reward. Consequently, children did not see parents as a source of frustration and therefore did not develop mixed feelings of love and resentment toward them. The result, typically, was a self-confident and aggressive adult, secure in his ability to deal with his environment and determined to achieve the goals set by his culture through the use of his own initiative. His dealings with the supernatural were not based on helplessness, recognition of sinfulness, and need for forgiveness, but rather on a direct appeal for personal power and for the qualities that would make him worthy of possessing it.

In contrast, it has been found that the children of the Alor Islanders of Indonesia are subjected to strikingly different treatment. When there is work to be done in the vegetable gardens, mothers place their children, even those only a few weeks old, in the care of other members of the family and go out to the gardens. Under such circumstances, the newborn child may remain hungry for long periods of time. Children are also subjected to frequent teasing and ridicule and are alternately praised or physically punished with little, if any, consistency. The child has scarcely any opportunity to develop a strong relationship to his father or mother, and the general atmosphere of uncertainty prevents him from developing self-assurance, self-esteem, and confidence in his ability to handle the world around him. Alorese supernatural beliefs faithfully reflect these attitudes. The spirits of ancestors are given offerings and are feared. But instead of being shown reverence, they are obeyed with reluctance and even resentment.

Abram Kardiner, a psychiatrist who worked on some of the pioneering studies of culture and personality, has termed the patterns of child treatment that characterize a society its **primary institutions.** Primary institutions, which vary in their particulars from society to society, include such things as patterns of child feeding, the attention and amount of freedom given a child, and the reward or punishment that follows a child's actions. A child usually comes into contact with the primary institutions within his own family, which is the foremost agent of initiation into any culture. According to Kardiner, the pleasures and frustrations a young child faces contribute decisively to the formation of his **basic personality structure,** which in turn affects his adult behavior. The behavior of the many adults within a society ultimately determines the forms of economic, religious, and other cultural activities that characterize the society. These Kardiner refers to as the **secondary institutions.** In terms of the Alorese culture, Kardiner's ideas would be applied as follows: poor maternal care and neglect create in the child a deep sense of insecurity and distrust of others that result later, in the adult, in a feeling of helplessness before the deity and a lack of enterprise in other matters.

The Concept of the World View

The study of culture, if it aims at penetrating below the surface of readily observable behavior, becomes a formidable task. Yet if the anthropologist is to predict the reactions of members of a society in a given set of circumstances, he must first ask why these people behave as they do. The explanation will often lie in the particular ideology, or world view, that the members of any normally functioning society share. The anthropologist defines **world view** as the characteristic way in which the members of a culture perceive and respond to their total environment.

The world view of a people is reflected in many aspects of their culture. How a people conceive of their relationship to both natural and supernatural forces, how they define their mutual relationships within society, and what they consider their ultimate goals as individuals and as members of a group all are part of their world view. In advanced literate civilizations, both ancient and modern, the merits of differing world views have quite commonly been debated by philosophers, historians, and religious leaders. Such discussion implies an awareness on the part of some members of a society that a particular world view guides their way of thinking. In most cultures, however, the assumptions about man and the universe that determine individual actions have been learned indirectly and accepted so completely that members of the society are not consciously aware of them. The anthropologist tries to discover these fundamental assumptions by closely observing a particular culture over a period of time. He notes what people say and do in times of crisis, what they particularly value and what they scorn, and what their attitude is toward outside cultural influences.

As an example, let us consider several contrasting attitudes that members of different cultures have toward time. Time may be considered a valuable commodity, as in American culture, where people often equate it with money ("Time is money"). The activities of Americans are for the most part rigidly scheduled, and people try to meet their appointments and discharge their obligations promptly. The time-consciousness of the average American is also closely correlated with a pronounced orientation toward the future. Members of American society are forever setting goals for themselves, only to set new ones once the original goals have been achieved. High school students eagerly anticipate their next experiences, college students their first jobs or advanced studies, and people in occupations their future assignments. Americans seem always to be looking forward to better times. This is reflected in their concern with political, social, and economic progress.

In contrast, traditional Chinese society was firmly rooted in the past. In traditional Chinese society, it was not usual for an individual to rush headlong into one new activity after another. People tended to follow the ways of their ancestors and to seek the advice of their elders before beginning any new undertaking. Politically, too, the Chinese looked to the past, following the rules of government set down by scholars many centuries earlier. This may help to explain the stability of the Chinese

political system, which managed to sustain itself over thousands of years despite the periodic overthrow of ruling dynasties in times of internal crisis. This description does not fit the present Communist society of mainland China, which, in its attempt to shortcut the process of economic development, has imposed methods that conflict with traditional Chinese values and attitudes. The result has been much turmoil and confusion.

The Navaho World View

The Navaho Indians, whose growing number has already exceeded the hundred-thousand mark, have been studied in more detail than any of the other original inhabitants of North America. Perhaps the most knowledgable student of Navaho culture was Clyde Kluckhohn, who analyzed the Navaho world view and expressed it in terms of a series of "keystones on which the Navaho view of the world appears to rest." He found that the Navaho considers the universe to be a well-ordered system in which all events are related to each other and are the result of a specific cause. In order to live in harmony with the universe, the Navaho must avoid extreme behavior and continually seek and maintain balance and order in his personal life as well as in his environment. If harmony should become upset, it must be reestablished by appropriate orderly procedures. We have already seen how illness, which to the Navaho reflects disharmony of some kind, is treated in the Night Way ceremonial by ritual activities characterized by orderly repetition.

The childhood activities encouraged by different societies are not chosen at random, but help to prepare children for their roles in adult life. Both the Indian boy at work (above) and the American Indian boy at play (below) are developing skills valued in their cultures. The Nepalese girl carrying a basket has assumed an adult task at an age when children in many societies are just beginning their schooling.

It is also the unstated conviction of the Navaho that nature is more powerful than man and that it is man's duty to adjust to nature rather than to try to master it. By comparison, the usual American view of nature is quite the opposite. While this viewpoint may recognize some of nature's forces as overwhelming, it nevertheless considers it possible to restrain or redirect most of them. In fact, the American past is to a large extent the story of man's struggle to exploit this continent's natural riches with ever-increasing effectiveness.

Much of the education of Navaho children has shifted from the traditional family dwelling, the hogan, to modern boarding schools which the federal government has established on the vast Navaho reservation. As a result, the basic ideas of the Navaho people are weakening or blending with those of mainstream American culture. It is not easy to say whether or not this is a desirable development. If there are Navaho Indians who wish to compete economically on the same terms as the majority of American citizens, such a change of basic values and outlook becomes inevitable. But an individual cannot maintain two sets of values, some of which are completely opposed to each other. Many of those who try to do so find themselves suspended between two cultures, unable to derive from either the necessary support or refuge in times of anxiety or of crisis.

Trends in Cultural Anthropology

The rapidly growing collections of data about human groups from every part of the world at last make it possible for anthropologists to attempt cross-cultural comparisons. These collections contain statistical information concerning relationships among various aspects of culture. For example, among the seventy or so animal-herding societies represented in one sizeable sample, nearly four fifths trace descent through the father and his ancestry. This seems to suggest a definite relationship between a basic economic activity and a particular type of kinship organization.

While comparisons are useful and are important goals of every scientific inquiry, a number of young American anthropologists have begun to question the validity of cross-cultural comparisons. They argue that the approach of the natural sciences, where it is possible to locate what is already known or to discover universally applicable principles, cannot be applied to the study of human cultures. For example, using this approach, one might assume that the various kinds of diseases identified by medical research, or the various species and varieties of plants established by botanists, have the same objective existence and hold the same meaning for a Navaho Indian as they do for those who accept modern science. According to these anthropologists, such a view is but another form of old-fashioned ethnocentrism. The supporters of the "new ethnography" claim that each culture has its own set of basic values and one must be careful, when discussing mankind, not to endow it with the prejudices of one particular culture—most commonly Western culture.

This view places considerable demands on anthropological field work. The importance of an extended period of living among the people one studies and frequent revisits cannot be overemphasized. Of equal importance is the ethnographer's need to understand and to make use of the language of the people he studies. A language enables the members of a society to talk about what they consider culturally significant and thus reflects many of the characteristic features of their particular culture. Moreover, this view sees culture as the source which determines how the members of a society decide what is and what can be, what attitudes one should take and how one should carry out his decisions. This so-called **cognitive approach,** or method aiming to discover the relevant features of the "cultural knowledge" which members of any society share, is the subject of much current discussion. There are those who point out that above all anthropology should strive to uncover universally applicable cultural laws. They feel that the cognitive approach to the study of man frustrates these goals by emphasizing the uniqueness of every individual culture. One is tempted to answer that indeed mankind is one, but the ways of mankind are many. Therefore, there should be room for a variety of approaches to the study of mankind.

Cultural Ecology

Ecology is the study of the interrelationship between organisms and their environment. **Cultural ecology** is concerned with the interaction between human societies and the environments in which they live. In recent years, the ecological orientation in the study of man has been gaining ground rapidly.

This approach is based on the recognition that any particular culture is the result of adaptations which members of that society have made to a particular environment. Here, environment must be understood to refer not only to the natural setting, but to tools, weapons, and other technology, as well as to the nature of the interactions which exist among the members of a society, and between them and other societies with whom they have contact.

The remarkable adaptability of man —his genius for adjusting to a variety of changing environments rapidly and effectively—has been responsible for the rapid evolution of his culture and for his dominant position in the world. In our earlier discussion of man's prehistory, the sharply rising curve of man's cultural accomplishments was drawn in some detail. The major question now is whether, given the dramatic rate of population growth and man's destructive exploitation of natural resources, his successful adaptations can continue indefinitely into the future. Could it be that man at last has reached the limits of the potential which brought him to his present preeminence? This problem is of such magnitude that in the future the ecological orientation in the study of man will become even more important to cultural anthropologists.

SUMMARY

The growing amount of knowledge that has been accumulated about human cultures has made anthropology a more exacting study. Broad generalizations about the evolution of human culture have given way to the more scientific analysis of culture in its various aspects. The application of the scientific method to the study of culture received impetus during the first half of the twentieth century from a number of anthropologists. First among them was Franz Boas, who insisted upon the necessity of performing extensive field work before attempting to draw any broad conclusions about human cultural development. Anthropologists today still seek to discover what is universal in human culture, but their scientific attitude tends to discourage any generalizations which can not be fully confirmed by facts.

Many anthropologists today strive to understand "why" the members of a particular culture act as they do. Some base their explanation on the close ties between culture and personality. Culture helps to shape personality. A child born into a particular culture develops attitudes and emotional responses that are just as important as the things he is taught directly by other members of his culture. He absorbs from his culture a particular outlook on life, or world view, which he in turn helps to perpetuate as an adult member of his society. Other anthropologists try to discover the unwritten rules of a group's behavior, their mutual expectations, and their shared understandings and values. Still others consider a culture as the particular adaptation the members of a society have made to the total environment in which they live.

The goals of modern anthropology are broad. The anthropologist hopes, by pointing up variations in human behavior in different societies, to make people more aware of how their own behavior is shaped by their culture. At the same time, the anthropologist considers the differences among man's cultures to be slight when weighed against the basic similarity in human needs and aspirations. He hopes to make all of mankind aware not only of its common heritage but of its common destiny.

Chapter Review

Terms in Anthropology

basic personality structure

cognitive approach

cultural ecology

cultural evolution

personality

primary institution

secondary institution

world view

Questions for Review

1. What is meant by the term "cultural evolution"? What technological advancements marked each stage of human cultural evolution as described by Lewis Henry Morgan?
2. Why does Morgan's scheme of cultural evolution apply less well to social and other forms of cultural activity than to human progress in technology?
3. Describe the contribution of Franz Boas to the methods of anthropological study.
4. What method did Malinowski propose for the study of human culture? How was this method previously applied in our study of the Navaho Night Way ceremonial?
5. Why are anthropologists today hesitant to make broad generalizations about human cultural development?
6. How would your childhood experiences have differed if you had been the child of Comanche parents? of Alorese islanders?
7. In your own terms, explain Abram Kardiner's theory of the relationship between culture and personality.
8. What is meant by "world view"? Describe what you think are the most important attitudes making up your cultural world view.
9. What are the basic assumptions of the cognitive approach to cultural anthropology?
10. Explain the reasons for the increasing interest in the ecological approach to the study of man.

Chapter **17**

Language in Culture and Society

Since language is largely a self-contained unit within the whole of culture, anthropologists are frequently heard to discuss "language and culture" when they actually mean "language in culture" or "language and the rest of culture." Most anthropologists agree that the relationship between language and culture is not only of great interest but of deep significance as well. It is therefore important that we become acquainted with some of their findings.

Language Acquisition

Children everywhere are first initiated into their respective societies by learning the language of their parents. This is usually accomplished during the first six years of life. How much do we know about the child's capacity for language acquisition? Let us look briefly at the stages of this process.

An infant first makes its presence heard by crying and by cooing. After these very early stages of vocalization, the infant begins to babble.

Babbling may well be biologically determined, for it occurs even in some children who are congenitally deaf. Since a normal infant begins to acquire simple patterns of intonation during this stage, babbling may be said to be a transition toward a true language.

From the beginning of the second year of life, a child responds to simple commands and begins to produce speech sounds approximating the significant sounds, or phonemes, of the language spoken by his family. The two-word combinations which follow next reflect a child's acquisition of simple syntactic patterns, not unlike the common subject-predicate construction. For example, a child may say, "allgone milk" for "The milk is all gone" and "Daddy bye-bye" for "Daddy isn't here." During the third and fourth year of life, grammatical patterns are acquired so readily that generally well before the age of six, normal children in all known societies have developed an effective command of their language.

Children in all known societies develop an effective command of their language before the age of six. These Pakistani children are learning to read—the next process of language acquisition in literate societies.

Think of it this way. During these few years a child builds up a vocabulary not only of several thousand words that distinguish the common features of his natural and cultural environment, but also of those morphemes necessary for the production of grammatical constructions such as plural endings and the like. How he does it linguists are still trying to find out! Consider for a moment the difficulties most students experience in their study of a foreign language. Yet young children are capable of using new words in fully grammatical constructions with a minimum of error. Somehow the child must be constantly performing—unconsciously, of course—a remarkably effective linguistic analysis of what he hears, and with it achieving superior results in a very short time.

Because anthropologists and linguists have observed that children everywhere achieve mastery of their language at about the same age, they have come to the conclusion that there is most probably a biological basis for speech acquisition common to all mankind. Moreover, this observation supports their contention that no language is intrinsically more difficult than any other. When we say, as we often do, that some foreign languages are harder to learn than others —for example, Chinese as compared with French, or Russian as compared with Spanish—we are expressing our awareness that some languages employ sounds and grammatical patterns very different from our own. Such languages make extraordinary demands on our speech habits, which by the age of six have become automatic.

The problems we experience in trying to master some of the "strange" sounds or constructions of a new language do not arise from the nature of the sounds or constructions themselves, but from our own natural resistance to changing our well-established speech habits. Similarly, most people find it difficult or impossible to do certain things with the left hand once they have become used to employing the right hand for the task.

Language as a Mirror

Since languages are learned and used for communication, it is essential that the speakers of a language agree upon the pronunciation and usage of a majority of the words in the language. But the larger and more complex a society, the more diversified it tends to become. As one would expect, this diversity is faithfully mirrored in the language, where it gives rise to many different occupational and social dialects. Some dialects make use of so many special terms that they are understood only by the particular group speaking the dialect. One has to be a golfer to appreciate the full meaning of such a description as "her last birdie came at the fifteenth, where she tapped in a curling eight-foot downhiller." One would have to know his way around a carpentry shop quite well to follow a manual which gives the following instructions: "To cut tenons, insert spacing collars between dado blades and set motor as for rabbeting."

In our discussion of language as the primary means of human communication, we observed that the Dinka people of Sudan have a great number of words for "cattle." This we explained by the fact that the Dinka economy is dependent upon cattle-raising. As a rule, those aspects of the natural and social environment that a society considers particularly significant are singled out for elaboration in the vocabulary of the language.

Let us consider another example. An Eskimo's survival is dependent much of the year on how successfully he can cope with snow conditions. For an Eskimo, therefore, an overall term designating the variety of frozen water we call "snow" would be of little if any use. The Eskimo vocabulary contains, instead, a great many words specifying distinct qualities of snow. Different words describe its suit-

ability for travel, for igloo construction, and for tracking animals; the degree of packing; the nature of its surface; and so on. In American culture, considerations of physical comfort are responsible for a simple distinction being made between "snow" and "slush." But to American skiers—as to the Eskimos—snow has more meaning than this. Accordingly, skiers use several terms to refer to different varieties of snow. "Corn" refers to granular, refrozen snow; "powder" to light, dry snow; and "mashed potatoes" to heavy, wet snow resulting from warm weather.

Here is still another example. The traditional Japanese concern with etiquette, closely linked to respect for age and social rank, is reflected in distinct speech styles appropriate to different social situations. Thus, social superiors and older people are spoken to in the deferential style, cultivated company in the polite style, and friends in the informal style. Each style is distinguished according to its own special set of verb forms.

Societies as complex and as specialized as that of the United States need to differentiate among a great many concepts and material objects. It is to be expected, therefore, that the stock of words in American English should be comparatively large. Language is a remarkably sensitive instrument of human culture and mirrors faithfully the purpose and circumstances of those who use it.

Language as a Map

Another aspect of the relationship of language to the rest of culture has been challenging linguistic anthropologists for more than a quarter of a century. This involves the idea that language may act as a kind of map of reality or, to put it differently, as a filter through which the members of a society perceive the world.

Some languages force people to express features of meaning that are optional in other languages. An American child may return home after the first day of school and say, "Mother, I think I'm going to like my new teacher." From what has been spoken, there is no way of knowing whether or not the reference is to a male or a female instructor. But a German pupil has no choice but to indicate the sex of the teacher by using either the word *Lehrer*, denoting a man, or *Lehrerin*, referring to a woman. What in English is only occasionally indicated by paired forms, such as "prince" and "princess," "sculptor" and the optional "sculptress," is an inescapable distinction in German.

The kinship terms used in different societies provide another rich area of contrast. In American culture, we normally use the term "father" to mean only the male parent. Among the Arapaho Indians, by contrast, the word for one's biological father extends equally to the father's brother and to the mother's sister's husband. We use the term "uncle" to refer to both of these relatives. This difference between English and Arapaho cannot be viewed as merely a terminological peculiarity of either language. Kinship terminology closely reflects our patterns of behavior toward specific relatives and thus, in turn, greatly affects the nature of these social relationships.

Another example of the contention that language is a filter for our perceptions may be drawn from the science of physics. The perception of light seems to be the same for humans with normal vision everywhere. Yet some interesting differences in color classification have been discovered among different peoples. Most native speakers of English will distinguish among the colors green, blue, and purple, even though they may have difficulty assigning certain shades along the continuous spectrum to one color or another. The Navaho Indians, on the other hand, make fewer distinctions among colors. Although they have a word which corresponds to our "green," it is used infrequently, and the word usually employed for "green" corresponds roughly to the entire range of green through purple. It is not farfetched to say, then, that the same physical world of color is charted differently in the English and Navaho languages. The Navaho speak of their world in terms of a somewhat different color scheme and hence perceive it culturally in a somewhat different manner.

Similarly, American men and women demonstrate varying degrees of color perception. Since women are generally more conscious than men of clothes and interior decoration, they make use of a substantially larger color vocabulary. What to a man is simply "blue-green" may range for a woman from "robin's egg blue" to "aqua green," through such intermediate hues as "turquoise blue," "turquoise green," and others.

As a final example of how language may chart human action—action of the simplest kind—let us examine the case of the "empty" gasoline containers. One of the pioneers in the

Until recently, all Japanese children practiced the strict rules of etiquette that were to govern their behavior in different social situations throughout their lives. Their language still mirrors the traditional culture: they address each other in the informal style, their parents and elders in another style, and their teachers and social superiors in still other styles.

study of the effects of language on culture, Benjamin Lee Whorf, became interested in this study when employed by an insurance company to discover the cause of several recent gasoline fires. Whorf observed that men working around gasoline containers frequently made the mistake of throwing matches into "empty" containers—containers in fact still containing gasoline vapors. The "empty" containers gave rise to very real fires, whose damages were costly not only in materials but in human lives. Here a word had provided its speakers with a very poor map of reality indeed.

Language and Meaning

The study of meaning can never keep pace with the study of forms in language. If you have a good, up-to-date dictionary, you may keep well abreast of small changes in the **denotations,** or specific meanings, of words. But no dictionary can possibly list all the **connotations,** or emotional associations, of all the words in a language.

The meaning of a word may vary even from one speaker to another. The word "horse" may have totally different connotations for two sisters, if one has experienced a painful fall from a horse and as a result fears all horses, while the other loves horses and prefers riding to any other form of outdoor activity. Words also may acquire distinct connotations for various groups of people. For teen-agers, "electric guitar" carries the pleasant connotation of a type of music they particularly like. But for the parents of these same teen-agers, the instrument more likely than not suggests a type of excessively loud music to be avoided at all costs!

Agreement upon the meaning of words may acquire great importance at the international level. Some of the words commonly used to describe systems of government and society have taken on quite different meanings among different groups of people. Many times the inability of nations to communicate meaningfully at conference tables results from the fact that certain words used by all parties, such as "communism," "democracy," "dictatorship," "freedom," and "socialism," have come to have meanings or connotations almost diametrically opposed.

To improve the habits of response of people to each other through a more critical use of words is therefore a well-recognized and urgent need. One must always keep in mind that words should never be confused with things and ideas, and that our thoughts and actions derive to a large measure from the particular manner in which each of us has labeled the world around him. Many people who "don't like fish" will also avoid lobsters, abalone, and oysters, though these are no more closely related to fish than snails are to chickens. Their working label of "fish" when referring to food includes most of the organisms that live in water, and they act accordingly.

Language Families of the World

We have already defined a language family as a group of languages whose relationship and common ancestry have been clearly established. Such is the case with the Indo-European languages, and there are many other comparable language families the world over. The ones mentioned below are but a small sample of the total number.

A language map of Europe would show us a few areas where the dominant language is not Indo-European. The language spoken in one small pocket of the western Pyrenees (in France and Spain) is Basque, a one-language family of unknown origin and relationship. The widespread Finno-Ugric family, which extends from eastern Europe into Asia, includes three important languages spoken in Europe—Hungarian, Finnish, and Estonian. The Finno-Ugric languages bear some resemblances to the Altaic language family of Asia, one branch of which includes Turkish. Because of a number of structural features they hold in common, the Finno-Ugric and Altaic languages are frequently grouped together under the combined term Ural-Altaic.

At the opposite end of the Asian continent exists a language family second only to Indo-European in the number of speakers. This Sino-Tibetan family includes among its member languages Burmese, Tibetan, and the various languages of China—Mandarin, Cantonese, and others. The Chinese languages are frequently spoken of as dialects even though they are not mutually intelligible. Another Asian language group, the Malayo-Polynesian family, includes languages spoken throughout the Malay archipelago and most of the islands of the Pacific. Two other important Asian languages, Japanese and Korean, do not seem to bear relationship to any other language groups.

Northern Africa and southwestern Asia are occupied by speakers of languages belonging to the Afro-Asiatic family. The most important branch of this family is the Semitic, which includes Hebrew and several varieties of Arabic. Most of the remainder of Africa may be assigned to the Niger-Congo language group, of which the best known are the Bantu languages generally spoken south of an imaginary line connecting the Cameroon Republic in the west and Kenya in the east.

The Americas are continents of extraordinary linguistic diversity when native Indian languages are considered. Several dozen language groups of family status have been established. Many of the Indian languages of North America have been very well described by linguists in recent decades. The result is that several language families—Algonquian, Athabascan, Iroquoian, Siouan, and Uto-Aztecan, for example—are now known in surprising depth and detail.

There are still a number of languages, however, whose structures we do not know in satisfactory detail. As additional information becomes available, classifications may have to be revised. It has already been necessary to reassign certain languages from one group to another or to consolidate several small groups into one larger group. If you are puzzled by the apparent disagreement among scholars concerning the classification of languages, remember that linguists themselves are still trying to fit all the pieces of this puzzle together.

How Languages Differ

All languages have a characteristic set of significant sounds, or phonemes, which combine to form its meaningful units, called morphemes. When people speak, these morphemes are being arranged and rearranged in sequences according to the patterns peculiar to a particular language. Within this overall plan, the linguist encounters an astonishing amount of variation.

Most languages distinguish between two grammatical numbers, the singular and the plural, as in English "dog" and "dogs" or "leaf" and "leaves." Some languages also have a special form to represent the notion of two of a kind, as in the Greek *anthrōpos,* "(one) man," *anthrōpō,* "two men," and *anthrōpoi,* "(more than two) men." Still other languages have additional number distinctions.

Languages differ from each other in their verb forms. Inflected forms for two voices, the active and the passive, occur in Latin, as in *laudo,* "I praise," and *laudor,* "I am praised." Greek has a three-way contrast, adding to the two a middle voice with reflexive meaning.

Some languages, Latin included, make extensive use of suffixes—that is, they attach endings to word bases. Other languages express grammatical relationships by prefixes—morphemes occurring before the word bases. And then there are many instances of changes within the word, as in the English forms "sing," "sang," "sung" and "ring," "rang," "rung." In Po-

United Nations diplomats must overcome a language barrier before they can begin to discuss the problems that divide their nations. Would the adoption of an international language help to solve these problems?

comchi, a Mayan language of Guatemala, intensity is regularly expressed by means of **reduplication,** or the repetition of a form. If *suk* is "good," *suksuk* is "delicious"; and whereas *nim* is "big," *nimnim* is "enormous."

Given this variety among languages, of which our examples are only the barest sampling, linguists have occasionally chosen to compare or contrast languages from the point of view of their structures. They may observe, for instance, the way that verbs operate in different languages. The Turkish equivalent of the English verb form "were they not broken?" is the form *kırılmadılarmı,* consisting of six morphemes, *kır-ıl-ma-dı-lar-mı.* These morphemes mark, successively,

the root meaning "break," the passive, the negative, the past, the third person plural actor, and the interrogative. A language such as Latin, in contrast, may compress several grammatical meanings into one element. For instance, the Latin *amor,* "I am loved," expresses in addition to the meaning "love," the first person singular, the passive, the present tense, and the indicative mode, all with the utmost economy. The English constructions "I am loved" or "were they not broken?" clearly represent still another type of morphemic arrangement. The classification of languages that disregards relationships and origin and concerns itself only with types of structure is known as **linguistic typology.**

International Languages

As people of different nations are coming into more and more frequent contact, the variety of their languages is proving a barrier to mutual understanding. Some people have felt that a good solution to this problem would be the adoption of an artificial language for international communication. Several hundred such systems have been designed over the last few centuries. Of these, Volapük, Interlingua, and Esperanto, all drawing on root words common to the leading languages of western Europe, have won supporters and been put to limited use. But centuries of experience indicate that it is unrealistic to hope that the major countries of the world will ever settle on a single language to be used universally.

However, just as Latin was the common language of educated Europeans during the Middle Ages and French the language of diplomacy for the past several hundred years, so English has gained ascendancy as the language of commerce and science during the current century. Now that people in many countries of the world are studying English as their second language, Americans should also feel a responsibility for learning a language other than their own. If it is unlikely that the peoples of the world will ever agree on a common language, it is at least reasonable to urge that they have command of more than one.

SUMMARY

Language is acquired by children everywhere at about the same rate, and becomes an automatic habit around the age of five or six. Once acquired, language exerts a powerful hold and influence on its speakers, for it not only mirrors the culture of the society it serves but also provides its speakers with a map of the world in which they live. With the growth of communications media and the increased contact among people of diverse cultural and language backgrounds, the study of linguistics and of individual languages has been receiving the heightened attention it deserves.

Chapter Review

Terms in Anthropology

connotation	linguistic typology
denotation	reduplication

Questions for Review

1. What are the major stages in a child's acquisition of language?
2. Why do people generally find some foreign languages harder to master than others?
3. What is meant by the statement "Language is a mirror"?
4. What is illustrated by the fact that the Eskimos have a very specialized vocabulary dealing with "snow"?
5. What does the comparatively large vocabulary of English suggest about the societies in which it is spoken?
6. What is meant by the statement "Language is a map"?
7. What examples does this chapter give of how language may affect one's perception of reality? What examples can you think of to illustrate this quality of language?
8. Why is it that the definitions of words in dictionaries can only approximate the meanings of the words?
9. What are the major language families of the world? Where are the languages within these families spoken?
10. What are some of the ways in which languages may differ?

Chapter **18**

Anthropology in Today's World

Today, one hears a great deal about the need for "relevance," particularly the need for the educational experience to be socially useful. In a world facing many unprecedented perils, such a goal cannot be dismissed lightly. At the same time, one must keep in mind that any social activity, if it is to be truly useful, must be based on relevant knowledge. Increasingly in the future, when interaction will no longer be limited to individuals within a society but will take place among human groups on a global scale, relevant knowledge can come from the lessons taught by anthropology.

Studies of the effects of culture change have identified several tendencies which will require careful attention: the influence of cities as focal points of change is rapidly growing; basic changes in economy affect the patterns of family organization; the growing of crops for the market and increased use of money disrupt traditional patterns of rural cooperation and promote rivalries and disputes;

sudden or profound changes in subsistence patterns are commonly accompanied by dietary deterioration; and the raising of cultural expectations sets into motion forces which strive to realize these expectations.

Anthropology and its concern with culture change can perhaps help us to understand these disruptive tendencies. The use of research methods, theoretical concepts, and factual knowledge in programs designed to improve the social and economic conditions of human groups is referred to as applied anthropology. It is appropriate that we devote a separate chapter to this aspect of anthropology to indicate how anthropology can serve mankind.

Directed Culture Change

Understanding the process of social and cultural change involves three major considerations. What are the chances of a community's accepting

These young Indian boys carrying posters that urge people to be vaccinated illustrate the tendency that rising cultural expectations set into motion forces to achieve these expectations.

an innovation? What are the forces that are likely to act as barriers to change? And, what effects may the acceptance of an innovation be expected to have on the culture as a whole?

In recent decades, anthropologists have been able to observe the process of culture change, both directed and unplanned, in hundreds of field situations. Yet, for a variety of reasons, man has not used this cumulative experience to ease the stress and anxiety of humans when bringing about desired changes. Technical improvements designed to help a group may not be beneficial if a problem is approached without understanding the culture of those

who are expected to benefit. Two examples reported by George M. Foster, an anthropologist with experience in applied work, will illustrate the point.

To improve the yield of the basic food crop of Nepalese farmers, agricultural specialists introduced a Japanese rice. This rice made it possible for farmers in Nepal to at least double their rice yield. While this achievement may seem considerable, it turned out to be a disappointment to the Nepalese farmers. One reason was that the Japanese rice grows on dwarf stalks. These stalks provide considerably less fodder than the native rice for the livestock on which the Nepalese farmers also depended. Moreover, in this variety of rice the seeds cling tightly to the stalks, so that harvesting requires the use of special threshing machines which are not readily available to Nepalese farmers.

The second example comes from Mexico. To improve the sanitary conditions in rural areas, government officials have been working for years to provide remote villages with a regular water supply. One of the by-products of their efforts was the construction of communal centers designed to eliminate the necessity of bathing and laundering in the cold water of nearby streams. The layout of the laundries was simple and quite sound from an engineering point of view. The washtubs were attached in a single row to one side of a wall, the other side of which was used for shower baths. Yet instead of welcoming this new arrangement, the village women bitterly complained about it. Used to talking and gossiping while doing their laundry in the streams, the women suddenly found themselves facing a

Useful inventions or innovations usually spread rapidly from their place of origin into other cultures. However, in this process of cultural diffusion, the invention may be adapted to the new culture. The young Indian women above, who are part of a nutrition program, use bicycles to travel to villages and to bring information to the villagers. Below, a Chinese man uses an ox and a cart mounted on Western truck tires to pull his load of wood.

Mexican farmers and an agricultural expert compare an improved variety of corn plant to the old variety grown in the village. The farmers in the village now plan to start growing the new variety.

cement wall which hindered this social custom.

The lesson which can be drawn from these two examples is simple. Technical improvements may not be appreciated unless they are introduced with an understanding of the cultural and social implications for those who are supposed to benefit from them. It is impossible for anthropologists to predict always what the effects of changes will be in any given situation. However, the theory and methods of anthropology are sufficiently developed today to permit us to anticipate which aspects of a culture will bear the heaviest stress under changing conditions.

Contributions in Curbing Disease

One way in which modern science can significantly contribute to the well-being of human groups is through medicine. Techniques designed to pre-

A Vietnamese woman uses water pumped from the Mekong River in a new irrigation system to wash her clothes and to bathe. The irrigation system is also used to provide water for farming and electricity.

vent or to cure diseases are found in all societies, but it would be foolish to claim that they are equally effective. Yet one must keep in mind that illnesses and diseases are biological as well as social phenomena. For many peoples, disease is defined primarily in cultural terms. For example, a person who is in pain or has a fever may be thought to be ill not because of insufficient bodily defenses against some invading organisms but because he violated a taboo or became be-

witched. Among the Navaho Indians, to offend or kill a snake is likely to be followed by "snake sickness." Another source of disease among the Navahos may be an attack by a ghost, native or foreign, and if the usual treatment does not restore the patient to health, witchcraft is likely to be suspected.

For physicians serving in hospitals on the Navaho reservation, native attitudes toward disease have been a source of considerable frustration. Yet to meet the native beliefs head

A woman in Northern India explains a good luck sign on her house to a visiting doctor. The doctor who is bringing Western medicine to the village is accepting the cultural practices of the village.

on would be the same as asking an American to give up his religious beliefs or his trust in the effectiveness of modern medicine. What, then, can be done?

The cooperation of anthropologists in the Navajo-Cornell Field Health Project established in 1956 at Many Farms, Arizona, turned out to be a step in the right direction. The anthropologists, well acquainted with the Navaho culture, acted as inter-

mediaries between the Indians and the physicians, explaining the one to the other. This program was so successful that it was not unusual for Navaho curers, or singers, themselves to suggest "white medicine" to their patients.

A classical example of anthropological insight is revealed in the treatment of the Papuan people of New Guinea at the time of World War I. In 1914, smallpox threatened the

Papuans. Hubert Murray, the lieutenant governor of the territory, realized that forcible vaccination would be opposed by the Papuans. However, he gained the Papuans' acceptance of the vaccination program by explaining it in their own cultural terms: "We told them that there was a very dangerous and powerful sorcerer . . . and that this sorcerer had conjured up a very bad sickness which might come along at any moment. But, though the sorcerer was strong, the Government was stronger, and would protect all who claimed its protection. A mark would be put on the arm of all those who trusted themselves to the Government; the sorcerer when he came would see the Government mark, would realize that he was powerless, and would retire foiled and baffled. . . . But for those who would not receive the mark the Government could, of course, do nothing." The inoculation program became a great success, and it was the Papuan without the vaccination scar who was considered odd.

Today, Murray's handling of the case may strike us as somewhat paternalistic. But the situation was an emergency, and Murray did not have the time to develop an educational program to explain the smallpox virus and the development of immunity by vaccination.

Other Applications of Anthropology

We shall not discuss all of the possible applications of anthropology. Some have already been mentioned in the preceding chapters—for example, emergency, or salvage, archaeology, to preserve man's past accomplishments, and urban anthropology, to study sociocultural problems associated with ethnically heterogenous concentrations.

The participation of anthropologists as witnesses in cases involving the settlement of claims of Indian tribes against the United States Government is still another example of applied anthropology. Archaeological investigations, and particularly ethnohistorical information, help clarify such matters as the identification of tribes and the original boundaries of their lands. The many injustices perpetrated upon the Indian peoples over the last centuries cannot be erased. But some of the financial or land settlements awarded under the provisions of the Indian Claims Commission Act passed in 1946 at least make it possible for their descendants to provide for some of their needs.

Anthropology has also been used to help train United States diplomatic or business personnel assigned to foreign posts. The representatives of a nation should be acquainted with the cultural differences of the host country, if they are to carry out their assignments with understanding. Anthropology can help to inform them of cultural differences which will affect their official and social duties. For example, the distance at which people carry on a conversation varies. American men talking face to face generally maintain a distance of about twenty inches. When one member of a pair is a woman, the distance tends to increase by about four inches. In some parts of the Middle East or Latin America, the corresponding distance is only a little more than half of the "American" distance. Americans generally place business obligations

Anthropology can help acquaint us with important cultural differences. One cultural difference we may be aware of is the difference in forms of greeting. In the United States people often shake hands when meeting. In many European, African, and Middle Eastern countries an embrace is the common form of greeting, while in the Far East bowing is the accepted tradition.

ahead of claims on their hospitality. But an Arab feels that hospitality and loyalty to friends comes first. Consequently, most Americans would feel free to attend a previously scheduled business meeting even though friends from some distance had dropped in for a visit. Most Arabs would feel that the demands of friendship and hospitality take precedence over a business meeting. While some of these differences may seem unimportant, they have caused discomfort and even misunderstanding, sometimes with serious effects.

Other applications of anthropology may help nations to develop their educational systems, medical services, administrative organization, and the like. This is not to suggest that the anthropologist is competent to assume all of these tasks by himself, but rather that the anthropologist's insight may mean the difference between success and failure.

In all these various endeavors and programs, anthropologists have served as consultants rather than as administrators. Working in just about every part of the world in close personal association with the peoples and situations they study, their professional position is uniquely varied and complex. Responsible conduct is therefore paramount, and recently, anthropologists have discussed setting down comprehensive guidelines for their professional activity. Above all, the anthropologist bears responsibility to the people he studies. He must always do his utmost to protect their physical, social, and psychological welfare and to respect their dignity and privacy. To those who may utilize his findings, the anthropologist has a commitment to truth as he makes public the results

of his research. Besides these, the anthropologist also has responsibilities toward his students, his sponsors, and the governments of both his own and the host country. In short, the well-being of mankind in general, and of the group being studied in particular, should be the foremost objective of any undertaking in anthropology.

The Nature of Human Nature

The subject of the nature of human nature has recently been receiving much attention, largely as a result of several influential books written by students of animal behavior. These books assert that man is instinctively, or innately, an aggressive creature—one for whom violence is by nature an unalterable way of life. We shall not discuss the selective use of data concerning subhuman animals with which the authors of these books support their theories. Nor shall we discuss the unwarranted analogies they make concerning the behavior patterns of animals and humans. Rather, we shall investigate a question of tremendous consequence: Is man doomed to constant warring and to the indiscriminate killing of his own kind? The evidence from anthropology points to the contrary.

The anthropologist feels justified in operating on the assumption that all of adult human behavior is thoroughly controlled by custom rather than by inborn instinctive forces. This is not to deny that some of our habits, and unfortunately the less desirable ones in particular, are annoyingly deep-seated. Nor does the assumption deny that humans engage both in personal acts of violence and collectively in

Most anthropologists feel that aggression in man is learned rather than instinctive behavior. If aggression is indeed learned, young children playing with guns may provide a learning situation for aggressive forms of behavior.

bloody and protracted wars. But the assumption allows, and even invites, the search for the sources of man's aggressive behavior. There is no doubt that these sources vary: frustrations induced by a society in some of its members; the teaching of, and the belief in, a particular group's superiority over other groups; feelings of anxiety or uncertainty brought about by some unusual and unexpected circumstances; unfulfilled cultural expectations; and many others. The viewpoint of the anthropologist—that man is not aggressive by nature—not only reflects more adequately our knowledge of man's behavior but keeps paths open to inquiry, which may help to alleviate the sources of aggression. Much work in this area is yet to be done, and its importance cannot be overemphasized.

Anthropology and the Future

"It would hardly be fish who discovered the existence of water," Kluckhohn wrote concerning the value of studying other cultures. This remark aptly points up both the goals and the method of anthropology. The immediate goal of anthropology is to develop ways of thinking about culture that make it possible to examine critically one's own culture and society. The method by which this goal can best be reached is the open-minded and detailed study of different cultures and societies, whose members share the same fundamental human needs but satisfy them in different ways. The ultimate goal, and the very special reward which the study of anthropology promises, is a view of humanity as an indivisible whole. Such a view, rather than the fragmented view which sees mankind as a motley collection of exotic populations of both the past and the present, is no longer merely desirable, but urgently necessary.

Mankind's recent astounding advances in communications and weaponry have been such that, within a single generation, decisions and actions taken by the powerful nations of the world have come to hold the most profound consequences for mankind everywhere. The alternatives which the world faces today are clear enough. On the one hand, the scientific genius of man can be used to destroy the results of thousands of years of patient striving; on the other, man's stupendous accomplishments can be placed in the full service of peace and the elimination of human misery.

Since an individual forms his overall cultural perspective before he has reached adulthood, schools are among the principal transmitters of culture in most societies. It follows, therefore, that one effective means of preparing future generations for a world intent upon cooperation rather than destruction would be to make the study of mankind part of all early education. If we are to eliminate warfare as one of the methods of solving conflicts within or between human societies, we must earnestly study the conditions which produce conflicts, and we must employ all of our energies in developing means for solving such conflicts peacefully. At the same time, the ethnocentric attitudes that characterize the educational systems of most nations will have to be overcome. Mankind needs to achieve in every sphere of activity the international co-

operation that is already taken for granted in such fields as transportation and communications.

The tremendous inventiveness and adaptability of mankind during its relatively short but rich history has often been asserted by anthropologists. Since it has been traditional for most Americans to trace their heritage to the ancient civilizations of Greece and Rome, it is easy to forget that splendid civilizations existed in the Near East and northern Africa three thousand years ago. At a time when philosophy and poetry flourished in the Far East, most of Europe would have had to be included among the "underdeveloped" or "backward" areas of the world. One also needs to remember that the original biocultural transition toward humanness took place in that part of the world which, despite all evidence to the contrary, some people still dismiss as unproductive and savage. If the anthropologist has a lesson to teach through his knowledge of man's cultural development, it is this: civilization is not the exclusive achievement of a particular people or "race," but belongs to all humanity. Any society which today is rich and powerful as the result of a favorable combination of circumstances—such as the opportunity to draw on a variety of different cultural traditions or a natural environment replete with resources—must be just as ready to give of its talents and resources as it once was ready to accept the best of the creative talents and accomplishments of mankind.

In short, man's hope rests on his increasing ability to understand the sources of his behavior and the nature of the social relationships in which

Man's knowledge has often been turned to creating destructive forces, such as the atom bomb. War has caused untold suffering, killed thousands, and left millions homeless. If men can learn to cooperate with one another, perhaps warfare can be eliminated. Teaching children about people of other cultures and international cooperation may help in this goal.

he participates. If human accomplishments are overwhelmingly the result of the cooperative tendencies in human societies, mankind's goal must be to effect cooperation between individuals and societies on a worldwide basis. The study of anthropology cannot help but illuminate the path leading to this goal.

SUMMARY

The lessons taught by anthropology can provide us with highly relevant knowledge, especially in the area of cultural change. The knowledge and concepts developed by anthropologists should be used when programs to improve the social and economic conditions of various human groups are established. For programs designed with the aid of anthropological insights are more likely to achieve their goals without producing tensions and anxieties in human societies.

More specific instances of the uses of applied anthropology can be seen in the training of diplomatic or business personnel assigned to foreign posts, in the presentation of modern medical practices in areas where they are unfamiliar, in helping other nations to develop educational systems which will best serve their particular needs, and in assisting economically struggling populations to raise their level of subsistence. In all of these situations the anthropologist should be asked to contribute his expertise, for his knowledge can assure that the desired changes are brought about with the least possible stress on both the society as a whole and its individual members. In the future, anthropology will make still greater contributions toward our understanding of man and his cultures. It will help us understand that no matter how different the ways in which men may satisfy basic human needs, humanity is indeed one indivisible whole.

Chapter Review

Questions for Review

1. Give some additional examples of directed culture change in which anthropological insight could be helpful.
2. What are the major considerations necessary for understanding the process of sociocultural change?
3. How can anthropological knowledge aid the administration of medical services to nonliterate peoples?
4. Discuss the importance of emergency (salvage) archaeology.
5. How can persons serving in foreign countries profit from the findings and teachings of anthropology?
6. What do you think is the most important responsibility the anthropologist assumes when he studies a population? Why do you think so?

7. No one questions the statement that men commit aggressive acts, but there is disagreement concerning the sources of man's aggression. What is the consensus of anthropologists in this matter?

8. Do you think that anthropology should be taught to students in elementary school? Why?

9. Jokes and cartoons frequently appear concerning the behavior of American tourists abroad. Comment on the reasons for this subject matter, making use of what you have learned in your anthropology course.

10. What does anthropology teach us about the development of what we call civilization?

Suggestions for
Further Reading

Chapter 1

Ashley Montagu, M. F., *Man: His First Million Years* (Cleveland: World Publishing Company, 1957).**

Casagrande, Joseph B., ed., *In the Company of Man: Twenty Portraits by Anthropologists* (New York: Harper & Row, 1960).*

Coon, Carleton S., *The Story of Man: From the First Human to Primitive Culture and Beyond,* 2nd rev. ed. (New York: Alfred A. Knopf, 1962).

Edel, May, *The Story of People: Anthropology for Young People* (Boston: Little, Brown, 1953).

Hayes, H. R., *From Ape to Angel: An Informal History of Social Anthropology* (New York: Alfred A. Knopf, 1958).

Kluckhohn, Clyde, *Mirror for Man: The Relation of Anthropology to Modern Life* (New York: McGraw-Hill, 1949).*

Lisitzky, Genevieve, *Four Ways of Being Human: An Introduction to Anthropology* (New York: Viking Press, 1956).*

Mead, Margaret, *et al.,* eds., *War: The Anthropology of Armed Conflict and Aggression* (Garden City, N.Y.: Doubleday, 1968).

Oliver, Douglas L., *Invitation to Anthropology* (Garden City, N.Y.: Doubleday, 1964).**

Chapter 2

Benedict, Ruth, *Patterns of Culture* (Boston: Houghton Mifflin, 1934).*

Brown, Ina Corinne, *Understanding Other Cultures* (Englewood Cliffs, N.J.: Prentice-Hall, 1963).**

Cutler, Charles, *et al.,* eds., *Anthropology in Today's World: Case Studies of People and Cultures* (Columbus, Ohio: American Education Publications, 1965).

Goldschmidt, Walter R., ed., *Exploring the Ways of Mankind* (New York: Holt, Rinehart and Winston, 1960).*

Herskovits, Melville J., *Acculturation: The Study of Culture Contacts* (Gloucester, Mass.: Peter Smith Reprints).

* also available in paperback
** paperback edition

Linton, Ralph, *The Tree of Culture* (New York: Alfred A. Knopf, 1955).*

Mead, Margaret, *People and Places* (Cleveland: World Publishing Company, 1959).

Turnbull, Colin M., *The Lonely African* (New York: Simon and Schuster, 1962).*

Weyer, Edward, Jr., *Primitive Peoples Today* (Garden City, N.Y.: Doubleday, 1959).**

Chapter 3

Kroeber, Theodora, *Ishi in Two Worlds; A Biography of the Last Wild Indian in North America* (Berkeley: University of California Press, 1961).*

Lowie, Robert H., *Social Organization* (New York: Holt, Rinehart and Winston, 1948).

Mumford, Lewis, *The Myth of the Machine: Technics and Human Development* (New York: Harcourt, Brace & World, 1967).

Spencer, Robert F., and Elden Johnson, *Atlas for Anthropology* (Dubuque, Iowa: William C. Brown, 1960).

Winick, Charles, *Dictionary of Anthropology* (New York: Philosophical Library, 1956).*

Chapter 4

Barnett, Lincoln, and the editors of *Life* Magazine, *The Wonders of Life on Earth* (New York: Golden Press, 1961).

Oparin, A. I., *Life: Its Nature, Origin and Development* (New York: Academic Press, 1962).**

Sullivan, Walter, *We Are Not Alone: The Search for Intelligent Life on Other Worlds,* rev. ed. (New York: McGraw-Hill, 1966).*

Chapter 5

Beadle, George and Muriel, *The Language of Life* (Garden City, N.Y.: Doubleday, 1966).*

Darwin, Charles, *The Origin of Species; The Descent of Man* (New York: Modern Library, 1948).*

Darwin, Charles, *The Voyage of the Beagle* (New York: Harper & Row, 1959).*

Eiseley, Loren, *Darwin's Century: Evolution and the Men Who Discovered It* (Garden City, N.Y.: Doubleday, 1958).**

Moore, Ruth, *The Coil of Life: The Story of the Great Discoveries in the Life Sciences* (New York: Alfred A. Knopf, 1961).

Moore, Ruth, and the editors of *Life* Magazine, *Evolution* (Morristown, N.J.: Silver Burdett, 1964).

Romer, Alfred S., *Man and the Vertebrates,* 2 vols. (Baltimore: Penguin Books).**

Watson, James D., *The Double Helix* (New York: Atheneum, 1968).

Chapter 6

Ardrey, Robert, *African Genesis: A Personal Investigation into the Animal Origins and Nature of Man* (New York: Atheneum, 1961).*

DeVore, Irven, Eimerl, Sarel, and the editors of *Life* Magazine, *The Primates* (Morristown, N.J.: Silver Burdett, 1965).

Dobzhansky, Theodosius, *Mankind Evolving: The Evolution of the Human Species* (New Haven: Yale University Press, 1962).*

Flint, Richard F., *Glacial and Pleistocene Geology* (New York: Wiley, 1957).

Hayes, Carleton, *The Ape in Our House* (New York: Harper & Row, 1957).

Moore, Ruth, *Man, Time, and Fossils: The Story of Evolution,* rev. ed. (New York: Alfred A. Knopf, 1961).

Reynolds, Vernon, *The Apes: The Gorilla, Chimpanzee, Orangutan, and Gibbon—Their History and Their World* (New York: Dutton, 1967).

Schaller, George B., *The Year of the Gorilla* (Chicago: University of Chicago Press, 1964).*

Chapter 7

Campbell, Robert, Howell, F. Clark, and the editors of *Life* Magazine, *Early Man* (Morristown, N.J.: Silver Burdett, 1965).

Clymer, Eleanor, *The Case of the Missing Link* (New York: Basic Books, 1962).

Dart, Raymond A., with Dennis Craig, *Adventures with the Missing Link* (New York: Harper & Row, 1959).

Edel, May, *The Story of Our Ancestors* (Boston: Little, Brown, 1955).

Gregor, Arthur S., *The Adventure of Man: His Evolution from Prehistory to Civilization* (New York: Macmillan, 1966).

Howells, William W., *Mankind in the Making: The Story of Human Evolution,* rev. ed. (Garden City, N.Y.: Doubleday, 1967).

Chapter 8

Ashley Montagu, M. F., *Man's Most Dangerous Myth: The Fallacy of Race,* 4th rev. ed. (Cleveland: World Publishing Company, 1964).*

Coon, Carleton S., *The Origin of Races* (New York: Alfred A. Knopf, 1962).

Dobzhansky, Theodosius, *Mankind Evolving* (New Haven: Yale University Press, 1962).*

Garn, Stanley M., *Human Races,* 2nd ed. (Springfield, Ill.: Thomas, 1965).

Turnbull, Colin M., *The Forest People* (New York: Simon and Schuster, 1961).*

Chapter 9

Braidwood, Robert J., *Archeologists and What They Do* (New York: F. Watts, 1960).

Ceram, C. W., *Gods, Graves, and Scholars: The Story of Archaeology,* 2nd rev. ed. (New York: Alfred A. Knopf, 1967).

Ceram, C. W., *The March of Archaeology* (New York: Alfred A. Knopf, 1958).

Deetz, James, *Invitation to Archaeology* (Garden City, N.Y.: Doubleday, 1967).*

Editors of *Life* Magazine, *The Epic of Man* (New York: Time Book Division, 1961).

Fortiner, Virginia J., *Archaeology as a Hobby* (Maplewood, N.J.: C. S. Hammond, 1962).

Meighan, Clement W., *Archaeology: An Introduction* (San Francisco: Chandler, 1966).*

Piggott, Stuart, ed., *The Dawn of Civilization: The First World Survey of Human Cultures in Early Times* (New York: McGraw-Hill, 1961).

Rapport, Samuel, and Helen Wright, eds., *Archaeology* (New York: New York University Press, 1963).*

Robbins, Maurice, with Mary B. Irving, *The Amateur Archaeologist's Handbook* (New York: Crowell-Collier, 1965).

Chapter 10

Bacon, Edward, ed., *Vanished Civilizations of the Ancient World* (New York: McGraw-Hill, 1961).

Breuil, Abbé Henri, *Four Hundred Centuries of Cave Art* (New York: Graphic Society, 1950).

Clark, J. Desmond, *The Prehistory of South Africa,* 2nd ed. (Baltimore: Penguin Books, 1959).**

Clark, John G., and Stuart Piggott, *Prehistoric Societies* (New York: Alfred A. Knopf, 1965).

Cole, Sonia, *The Prehistory of East Africa* (New York: Macmillan, 1963).*

Cottrell, Leonard, *Quest for Sumer* (New York: Putnam, 1965).

Editors of *Life* Magazine, *The Epic of Man* (New York: Time Book Division, 1961).

Hawkes, Jacquetta, and Leonard Woolley, *Prehistory and the Beginnings of Civilization,* Vol. I, *The History of Mankind,* prepared for UNESCO (New York: Harper & Row, 1962).*

Howells, William W., *Back of History: The Story of Our Own Origins* (Garden City, N.Y.: Doubleday, 1954).

Kenyon, Kathleen, *Digging Up Jericho* (London: Benn Bros., Ltd., 1957).

Kramer, Samuel, *History Begins at Sumer* (New York: Doubleday Anchor Book, 1959).**

Maringer, Johannes, and Hans-Georg Bandi, *Art in the Ice Age* (New York: Praeger, 1953).

Mellaart, James, *Çatal Hüyük: A Neolithic Town in Anatolia* (New York: McGraw-Hill, 1967).

Parrot, André, *Sumer: The Dawn of Art* (New York: Golden Press, 1961).

Piggott, Stuart, ed., *The Dawn of Civilization* (New York: McGraw-Hill, 1961).

Chapter 11

Diaz del Castille, Bernal, *The Discovery and Conquest of Mexico, 1517–1521* (New York: Farrar, Straus, 1956).*

Edwards, I. E., *The Pyramids of Egypt,* rev. ed. (Baltimore: Penguin Books, 1961).**

Gallenkamp, Charles, *Maya: The Riddle and Rediscovery of a Lost Civilization* (New York: D. McKay, 1959).

Macgowan, Kenneth, and Joseph A. Hester, Jr., *Early Man in the New World,* rev. ed. (Garden City, N.Y.: Doubleday, 1962).**

Piggott, Stuart, ed., *The Dawn of Civilization* (New York: McGraw-Hill, 1961).

Stephens, John L., *Incidents of Travel in Central America, Chiapas, and Yucatán* (New Brunswick, N.J.: Rutgers University Press, 1956).

Stephens, John L., *Incidents of Travel in Yucatán,* 2 vols. (Norman: University of Oklahoma Press, 1962).*

Thompson, J. Eric, *The Civilization of the Mayas* (Chicago: Natural History Museum Press, 1953).

Vaillant, George C., *The Aztecs of Mexico: Origin, Rise and Fall of the Aztec Nation,* rev. by Suzannah B. Vaillant (Garden City, N.Y.: Doubleday).*

Von Hagen, Victor W., *The Ancient Sun Kingdoms of the Americas: Aztec, Maya, Inca* (Cleveland: World Publishing Company, 1961).

Von Hagen, Victor W., *The Aztec: Man and Tribe* (New York: New American Library, 1958).**

Von Hagen, Victor W., *Maya Explorer: John Lloyd Stephens and the Lost Cities of Central America and the Yucatán* (Norman: University of Oklahoma Press, 1954).

Von Hagen, Victor W., *Realm of the Incas,* rev. ed. (New York: New American Library, 1957).**

Von Hagen, Victor W., *World of the Maya* (New York: New American Library, 1960).**

Wissler, Clark, *Indians of the United States: Four Centuries of Their History and Culture,* rev. by L. W. Kluckhohn (Garden City, N.Y.; Doubleday, 1966).*

Chapter 12

Lowie, Robert H., *Social Organization* (New York: Holt, Rinehart and Winston, 1948).

Mead, Margaret, and Ken Heyman, *The Family* (New York: Macmillan, 1965).

Mead, Margaret, *Growing Up in New Guinea: A Comparative Study of Primitive Education* (New York: Morrow, 1930).*

Underhill, Ruth, *First Came the Family* (New York: Morrow, 1958).

Westermarck, Edward, *A Short History of Marriage* (New York: Macmillan, 1926).

Chapter 13

Hoebel, E. Adamson, *The Law of Primitive Man: A Study in Comparative Legal Dynamics* (Cambridge, Mass.: Harvard University Press, 1954).

Hutton, J. H., *Caste in India: Its Nature, Function, and Origin,* 4th ed. (London: Oxford University Press, 1963).

Lewin, Julius, *Studies in African Native Law* (Philadelphia: University Museum, 1947).

Lowie, Robert H., *Social Organization* (New York: Holt, Rinehart and Winston, 1948).

Mead, Margaret, *Coming of Age in Samoa: A Psychological Study of Primitive Youth for Western Civilization* (New York: Morrow, 1928).*

Mead, Margaret, *Male and Female: A Study of the Sexes in a Changing World* (New York: Morrow, 1949).*

Chapter 14

Durkheim, Émile, *Elementary Forms of the Religious Life* (New York: Macmillan, 1915).*

Frazer, James G., *The Golden Bough: A Study in Magic and Religion* (New York: Macmillan, 1924).*

Howells, William W., *The Heathens: Primitive Man and His Religion* (Garden City, N.Y.: Doubleday, 1948).

Malinowski, Bronislaw, *Magic, Science and Religion and Other Essays* (Garden City, N.Y.: Doubleday Anchor Book, 1954).**

Norbeck, Edward, *Religion in Primitive Society* (New York: Harper & Row, 1961).

Starkey, Marion Lena, *The Devil in Massachusetts* (Gloucester, Mass.: Peter Smith Reprints).*

Tylor, E. B., *Primitive Culture* (Gloucester, Mass.: Peter Smith Reprints).

Chapter 15

Boas, Franz, *Primitive Art* (New York: Dover, 1955).

Inverarity, R. B., *Art of the Northwest Coast Indians,* 2nd ed. (Berkeley: University of California Press, 1967).*

Nettl, Bruno, *Music in Primitive Culture* (Cambridge, Mass.: Harvard University Press, 1956).

Thompson, Stith, *Tales of the North American Indians* (Cambridge, Mass.: Harvard University Press, 1929).

Chapter 16

Boas, Franz, *Anthropology and Modern Life,* rev. ed. (New York: Norton, 1932).*

Du Bois, Cora, *The People of Alor* (Cambridge, Mass.: Harvard University Press, 1960).*

Kardiner, Abram, ed., *The Individual and His Society* (New York: Columbia University Press, 1939).

Kardiner, Abram, *et al., Psychological Frontiers of Society* (New York: Columbia University Press, 1945).*

Kluckhohn, Clyde, and Dorothea Leighton, *The Navaho* (Cambridge, Mass.: Harvard University Press, 1946).*

Malinowski, Bronislaw, *A Scientific Theory of Culture* (Chapel Hill, N.C.: University of North Carolina Press, 1944).*

Mead, Margaret, ed., *Cultural Patterns and Technical Change* (Paris: UNESCO, 1953).*

Morgan, Lewis Henry, *Ancient Society,* ed. by L. A. White (Cambridge, Mass.: Harvard University Press, 1964).*

Chapter 17

Malmstrom, Jean, *Language in Society* (New York: Hayden Book Company, 1965).*

Sapir, Edward, *Culture, Language, and Personality,* ed. by D. G. Mandelbaum (Berkeley: University of California Press, 1949).**

Whorf, Benjamin Lee, *Language, Thought, and Reality,* ed. by John B. Carroll (Cambridge, Mass.: M.I.T. Press, 1956).*

Chapter 18

Downs, James F., *Cultures in Crisis* (Beverly Hills, Calif.: Glencoe Press, 1971).**

Foster, George M., *Applied Anthropology* (Boston: Little, Brown and Company, 1969).

Goodenough, Ward Hunt, *Cooperation in Change: an Anthropological Approach to Community Development* (New York: Russell Sage Foundation, 1963).

Levine, Stuart, and Nancy O. Lurie, eds., *The American Indian Today* (Baltimore: Penguin Books, 1968).**

Mead, Margaret, ed., *Cultural Patterns and Technical Change* (New York: UNESCO, 1955).*

Paul, Benjamin D., ed., *Health, Culture and Community: Case Studies of Public Reactions to Health Programs* (New York: Russell Sage Foundation, 1955).

Glossary

A

absolute (direct) chronology: the dating of archaeological remains within a specific period of years in the past.

acculturation: the proces by which a society undergoes profound cultural change as a result of prolonged contact with another culture.

achieved status: status which an individual gains through his own efforts.

a culture: the traditional ways of doing things in a particular society.

affinity: kinship relationship by marriage.

age-grade: an association of persons of the same sex and approximately the same age.

age-village: a village built by Nyakyusan boys of the same age-grade.

amino acids: the chemical substances whose molecules combine in countless possible arrangements to make up proteins.

Anasazi culture: the most fully developed regional culture within the Southwestern (Indian) tradition; it centered in the broad plateau region where Arizona, New Mexico, Colorado, and Utah come together.

anatomy: the science that treats of the structures of plants and animals.

ancestor worship: worship of the spirits of dead relatives.

animal kingdom: one of the two major divisions of living nature (the kingdom Animalia).

animism: the belief in spiritual beings.

anthropoid: a member of the group of primates that includes monkeys, apes, and man (the suborder Anthropoidea).

anthropology: the study of man; the science that treats of the physical and cultural development of mankind.

anthropometry: the technique used by anthropologists to obtain human body measurements.

Antiquities Acts: an act of Congress (1906) to prohibit the appropriation, excavation, injuring, or destruction of any historic or prehistoric ruins situated on government lands.

anvil technique: an early method of percussion flaking that involved striking a stone repeatedly against a stationary boulder used as an anvil.

archaeology: the branch of anthropology that reconstructs past ways of life through careful examination of their remains.

Archaic tradition: an Indian tradition of eastern and midwestern North America that marked the transition from a hunting economy to an agrarian economy.

artifact: any object manufactured or used by man.

ascribed status: status which an individual possesses by reason of age, sex, race, or some other uncontrollable factor.

association: a social group whose members are joined in the pursuit of a common interest.

augur: a practitioner of divination in ancient Rome.

Aurignacian tradition: an Upper Paleolithic cultural tradition associated with Cro-Magnon people in Europe (*ca.*28,500 B.C.–22,000 B.C.).

Australopithecus: one of the two recognized genera of hominids; all known remains of *Australopithecus* have been discovered in southern and eastern Africa and dated in the Lower Pleistocene.

Australopithecus africanus: an australopithecine species whose members were relatively small and slender, walked upright, and made use of simple weapons.

Australopithecus robustus: an australopithecine species whose members were more rugged but probably less intelligent than *Australopithecus africanus.*

autocatalysis: the process by which a single molecule draws actively on its environment in order to manufacture more of its kind.

B

band: a group of wandering people comparable in size to a village.

basic invention: an invention that involves the application of a new principle.

basic personality structure: the total behavior of an individual, also termed "personality."

Big-Game Hunting tradition: an Indian tradition of North America dating from about 10,000 B.C. and thought to have begun in the Great Plains and then spread eastward and southward.

binocular vision: coordinated vision through both eyes, resulting in depth perception.

biocultural interaction: the process by which trends in biological and cultural evolution mutually affect and advance each other.

bipedalism: locomotion on two feet.

black magic (sorcery): magic performed with the intent to harm or kill.

blade technique: a method of producing blade tools by removing thin parallel flakes from a drum-shaped stone core.

blade tool: a stone tool made from a thin flake removed from a drum-shaped core.

brachiation: locomotion in trees using the forelimbs to swing from branch to branch.

bride-price (bridewealth): money or property given as compensation by a prospective husband to the bride's family.

bridewealth: *see* bride-price.

Bronze Age: the stage of man's cultural history which succeeded the Neolithic Age and was characterized by the use of bronze and the invention of writing.

burin: a blade tool with a chisel-shaped edge, used for cutting and engraving during the Upper Paleolithic period.

C

carbon-14 method: a method of dating organic fossil remains based on their content of carbon 14.

caste: a group or class within a society, such as (1) an occupational caste within a termite society, or (2) one of the hereditary castes of India.

caste system: a system of social classes characterized by hereditary status and by the practice of endogamy.

Cenozoic: the most recent geologic era, characterized by the formation of the modern mountain system and by the growing dominance of mammals.

cephalic index: the ratio of maximum head width to maximum head length.

ceremonial center: a center of religious, political, and sometimes commercial activity in Mesoamerican culture.

chordate: a member of the large group of animals that derive support at some stage in their development from the notochord (the phylum Chordata).

city: a unit of concentrated population larger than a village or a town.

civilization: a stage in the cultural development of a society generally marked by the keeping of written records, the building of large cities, and the use of advanced techniques in agriculture, industry, and the arts.

clan: a kinship group made up of several related lineages whose members claim common ancestry even though their relationship may be so remote as to be mythological.

Classic period: the period within the Mesoamerican tradition when most of the regional cultures of the area reached the highest stage of their development (A.D. 300–A.D. 900).

classical archaeology: the branch of archaeology that deals with cultures known through both material remains and written records.

Clovis point: a type of stone projectile point fluted at the base on both sides; associated with the Big-Game Hunting tradition.

collateral: referring to nondirect ties of kinship, such as the relationship between uncle and nephew.

compadre relationship: ceremonial kinship established between an adult sponsor and a godchild (and sometimes the child's parents) in many societies of Latin America.

component: in the Midwestern system of archaeological classification, the information about a past way of life found in a single site or just one level of a site.

confederacy: *see* league.

connotation: the emotional meaning conveyed by a word.

consanguinity: kinship relationship by blood.

contagious magic: magical practice based on the belief that things which have been in contact at one time continue to exert influence upon each other even when separated.

conventionalized (stylized) art: art which uses an accepted way of expressing the subject matter rather than striving for an exact likeness.

core tool: a stone tool made by chipping flakes off a stone core until it has reached the desired shape and size.

couvade: a religious custom whereby the father of a newborn infant acts as though he himself were experiencing the pains of childbirth.

cranial capacity: the capacity of the braincase, which is measured in cubic centimeters.

Cro-Magnon man: a variety of *Homo sapiens* whose members inhabited Europe during the late Upper Pleistocene and created several important cultural traditions (*Homo sapiens sapiens*).

cross-cousin: the child of one's father's sister or one's mother's brother.

cross dating: a method of determining absolute or relative chronology by comparing the distinctive traits of a site of unknown age with those of a site of known or relatively computed age.

crossing-over: the exchange of corresponding segments of paired chromosomes.

cultural anthropology: the branch of anthropology concerned with human culture and its development.

cultural ecology: the study of the interaction between human societies and the environments in which they live.

cultural evolution: the theory that human culture has progressed, and is constantly progressing, from simpler to more advanced stages.

culture: the enormous whole of learned, socially influenced behavior that has characterized mankind during the entire course of its history.

culture area: a geographical area within which several neighboring societies have made similar adjustments to the environment, thus sharing a number of culture complexes in common.

culture complex: a number of closely related culture traits centering in a particular interest shared by certain members of a society.

culture-free test: a test that could reliably compare the intelligence of peoples possessing wholly or partially different cultural backgrounds.

culture trait: any single characteristic of a culture, such as a pattern of behavior or a typical artifact.

D

decorative art: ornamental designs applied to an object of practical use for the sole purpose of enhancing its beauty.

dendrochronology: a method of determining the age of wood remains by reference to rings of growth in trees of known age.

denotation: the specific meaning of a word.

Desert tradition: an Indian tradition of western North America which marked the transition from a hunting economy to an agrarian economy.

dialect: a variety of spoken language peculiar to a community, a region, or a social group.

diffusion: the migration and borrowing of culture traits.

dig: another term for an archaeological excavation.

divination: a practice aimed at foretelling the course of future events by supernatural means.

DNA (deoxyribonucleic acid): a nucleic acid found in all living cells and thought to be the basic hereditary material.

dominant: referring to the characteristic observable in an offspring with contrasting genes for the same trait.

dowry: money or property given by the bride's parents to help a newly married couple establish a household.

drive: a bodily need that must be satisfied in order for an individual to survive.

Dryopithecus: a group of Miocene apes related to the Proconsul fossils and, like them, exhibiting certain manlike features of dentition.

E

ego: the person from whose point of view a kinship diagram is labeled.

embryonic development: the development of an organism during the earliest stages of its growth.

emergency archaeology: the salvaging of evidence of past cultures that is threatened by the modern upsurge in building construction.

endogamy: marriage within one's social group as required by custom.

epoch (geologic): a subdivision of time within a geologic period.

era (geologic): one of the six major divisions of geologic time.

ethnic appreciation: respect for one's own culture and for the institutions of one's own society.

ethnic group: a group of people identifiable by a common racial or cultural background.

ethnocentrism: the tendency to look upon other cultures with disfavor and to consider one's own culture superior.

ethnographic present: the time reference used by anthropologists to describe a culture stronger in a former period as though it were still fully functioning.

ethnography: the division of ethnology concerned with the description of cultures by anthropologists who have gathered their information firsthand.

ethnology: the branch of anthropology that studies culture, either one culture over an extended period of time or several cultures existing at the same time.

ethnomusicology: the branch of anthropology which studies musical behavior, especially that characteristic of nonliterate peoples.

Euglena: a one-celled organism ranked with plants according to its mode of nutrition, but ranked with animals according to its capacity for locomotion and absence of a solid cell wall.

evolution: the process by which an organism, or a group of organisms, develops such distinct characteristics as to form a new species.

excavation: the systematic unearthing of ancient ruins by digging out the soil, debris, or other materials superimposed on them over centuries.

exogamy: marriage outside one's social group as required by custom.

extended family: a family that has been extended beyond the nuclear group by the inclusion of near relatives or of another nuclear family.

F

feedback: the partial return of the effects of an evolutionary process back to the original source.

flagellate protozoa: simple one-celled organisms that move with the aid of one or more whiplike appendages (flagella).

flake tool: a stone tool made from a flake chipped off a stone core.

flaking: the removal of thin layers of flake from a stone core in order to produce tools.

fluorine test: a test of skeletal age based upon the fact that the fluorine content of bones buried in earth tends to increase through time at a rate particular to a given locality.

folklore: the oral traditions, beliefs, dances, and songs preserved by a people through custom over generations.

Folsom point: a type of stone projectile

point fluted almost the entire length of each side; associated with the Big-Game Hunting tradition.

formal art: art which emphasizes the form of an object rather than its meaning or likeness to something else.

G

gene: one of a pair of genetic units that determine one trait in the biological makeup of an organism.

genotype: the internal mechanism that controls the inheritance of a specific trait by an organism.

genus (pl. genera): the biological grouping which ranks next below the family and may include one or more species; the genus name forms part of the biological designation of any plant or animal.

geographical race: a collection of populations separated from other such collections by major geographical barriers, such as oceans or high mountain ranges.

geology: the science that treats of the earth's history and structure.

ghost dance: a religious movement widely spread among the Plains Indian tribes in the late nineteenth century, thought by many of its followers to promise the revival of Indian power.

glacial varve chronology: a method of determining geologic age by reference to layers of silt and clay that were deposited annually by the meltwaters of retreating glaciers.

go-between: the person chosen to mediate between parties to a dispute in Ifugao society.

group marriage: a rare marriage practice in which several husbands are married jointly to several wives.

H

hand ax: a core tool rounded at one end and pointed at the other, used for a variety of purposes during the Lower and Middle Paleolithic.

Hohokam culture: the regional culture within the Southwestern (Indian) tradition that centered in the Gila Valley of southern Arizona.

Holocene: the most recent geologic epoch, which began between ten and fifteen thousand years ago.

hominid: a member of the group of hominoids that includes both early and recent man (the family Hominidae).

hominoid: a member of the group of anthropoids that includes man, the apes, and certain forms intermediate between the two (the superfamily Hominoidea).

Homo: the only surviving member genus within the hominid family; it includes both extinct and recent forms of mankind.

Homo erectus: the fossil species of hominid that includes Java man, Peking man, and other extinct varieties of the Lower and Middle Pleistocene.

Homo habilis: a fossil hominid discovered in the Olduvai Gorge by L. S. B. Leakey, who considers the form to represent a third species of the genus *Homo*.

homology: a structural likeness between different types of organisms that is best accounted for by a common origin.

Homo sapiens: the only surviving species of hominid; it includes both extinct varieties and all of recent mankind.

household: a family group of varying size.

hybrid: possessing different genes for the same biological characteristic.

hybrid vigor: a term for the superior growth, fertility, and resistance to disease observed in hybrid offspring produced under experimental control.

I

imitative magic: magical practice based on the belief that a desired result can be brought about by imitating it.

incest taboo: a social regulation that prohibits marriage among certain close relatives.

independent invention: an invention arrived at independently, even though another group of people may have made this invention earlier.

instinct: a biologically inherited pattern of complex behavior that helps the members of a species to adjust to their environment.

intelligence quotient (IQ): a determination of general mental ability based upon dividing a person's mental age (as measured by an "intelligence test") by his chronological age (his age in years).

intonation: the rise and fall in the pitch of the voice in speech.

J

Java man: a variety of *Homo erectus* discovered in Java and dated between 700,000 and 500,000 years ago (*Homo erectus erectus*).

K

Kaaba: the shrine at Mecca which holds a sacred black stone worshiped by members of the Moslem religion.

kinship: the state of being related.

kiva: a circular subterranean chamber found in Anasazi dwellings and probably used for both ceremonial and social purposes.

L

language: the use of words for communication among people.

language family: a group of languages whose systematic resemblance to each other suggests their descent from a common ancestral language.

league (confederacy): several tribes loosely joined together, either for mutual protection or for aggressive purposes.

lineage: a kinship group made up of all the unilateral descendants of a common ancestor who can be named.

lineal: referring to direct ties of kinship, such as the relationship between father and son.

linguistic typology: the classification of languages on the basis of types of linguistic structure.

linguistics: the scientific study of language in all its aspects.

linkage: the tendency of certain biological traits to be inherited together, accounted for by the location of the genes for these traits on the same chromosome.

literature: written prose and verse, especially writings that are distinguished by excellence of form and universal appeal.

local race: a breeding population which is maintained by either natural or social barriers.

Lower Paleolithic: the period within the Paleolithic Age which extended from its beginning about 2,000,000 years ago up to about 150,000 years ago.

M

Magdalenian tradition: an Upper Paleolithic cultural tradition associated with Cro-Magnon people in Europe.

magic: any dealing with the supernatural which attempts to manipulate it for the benefit of some individual.

mammal: a member of the class of vertebrates characterized by a body covering of hair and by the nourishment of offspring with milk secreted by the mammary glands of females (the class Mammalia).

mana: an impersonal supernatural force that may be concentrated in persons or inanimate objects and acquired by a variety of means.

matrilineal: referring to descent traced through the mother's line.

matrilocal family: an extended family in which the husband joins the household of his wife's parents.

medicine man: the term for "shaman" among the American Indians.

Mesoamerican tradition: a cultural tradition of Middle America based on maize farming and including several important regional cultures; it dated from about 2,000 B.C. up until the Spanish conquest of Aztec Mexico.

Mesolithic (Middle Stone) Age: the stage in man's cultural prehistory that marked the transition from Paleolithic hunting economies to Neolithic agrarian economies (*ca.* 12,000 to 10,000 years ago in the Middle East).

mestizo: a person of mixed European and American Indian ancestry.

metazoan: a member of the very large group of multi-celled animals (the subkingdom Metazoa).

microlith: a tiny blade tool, usually triangular in shape and set into a bone or wooden shaft, used for cutting during the Mesolithic Age.

microrace: a highly localized population which, though not geographically isolated, tends to be tightly inbred and subtly distinct.

Middle Paleolithic: the period within the Paleolithic Age which extended from about 150,000 to about 40,000 years ago.

Midwestern system: a system of archaeological classification developed by American archaeologists working in the central portion of the United States.

Mississippian tradition: an Indian tradition of eastern North America which evolved out of the Woodland tradition about A.D. 700.

Mogollon culture: the regional culture within the Southwestern (Indian) tradition that centered in southern Arizona and southwestern New Mexico.

monogamy: the practice of having only one wife or husband at a time.

monotheism: the belief in, or worship of, one god only.

morpheme: the smallest meaningful portion of an utterance.

Mousterian tradition: a Middle Paleolithic cultural tradition associated with Neanderthal people in Europe.

mutation: a sudden change in the genetic makeup of an organism.

N

nasal index: the ratio of maximum nose width to maximum nose length.

nation: a tribe or people organized into a relatively complex society whose limits are defined more by the existence of a strong central government than by a common racial or cultural background.

Natufian tradition: an early Neolithic cultural tradition of the Middle East.

naturalistic art: *see* realistic art.

natural selection: the Darwinian theory that evolution is based upon the long-term selection of traits that favor an organism's adaptation to a particular environment.

Navaho Night Way: *see* Yeibichai.

Neanderthal man: a variety of *Homo sapiens* whose members inhabited parts of Europe, Asia, Africa, and the Near East during the Upper Pleistocene (*Homo sapiens neanderthalensis*).

Neolithic (New Stone) Age: the stage of man's cultural prehistory characterized by the adoption of an agrarian economy and the earliest urbanization (*ca.* 8000 B.C.–3500 B.C.).

nonliterate: lacking a writing system, as opposed to failing to learn to read and write in a society where literacy is the norm.

nontribal fraternity: a male association whose membership is limited or carefully chosen.

notochord: the flexible internal rodlike structure that supports the body of a chordate at some stage during early development or throughout its lifetime.

nuclear family: a family group consisting of father, mother, and children.

nucleic acids: the chemical substances found in all cell nuclei which are responsible for controlling many important cell activities.

O

ordeal: a dangerous or painful test of innocence or guilt, supposed to be under supernatural control.

Oreopithecus: a fossil hominoid of the late Miocene or early Pliocene which in some respects evolved in a manlike direction, but apparently became extinct.

overproduction: the production of more offspring than are necessary to ensure the survival of a species.

P

Paleolithic (Old Stone) Age: the stage of man's cultural prehistory characterized by an economy based on hunting and gathering and the use of simple stone tools (*ca.* 2,000,000 to 12,000 years ago).

paleontology: the science that treats of past forms of life as observed through their fossil remains.

parallel cousin: the child of one's father's brother or one's mother's sister.

parasitic: dependent on another organism for nourishment and shelter.

patrilineal: referring to descent traced through the father's line.

patrilocal family: an extended family in which the wife joins the household of her husband's parents.

peasantry: persons deriving their subsistence by tilling the soil as laborers or small landowners.

pebble-tool tradition: a tool-producing tradition found in several parts of the Old World during the Lower Pleistocene; the tools produced had crudely shaped cutting edges.

Peking man: a variety of *Homo erectus* discovered near Peking, China, and dated in the Middle Pleistocene (*Homo erectus pekinensis*).

percussion flaking: a method of shaping stone tools by striking a stone either against, or through the use of, another object until flakes are chipped off.

period (geologic): a subdivision of time within a geologic era.

personality: the total behavior of an individual.

phase: in the Midwestern system of archaeological classification, a unit larger than a component and sometimes comparable to an entire culture.

phenotype: an observable biological characteristic of an organism.

phoneme: the smallest sound unit in a language capable of distinguishing one utterance from another.

physical anthropology: the branch of anthropology that studies human evolution and physical variation.

physiology: the science that treats of how animals and plants function under varied conditions.

Piltdown man: a fabricated fossil man exposed as a hoax in 1953 by British scientists who employed the fluorine test of skeletal age.

placental mammal: a member of the group of mammals whose early development is completed within the mother's womb (the subclass Eutheria).

plaintiff: the person who claims injury in a legal dispute.

Pleistocene: the epoch of the Cenozoic characterized by periods of intensive glaciation of the earth's surface and by the growing dominance of man (*ca.* 2,000,000 to 15,000 years ago).

polyandry: a form of polygamy that allows a wife to have more than one husband at a time.

polygamy: the practice of having more than one wife or husband at a time.

polygyny: a form of polygamy that allows a husband to have more than one wife at a time.

polytheism: the belief in, or worship of, more than one god.

polytypic: consisting of many different types.

pongid: a member of the group of hominoids that includes all the apes (the family Pongidae).

Postclassic period: the period within the Mesoamerican tradition marked by a general decline in cultural activity throughout the area, ending with the Spanish conquest of Mexico (*ca.* A.D. 900– A.D. 1519).

Preclassic period: the period within the Mesoamerican tradition marked by the adoption of an agrarian economy (*ca.* 2000 B.C.–A.D. 300).

pre-Columbian: prior to the arrival of Columbus in the New World.

preferential mating: marriage according to the guidelines set by a society.

prehistoric archaeology: the branch of archaeology that deals with cultures known through material remains only.

pressure flaking: a method of shaping stone tools by pressing against a stone with a blunt tool until flakes are forced off.

priest: a person who through special ability or training acts as an intermediary between the supernatural and the members of a religious group.

primary institution: a customary pattern of child treatment in a society.

primate: a member of the highly developed group of mammals that includes prosimians, monkeys, apes, and man (the order Primates).

Proconsul: a group of apes dated in the Miocene epoch and thought to be ancestral to the modern chimpanzees and gorillas.

prosimian: a member of the group of primates that includes such tree-dwelling forms as tarsiers, lemurs, and tree shrews (the suborder Prosimii).

proteins: the class of chemical compounds most important in the makeup of living cells.

protozoan: a microscopic animal of single-celled body.

R

race: a human population whose members breed among themselves and have become distinct from other populations by sharing a number of inherited physical traits.

Ramapithecus: a fossil hominoid of the late Miocene or early Pliocene some of whose features suggest that he may be ancestral to man.

realistic (naturalistic) art: art which deliberately strives for faithful representation of an object.

recessive: referring to the characteristic which tends to be hidden in an offspring with contrasting genes for the same trait.

reduplication: the repetition of a word form in order to express additional meaning, such as intensity (Pocomchi language).

reflex: an automatic bodily action, such as grasping or sucking in newborn infants.

relative (indirect) chronology: the dating of archaeological remains in terms of whether they are older or more recent than other objects.

religion: man's concern with the supernatural as expressed in his beliefs, attitudes, and actions.

replication: reproduction at the molecular level.

representative art: art which emphasizes the portrayal of nature or life.

rites of intensification: religious ceremonies associated with periodic or seasonal events of importance to a society.

rites of passage: religious ceremonies which mark changes in an individual's position in society at certain important stages in his life.

role: the way of behaving considered appropriate to a particular status.

S

sand painting: a painting made from colored sands and used in curative ceremonies among the Navaho Indians.

Sandia point: a type of stone projectile point characterized by only a semblance of fluting; associated with the Big-Game Hunting tradition.

secondary institution: an economic, religious, social, or other cultural activity that characterizes a society.

secondary invention: an invention derived from the principle underlying a basic invention.

self-help: the right of redressing an injury by one's own action without judicial intervention.

sequence: in the Midwestern system of archaeological classification, a set of components or phases occurring successively in time.

shaman: a magical practitioner whose power to cure is based on direct dealings with the supernatural.

sibling: a brother or sister.

site: the smallest significant unit of space studied by an archaeologist.

slash-and-burn: the agricultural technique which consists of cutting down trees and brush and burning them in order to create arable land.

social class: one of two or more groups in a society whose members derive a sense of unity from possessing a number of statuses in common.

society: (1) a group of people, regardless of size, who share a common culture and a sense of common identity, and (2) the system of interpersonal relationships among the members of such a group.

sorcery: *see* black magic.

Southwestern tradition: a cultural tradition of southwestern North America characterized by maize farming and including several regional cultures; it dated from about A.D. 500 until near the end of the thirteenth century.

species (pl. species): a group of animals or plants whose members have the same structural characteristics and mate with each other to produce fertile offspring.

spontaneous generation: the theory that living organisms may proceed under certain circumstances from lifeless matter; the original theory, now discredited, held this to be possible under present conditions on earth.

status: the position of an individual in relation to others within his society.

Steinheim man: an early variety of *Homo sapiens* discovered at Steinheim, Germany, and dated in the late Middle Pleistocene (*Homo sapiens steinheimensis*).

struggle for existence: the competition of organisms for space and food which serves as a natural check on overpopulation.

style: a characteristic mode of artistic expression.

stylized art: *see* conventionalized art.

subculture: a pattern of culture sufficiently different as to be distinct from the overall culture of a society.

subspecies: a subdivision within a species, also termed a "race" or a "variety."

Sumerian city-states: a group of city-states established in ancient Mesopotamia between about 3200 B.C. and 2500 B.C.

supernatural: that which cannot be explained as resulting from natural causes, or that which is beyond or above human reason.

survival of the fittest: Darwin's theory that organisms possessing variations which make them especially well adapted to their environment have the best chance for survival in the struggle for existence.

Swanscombe man: an early variety of *Homo sapiens* discovered at Swanscombe, England, and dated in the late Middle Pleistocene (*Homo sapiens steinheimensis*).

symbolic art: art which uses symbols to convey its meaning.

syntax: the study of how words and significant features of intonation are arranged in phrases, clauses, or sentences, and of how sentences relate to each other.

T

term of address: a term used to address someone to whom one is related.

term of reference: a term used to describe one's kinship relationship to someone.

tortoise-core technique: a method of producing flake tools by removing flakes from a stone core shaped to resemble a tortoise shield.

town: a unit of concentrated population larger than a village but smaller than a city.

trait-complex: *see* culture complex.

tribal fraternity: an association admitting all male members of a tribe after a required formal initiation.

tribe: a group of bands or villages sharing a common territory, language, and culture.

U

Ubaid phase: the first period of true urbanization, named for the site of Ubaid in southern Mesopotamia (*ca.* 4000 B.C.).

unilateral: referring to descent traced through one line of relatives only.

untouchable: a Western term for members of Hindu society who are outside the caste system.

Upper Paleolithic: the period within the Paleolithic age which extended from about 40,000 up to about 12,000 years ago.

urban anthropology: the study of ethnic minorities and their life-styles in urban areas.

V

variation: a difference in an inborn characteristic of an organism from the trait held by its parents or by other members of the species.

vertebrate: a member of the group of chordates in which the notochord is replaced by a cartilaginous or a bony vertebral column (the subphylum Vertebrata).

vestigial organ: a body part which no longer serves any useful function in members of a species.

village: a unit of several hundred or more people living together in a settled community.

virus: a form of matter which under certain conditions appears to be lifeless crystal, yet in other circumstances is capable of unlimited reproduction; its makeup is protein.

W

white magic: magic performed with the intent to do good.

witchcraft: the manipulation of harmful supernatural forces by someone who has inherited this power and may exercise it involuntarily.

Woodland tradition: an Indian tradition of eastern North America dating from about 1000 B.C. and characterized by an economy based on hunting and farming.

world view: the characteristic way in which the members of a culture perceive and respond to their total environment.

Y

Yeibichai (Navaho Night Way): a Navaho ceremony which combines painting, poetry, dance, and music to serve its primary function of an initiation rite or a curative ritual.

Z

Zinjanthropus: a fossil hominid discovered by Dr. and Mrs. Leakey in the Olduvai Gorge in 1959; it is generally thought to be either a variety of *Australopithecus robustus* or a third species of australopithecines.

zoology: the science that treats of the animal kingdom.

Index

Italicized page numbers refer to pictures. Such numbers preceded by *f*, *m*, or *t* refer to a figure (*f*), a map (*m*), or a table (*t*).

A

Component, 113
Confederacy, 24
Connotation, 225–26
Consanguinity, 154
Corbeled arch, 144, *f146*
Core tools, 120, *120*
Cortés, Hernando, 30, 140–41
Couvade, 187–88
Cro-Magnon man, 82, *f82*, 83, *t84–85;* cultural traditions of, 122–24, 179, 193
Cranial capacity, 65, 66, 72–73; in fossil men, 72, 78, 79, 80, 81, 82
Cross-cousins, 156; marriage among, 158, *f158*
Cross-cultural comparisons, 216
Cross dating, 111
Crossing-over, 57
Crow Indians, 24
Cultural anthropology, 4–5, 103–219; divisions of, 5–6; history of, 8–10, 207–11; trends in, 216–17; uses of, 10–11, 231–44
Cultural change, 29–30, 231–34; directed, 231–44
Cultural ecology, defined, 217
Cultural evolution, theory of, 208–09, 211
Culture, 4–5, 13–22, 103–219; a culture, 16; analysis of, 25–27; change in, 19, 27–28, 231–44; defined, 4, 16–18; ethnocentrism, 20–21; and language, 222–25; learned vs. instinctive behavior, 13–16; modern study of, 23–33, 209–11; as a mold, 18–19; and personality, 211–13; prehistoric of New World, 133–49; prehistoric of Old World, 117–31; "primitive," 31–32; and world view, 213–16
Culture area, 26–27, *27*
Culture complex (trait-complex), 26
Culture-free test, 99–100
Culture trait, 26
Cytoplasm, 39

D

Darwin, Charles, 10, 47, 53–54, *54*
Dating of archaeological finds, 7, 61–62, 111–12
Dawson, Charles, 61
Delphic oracle, 183–84, *184*
Dendrochronology, 7, 111, *f112*

Denotation, 225
Dentition, ape vs. human, 66, *f69*
Descartes, René, 38
Descent, tracing of, 157
Desert tradition, 136, *f137,* 138
De Vries, Hugo, 56–57
Dialect, 223
Diaz del Castillo, Bernal, 143
Diffusion, 29–30
Dig, *see* Excavation
Dinka people, language of, 223
Disease, curbing of, 234–37
Distance, cultural, 237
Divination, 183–84
DNA (deoxyribonucleic acid), 57–58, *f57*
Dog, domestication of, 124
Domestication of animals, 30, 124, 126–27, 149
Domestication of plants, 30
Dominant gene, 55–56, *f56*
Dowry, 159–60
Drives, modification of, 14–15, *15, see also* Instinct
Dryopithecus, 66, 68, *t84–85*
Dubois, Eugene, 76–77
Durkheim, Émile, 178

E

Earth, age of, 37; origin of life on, 41–44; *see also* Geologic time
Economy, types of, *210;* and kinship systems, 157, 211; and social classes, 167; *see also* Agriculture, Animal herding, Foraging, Hunting and gathering
Embryonic development, 48–49; of primates, 65
Emergency archaeology, 113, *114*
Endogamy, 169
Eocene epoch, 64, *t64,* 65
Epoch (geologic), 62
Era (geologic), 62, *t63*
Eskimo people, 21, 28, 122, 167, 209, 223; law of, 171–72, *172,* 175; local race, *90, 91, 96*
Ethnic appreciation, 21
Ethnic group, 25
Ethnocentrism, 20–21, 216

I

Ifugao law, 172–73
Incest taboos, 157–58
Indian Claims Commission Act, 237
Indian geographical race, *m94*, 95; local races within, 93
Indians, American, *see* American Indians
Initiation rites, of Ona tribe, 163–64; *see also* Yeibichai
Innovations, acceptance of, 231–34; in China, *233*; in India, *232-3, 236*; in Vietnam, 235
Instinct, 14–16
Intelligence Quotient (IQ), 98–100
Intonation, 221
Inventions, 28–30; of New vs. Old World, 148–49
Iroquois Indians, 9, 24, 157, 208

J

Japanese rice, introduction of, 232
Jarmo, *m125*, 126, 127, *ƒ128*
Java man, 76–77, *76, 77, t84–85;* a variety of *Homo erectus*, 78–79
Jaw, ape vs. human, 66, *ƒ69*
Jericho, *m125*, 126–27, *126, ƒ128*

K

Kaaba, 187
Kardiner, Abram, 213
Kariera people, 158, *ƒ158*
Kenyapithecus, see *Ramapithecus*
Kinship, 24, 154–57; American system of, 154–55, *ƒ156;* institutionalized, 166–67; *see also* Family, Marriage
Kiva, 147, *147*
Kluckhohn, Clyde, 11, 17, 214, 240
Kroeber, A. L., 31

L

Lamarck, Jean Baptiste, 52
Language, 5, 18, 221–30; acquisition of, 221–22; and culture, 222–25; differences,

227–28; international, 229; and meaning, 225–26; *see also* Grammar, Vocabulary, Writing
Lapps, 25
Law, 170–75
League, 24
Leakey, L.S.B. and Mary, 72, 80, 119
Life, defined, 39–41; origin of, 37–39, 41–44, *ƒ42*
Life span, of primates, 65
Lineage, 157
Linguistic typology, 228
Linguistics, 5, 221–30; *see also* Language
Linkage, 57
Literature, 198
Local races, 93–95
Lower Paleolithic, *t118,* 119, 121, *ƒ128*

M

Magdalenian tradition, 122, *ƒ128*
Magic, 178, 179, 180–83; contagious, 181, *182;* imitative, 123–24, 180–81, *181;* practitioners of, 182–83, *183;* vs. religion, 177, 180
Malayo-Polynesian language family, 226–27
Malinowski, Bronislaw, 211
Mammals, 50, *50, t52,* 62, 63–64
Man, anthropology is study of, 3–4; among the primates, 4, 50–51, 64–66; distinguished from apes, 66, *ƒ68, ƒ69, ƒ70;* evolution of, 71–73, 75–86, *t84–85;* place in animal kingdom, 49–51, *t52;* races of, 89–100; sole possessor of culture, 4–5, 14–16
Mana, 179–80
Marriage, 26, 157–60, *ƒ158, 159, 160;* and family system, 152–53
Masks, *183,* 197–98, *198*
Matrilineal descent, 157
Matrilocal family, 154
Maya Indians, 29, 133, 143–46, *144, 145, ƒ146*
Medicine man, 182; *see also* Shaman
Mediterranean local race, 94–95, *t97*
Melanesia, 179, 181
Melanesian-Papuan geographical race, *m94*, 95

Mendel, Gregor, 55–56
Mesa Verde, 147, *147*
Mesoamerican tradition, *f137*, 138–46, *m139*
Mesolithic (Middle Stone) Age, 118, *t118*, 124, *f128*
Mestizo (ladino), 98
Metallurgy, 130
Metazoans, 49
Mexican village, improving crops, *234*; modernization of, 232, 234
Microlith, 124, *f128*
Micronesian geographical race, *m94*, 95
Microraces, 93
Middle Paleolithic, *t118*, 119, 121, *f128*
Midwestern system, 113
Miller, Stanley L., 41–42, *42*
Miocene epoch, *t64*, 66, 68
Mississippian tradition, *f137*, 148
Moctezuma, 141
Mogollon culture, 146
Mongoloid racial stock, 92–93
Monkeys, 4, 50–51, 65
Monogamy, 152–53
Monotheism, 178
Monte Albán, *m139*, 143
Morgan, Lewis Henry, 10, 208–09
Morpheme, 227
Mousterian tradition, 121, *f128*, 179
Müller, Friedrich Max, 178
Music, 7, 194, 200–01; of Navaho, 204–05
Mutation, 57; cause of, 58

N

Nasal index, 91
Nation, 24–25
Natufian tradition, 125–26, *m125*, *f128*
Natural selection, 53–54
Navaho Indians, 147–48, 216, 224; arts of, 201–05; medicine among, 235–36; world view of, 214, 216
Navaho Night Way (Yeibichai), 201–05
Navaho-Cornell Field Health Project, 236
Neanderthal man, 81–82, *f81*, 83, *t84–85*; cultural traditions of, 81–82, 121, 179
Nea Nikomedeia, 127
Negroid racial stock, 92
Neolithic (New Stone) Age, 118, *t118*, 125–31, *f128*

Neolithic revolution, 125–28, 131
Nepalese farmers, 232
"New ethnography," 216
Newton, Sir Isaac, 38
New World, early man in, 83, 135; prehistoric cultures of, 133–49
Niger-Congo language family, 227
Nigeria, native courts of, *174*
Noble class, 167, *168;* among Northwest Coast Indians, 168
Nomadism, 24, 127
Nonliterate societies, 32
Nontribal fraternity, 164
North American Colored (American Negro) race, 95, 97–98
Northwest Coast Indians, art of, 196–98, *197, 198;* shamans among, *183;* social classes of, 167–68
Northwest European local race, 94, 95, *t97*
Notochord, 50
Nuclear family, 151–53, *152, f155*
Nucleic acids, 40, *t40*, 41
Nucleus, 39–40
Nyakyusa people, age-grading of, 165–66

O

Oldowan choppers, 119
Olduvai Gorge, 72, 79–80, 119
Old World, prehistoric cultures of, 117–31
Oligocene epoch, *t64*, 65
Ona tribe, 163–64
Oparin, A. I., 38–39, 41
Orangutan, *67, 76*
Ordeal, 173
Oreopithecus, 34, 66, 68–69, *t84–85*
Overproduction, 53

P

Paleocene epoch, 64, *t64*
Paleolithic (Old Stone) Age, 118–24, *t118*, *f128*
Paleontology, 7
Papuans, smallpox among, 236–37
Parallel cousins, 156; marriage among, 158
Pasteur, Louis, 38
Patrilineal descent, 157

Patrilocal family, 154
Peasantry, defined, 31
Peking man, 78, t84–85; a variety of *Homo erectus*, 78–79, f79
Period (geologic), 62
Personality, and culture, 6–7, 211–13
Phase, 113
Phenotype, 55; in racial classifications, 89–93
Phoneme, 221, 227
Physical anthropology, 4, 5, 7, 35–101; history of, 8–10; uses of, 98–100
Physiology, 7
Piltdown man, 61–62
Plains Indians, 30; art of, 195–96, *196;* culture area, 26–27; ghost dance of, 189–90
Pleistocene (Glacial) epoch, 62–64, t64; cultural periods of, 117–18, t118; and human evolution, 71–72, 79, 81, 82–83
Pliocene epoch, t64, 68
Polyandry, 152
Polygamy, 152–53
Polygyny, 152–53
Polynesia, 179–80
Polynesian geographical race, m94, 95
Polytheism, 178
Pongids, 51; *see also* Apes
Postclassic period, f137, 138
Preclassic period, f137, 138
Preferential mating, 157
Prehistoric cultures, of New World, 133–49, f137; of Old World, 117–31, f128
Priest, 187, *187*
Primary institutions, 211–13
Primates, 4, 50–51, t52; evolution of, 64–66, t64; *see also* Apes, Man, Monkeys, Prosimians
"Primitive," applied to a culture, 31–32
Proconsul, 68
Prosimians, 50–51, 64, 65, 65
Proteins, 40, 41
Protozoans, 48, 49
Pyramids, of Aztecs, 140; of Mayas, 144, *145;* of Teotihuacán, 139–40; Old vs. New World, 133–35, *134*

Q

Quaternary period, 62, t64
Quetzalcoatl (Kukulkan), 140, *140, 145*

R

Race, 4, 32, 51, 89–100; and American class system, 168–69; defined, 93; and ethnic groups, 25; and environment, *90, 91;* and mental endowment, 98–100; misconceptions of, 95, 97–98; mixture, 95, 97–98, *99;* modern classification of, 93–95, m94, 96; traditional classifications of, 89–93, f91, f92
Ramapithecus (Kenyapithecus), 66, 69–70, t84–85
Recessive gene, 55–56, f56
Reduplication, 228
Religion, 177–80, 185–90; defined, 177; origin of, 177–79; practices of, 185–87; in society, 187–88; vs. magic, 177, 180; *see also* Magic, Rites
Replication, 58
Rites (ceremonies and rituals), 177, 185, 187; curing, 182–83; initiation, 163–64; of intensification, 188; of passage, 188, *189;* of sacrifice, 185; *see also* Yeibichai
Role, 169

S

Sacrifice, 185
Sahagún, Bernadino de, 9, *10,* 143, 185
Sand painting, of Navaho, 201–03, *202*
Sandia point, 136
Scapegoat, 185
Scrapers, 121, f128
Secondary institution, 213
Self-help, 175
Sequence, 113
Shaman, 182–83, *183,* 197
Sino-Tibetan language family, 226
Sites, 106–07, *106, 107;* discovery of, 108; excavation of burial, 110–11, *110*
Skeletal structure, ape vs. human, 66, f70
Skull, ape vs. human, f68; of fossil men, 71, 79, 81, 82
Slash-and-burn method, 138
Slaves, 167; among Aztecs, 141; among Northwest Coast Indians, 168
Social class, 167–70
Social order, *see* Law
Social organization, *see* Associations, Kinship, Social class

Society, defined, 24; human vs. insect, 13–16; relationship to culture, 16–19; study of complex, 30–31
Song contest, 172, *172*
"Sorcerer," 179, *180*
Sorcery (black magic), 180
South African Colored race, 95
Southwestern tradition, *f137*, 146–48
Spallanzani, Lazzaro, 38
Species (pl. species), 51
Speech sounds, 221
Spontaneous generation, 38
Steinheim man, 80–81, *t84–85*
Stephens, John Lloyd, 133, 144
Struggle for existence, 53
Subculture, 25–26, *25*
Subspecies, 51
Sumer, city-states of, *m125, f128*, 129–31, *129, 130*
Supernatural, defined, 177; *see also* Magic, Religion
Survival of the fittest, 53
Swanscombe man, 81, *t84–85*
Symbolic art, 195, *196, 202*
Syntax, 221

T

Taboo, 180, 182; incest, 157–58
Tarsier, 64, *65*
Teeth, *see* Dentition
Tenochtitlán, 106, *m139*, 140–43
Teotihuacán, 138–40, *m139*
Terms of address, 155
Terms of reference, 155
Territorial units, 24
Tertiary period, 62, *t64*
Time, attitudes toward, 114; cultural divisions of, 117–19, *t118;* measurement of, 142–43, 144; *see also* Geologic time
Toltec Indians, 140, *141*, 144
Tools, of archaeology, 107–08, *107;* chimpanzee's use of, 66; and human evolution, 72–73, 78, 79, 80, 81–82, *t84–85;* making of stone, 120–21; metal, 130; of Mesolithic, 124; of Neolithic, 125, 127; of Paleolithic, 119–22, *119, 120, 122, f128;* prehistoric of New World, 136

Tortoise-core technique, 120
Totem pole, 196–97, *197*
Town, 24
Trait-complex (culture complex), 26
Trance, 178, 182–83
Tribal fraternity, 163–64, *165*
Tribe, 24; associations within, 163–66
Trickster, in American Indian folklore, 187, 199
Tswana law, 174
Tula, *m139*, 140, *141*
Tylor, Edward B., 10, 17, 178

U

Ubaid, *m125, f128*, 129
Underwater archaeology, 113–14, *115*
Unilateral descent, 157
Untouchables, 170, *171*
Upper Paleolithic, *t118*, 119, 121–24, *f128*
Ur, *m125*, 129, *129, 130*
Ural-Altaic languages, 226
Urban anthropology, defined, 31
Urbanization, 127–30, *210*
Urey, Harold, 41
Ute Indians, 30

V

Valley of Mexico, 138, *m139*, 140, *140*
Valley of Oaxaca, 138, *m139*, 143
Variation, 53–55, *54;* source of, 57
Vertebrates, 50, *t52*
Vestigial organ, 48
Village, 24
Virus, 43–44
Vocabulary, as mirror of culture, 223

W

Wallace, Alfred Russel, 53
Watson, James Dewey, 58
Wedding, *see* Marriage

White magic, 180
Whorf, Benjamin Lee, 224–25
Witchcraft, 184–85
Woodland tradition, *f137*, 148
World view, 213–14; of Navaho, 214, 216
Wovoka, 189
Writing, 5, 29, 30, 130–31

Y

Yagua Indians, 18, *19*, 24

Yeibichai (Navaho Night Way), 201–05
Yucatán, 133, 138, *m139*, 144, *145*
Yurok Indians, 183

Z

Zero, invention of, 29, 144–45
Zinjanthropus, 72, 80
Zoology, 7

Acknowledgments Positions are shown in abbreviated form as follows: *t*—top; *c*—center; *b*—bottom; *l*—left; *r*—right.

Key: Photo Researchers, P-R; Rapho-Guillumette, R-G; United Press International, UPI; The University Museum of the University of Pennsylvania, The University Museum.

UNIT I: M. and E. Bernheim from R-G; **p. 1**, Museum of Archeology, Ankara; **pp. 5–6**, courtesy of the American Museum of Natural History; **p. 8**, M. and E. Bernheim from R-G; **p. 9**, *The Royal Hordes* by E. D. Phillips, published by Thomas and Hudson, London and McGraw-Hill Book Co., New York; **p. 10**, courtesy of the American Museum of Natural History; **p. 15** *t*, The Bettmann Archive; *b*, European Picture Service; **p. 16**, M. and E. Bernheim from R-G; **p. 17**, UPI; **p. 19**, courtesy of Wenner-Gren Foundation for Anthropological Research, Inc., New York; **p. 20**, courtesy of Ford Foundation (Raghubir Singh); **p. 24**, Aktuell from Black Star; **p. 25**, Morath from Magnum; **p. 27** *t*, Luthy from De Wys, Inc., *b*, Cash from R-G; **p. 29**, Witlin from Black Star; **p. 30**, M. and E. Bernheim from R-G; UNIT II: Huzeler, Natural History Museum, Basel; **p. 35**, *Art in the Ice Age: Spanish, Levant Art, Arctic Art*, by Johannes Maringer and Hans-Georg Bandi, published by Frederick A. Praeger, Inc., New York, 1953; **p. 39**, Harbrace; **p. 42**, Miller from UPI; **p. 43**, Dr. Elso S. Barghoorn; **p. 50** *t*, Australian News and Information Bureau, photo Neil Murray, *c*, courtesy of the American Museum of Natural History, *b*, courtesy of Department of Public Information, Frankfort, Kentucky; **p. 54**, The Bettmann Archive; **p. 64**, New York Zoological Society; **p. 67** *tl*, Hess from Three Lions, *tr–bl*, New York Zoological Society, *br*, courtesy of the American Museum of Natural History; **pp. 76–78**, courtesy of the American Museum of Natural History; **p. 90** *l*, UNATIONS (from Belgian Gov't Inf. Center, N.Y.), *r*, Luthy from De Wys, Inc; **p. 96** *t* (*l–r*), Kosok from Black Star, Bosshard from Black Star, *c* (*r–l*), Sully from Black Star, R. Capa from Magnum, *b* (*l–r*), courtesy of National Film Board of Canada, Gerstle from P-R; **p. 99**, Hawaiian Visitors Bureau; UNIT III: Cartier-Bresson from Magnum; **p. 103**, courtesy of the Freer Gallery of Art, Smithsonian Institution, Washington, D.C.; **p. 106**, Ashmolean Museum; **p. 107**, The University Museum; **p. 109**, Brown Bros.; **p. 110**, courtesy of the American Museum of Natural History; **p. 114**, Reitz from De Wys, Inc.; **p. 115**, The University Museum–National Geographic Society Expedition; **p. 119**, courtesy of the British Museum; **p. 120**, The University Museum, photo Harbrace; **pp. 122–23**, courtesy of the American Museum of Natural History; **p. 126**, Jordan Ministry of Information; **p. 129**, Hirmer from Hirmer Verlag, Munich; **p. 130**, courtesy of the British Museum; **p. 134** *t*, The University Museum, *b*, Mandel from Black Star; **p. 136**, courtesy of the American Museum of Natural History; **p. 140**, courtesy of the Mexican National Tourist Council; **p. 141**, Holton from P-R; **pp. 142–44**, courtesy of the American Museum of Natural History; **p. 145**, Holton from P-R; **p. 147**, courtesy of the American Museum of Natural History; **p. 152**, Harbutt from Magnum; **p. 153**, M. and E. Bernheim from R-G; **p. 159**, Pan-Asia Photo News from Black Star; Lawson from R-G; **p. 165**, courtesy of the American Museum of Natural History; **p. 166**, M. and E. Bernheim from R-G; **p. 168**, Riboud from Magnum; **p. 171**, Cartier-Bresson from Magnum; **p. 172**, courtesy of the Danish Information Office; **p. 174**, M. and E. Bernheim from R-G; **p. 180**, photo, The University Museum; **p. 181**, Hamaya from Magnum; **p. 182**, Cole from R-G; **p. 183**, courtesy of the American Museum of Natural History; **p. 184**, Levy from P-R; **p. 186**, Haas from Magnum; **p. 187**, Glinn from Magnum; **p. 189**, Haas from Magnum; **pp. 194–95**, Exeter Photo; **p. 196**, courtesy of the American Museum of Natural History; **p. 197**, May from Black Star; **p. 198**, courtesy of Museum of American Indian, Heye Foundation; **p. 202**, courtesy of the American Museum of Natural History; **p. 204**, Dept. of the Interior; **p. 210** *t*, Bischof from Magnum, *c*, Luthy from De Wys, Inc.; **p. 215** *t*, Lion from Black Star, *b* (*l–r*), Matter from Black Star, United Nations; **p. 222**, United Nations; **p. 225**, Consulate General of Japan, N.Y.: **p. 228**, United Nations; **p. 232**, T. S. Satyan from World Health Organization; **p. 233** *t*, United Nations, *b*, Patrick Miller; **pp. 234–235**, United Nations; **p. 236**, Jack Ling from United Nations; **p. 238** *t* (*l–r*), A. Devaney Inc., N.Y., United Nations, *b*, René Burri from Magnum; **p. 240**, Clinton S. Bond from BBM Associates, Berkeley, Calif.; **p. 242** *t*, U.S. Army photo, *b* (*l–r*), United Nations.

A
B
C
D
E
F
G
H
I
J

274 *Acknowledgments*